C000110981

church 3.0

church 3.0

upgrades for the future of the church

Neil Cole

Foreword by Francis Chan

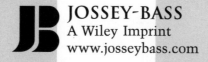

JOSSEY-BASS
A Wiley Imprint
www.josseybass.com

Copyright © 2010 by Neil Cole. All rights reserved.

Published by Jossey-Bass
A Wiley Imprint
989 Market Street, San Francisco, CA 94103-1741—www.josseybass.com

No part of this publication may be reproduced, stored in a retrieval system, or
transmitted in any form or by any means, electronic, mechanical, photocopying,
recording, scanning, or otherwise, except as permitted under Section 107 or 108 of
the 1976 United States Copyright Act, without either the prior written permission of
the publisher, or authorization through payment of the appropriate per-copy fee to the
Copyright Clearance Center, Inc., 222 Rosewood Drive, Danvers, MA 01923, 978-750-
8400, fax 978-646-8600, or on the Web at www.copyright.com. Requests to the publisher
for permission should be addressed to the Permissions Department, John Wiley & Sons,
Inc., 111 River Street, Hoboken, NJ 07030, 201-748-6011, fax 201-748-6008, or online at
www.wiley.com/go/permissions.

Readers should be aware that Internet Web sites offered as citations and/or sources for
further information may have changed or disappeared between the time this was written
and when it is read.

Limit of Liability/Disclaimer of Warranty: While the publisher and author have used
their best efforts in preparing this book, they make no representations or warranties
with respect to the accuracy or completeness of the contents of this book and specifically
disclaim any implied warranties of merchantability or fitness for a particular purpose. No
warranty may be created or extended by sales representatives or written sales materials.
The advice and strategies contained herein may not be suitable for your situation. You
should consult with a professional where appropriate. Neither the publisher nor author
shall be liable for any loss of profit or any other commercial damages, including but not
limited to special, incidental, consequential, or other damages.

Jossey-Bass books and products are available through most bookstores. To contact Jossey-
Bass directly call our Customer Care Department within the U.S. at 800-956-7739, outside
the U.S. at 317-572-3986, or fax 317-572-4002.

Scripture quotations taken from the New American Standard Bible®, Copyright © 1960,
1962, 1963, 1968, 1971, 1972, 1973, 1975, 1977, 1995 by The Lockman Foundation. Used
by permission. (www.Lockman.org)

Jossey-Bass also publishes its books in a variety of electronic formats. Some content that
appears in print may not be available in electronic books.

Library of Congress Cataloging-in-Publication Data
Cole, Neil, date.
    Church 3.0 : upgrades for the future of the church / Neil Cole ; foreword by
Francis Chan.—1st ed.
        p. cm.—(Leadership network)
    Includes bibliographical references and index.
    ISBN 978-0-470-52945-4 (cloth)
        1. Church. I. Title. II. Title: Church three point zero.
BV600.3.C63 2010
254'.5—dc22

                                                                        2009042687

Printed in the United States of America
FIRST EDITION
HB Printing   10 9 8 7 6 5 4 3 2 1

leadership network titles

The Blogging Church: Sharing the Story of Your Church Through Blogs, Brian Bailey and Terry Storch

Church Turned Inside Out: A Guide for Designers, Refiners, and Re-Aligners, Linda Bergquist and Allan Karr

Leading from the Second Chair: Serving Your Church, Fulfilling Your Role, and Realizing Your Dreams, Mike Bonem and Roger Patterson

The Way of Jesus: A Journey of Freedom for Pilgrims and Wanderers, Jonathan S. Campbell with Jennifer Campbell

Leading the Team-Based Church: How Pastors and Church Staffs Can Grow Together into a Powerful Fellowship of Leaders, George Cladis

Organic Church: Growing Faith Where Life Happens, Neil Cole

Church 3.0: Upgrades for the Future of the Church, Neil Cole

Off-Road Disciplines: Spiritual Adventures of Missional Leaders, Earl Creps

Reverse Mentoring: How Young Leaders Can Transform the Church and Why We Should Let Them, Earl Creps

Building a Healthy Multi-Ethnic Church: Mandate, Commitments, and Practices of a Diverse Congregation, Mark DeYmaz

Leading Congregational Change Workbook, James H. Furr, Mike Bonem, and Jim Herrington

The Tangible Kingdom: Creating Incarnational Community, Hugh Halter and Matt Smay

Leading Congregational Change: A Practical Guide for the Transformational Journey, Jim Herrington, Mike Bonem, and James H. Furr

The Leader's Journey: Accepting the Call to Personal and Congregational Transformation, Jim Herrington, Robert Creech, and Trisha Taylor

v

contents

about leadership network

Since 1984, Leadership Network has fostered church innovation and growth by diligently pursuing its far-reaching mission statement: to identify, connect, and help high-capacity Christian leaders multiply their impact.

Although Leadership Network's techniques adapt and change as the church faces new opportunities and challenges, the organization's work follows a consistent and proven pattern: Leadership Network brings together entrepreneurial leaders who are focused on similar ministry initiatives. The ensuing collaboration—often across denominational lines—creates a strong base from which individual leaders can better analyze and refine their own strategies. Peer-to-peer interaction, dialogue, and sharing inevitably accelerate participants' innovation and ideas. Leadership Network further enhances this process through developing and distributing highly targeted ministry tools and resources, including audio and video programs, special reports, e-publications, and online downloads.

With Leadership Network's assistance, today's Christian leaders are energized, equipped, inspired, and better able to multiply their own dynamic Kingdom-building initiatives.

Launched in 1996 in conjunction with Jossey-Bass (a Wiley imprint), Leadership Network Publications present thoroughly researched and innovative concepts from leading thinkers, practitioners, and pioneering churches. The series collectively draws from a range of disciplines, with individual titles offering perspective on one or more of five primary areas:

1. Enabling effective leadership
2. Encouraging life-changing service
3. Building authentic community
4. Creating Kingdom-centered impact
5. Engaging cultural and demographic realities

For additional information on the mission or activities of Leadership Network, please contact:

Leadership Network
(800) 765-5323
client.care@leadnet.org

foreword

For the past two years, the elders of Cornerstone Church have been talking about changes that need to happen at our church. The more we studied the Scriptures together, the more convinced we were that change had to take place. There was no doubt in our minds that the Lord wanted our church to look more like a "body."

For years, we emphasized each individual's "personal relationship with Christ." We gave little thought to how to become a collective witness. One person described it as "blackjack Christianity." In the game of blackjack, you care only about your relationship with the dealer. You don't really need to interact with anyone else seated at the table. Sunday services took on this mind-set as people came to work on their own relationships with God.

Personally, I enjoyed the old way of holding church services. I could hide in the back without having to interact with anyone. I even remember giving an illustration about ten years ago where I stood inside a refrigerator box with the top cut open. I told the congregation that we ought to worship like we're inside a refrigerator box—paying no attention to the others around us. This was between you and God, so just look up at Him. I didn't have any biblical support for this teaching, but no one challenged it. After all, it's easier to neglect those around us. It's rare that anyone challenges teaching that makes life easier.

I've long since repented for not just practicing isolationism but encouraging it. God's desire is that we see ourselves as a family. Just as God wanted to display His glory through Israel rather than just Israelites, so He wants us to use the church rather than individual Christians.

But you are a chosen race, a royal priesthood, a holy nation, a people for his own possession, that you may proclaim the excellencies of him who called you out of darkness into his marvelous light. 1 Peter 2:9

By myself, I can only speak of God's love. With others, I have the opportunity to actually "show" love, forgiveness, and patience. Rather than just hearing about Jesus, people can actually get a glimpse of Him.

No one has ever seen God; if we love one another, God abides in us and his love is perfected in us. 1 John 4:12

As the elders continued in their quest to turn our gathering of church service attendees into a body, we discovered others around the world pursuing the same thing! We thought we were alone and seeking to pioneer something new. What we discovered was that the Holy Spirit had been leading others down this same road. And some were much further down this road than we were.

I first read *Church 3.0* at a time when our leadership was struggling to find answers. The timing could not have been better. As a leadership team, we felt we had a good understanding of the big picture and God's desire for the church. Our struggle was seeing how it would flesh itself out. That's what I appreciated about this book. It's practical. It goes beyond concepts and gets us to consider another way of gathering. It spurs our thinking.

It would be beneficial for every pastor to read *Church 3.0*. I'm not saying that you have to agree with everything Neil writes. In fact, I think it would be unhealthy to merely copy his methodology (or anyone's, for that matter). I just believe it is in your best interest to wrestle with the thoughts he presents. It's hard for me to imagine anyone reading this book without making at least some adjustments to church gatherings.

I'm very excited about the potential future of our church gatherings in America. Neil is certainly not alone in his desire to see the church transformed into the beautiful bride she was intended to be.

Francis Chan

preface

I cannot say whether things will get better if we change; what I can say is they must change if they are to get better.
—GEORG C. LICHTENBERG

To be born is a good thing. To know why you were born is a better thing. To fulfill the reason you were born is perhaps the greatest thing.

My life is devoted to creatively releasing the reproduction of healthy disciples, leaders, churches, and movements to the ends of the earth until Christ returns or I die. I am pretty set in this purpose, and it is hard to get me away from it. There is little else that I see relevant to my calling. This is what gets me up in the morning and keeps me up at night. All of my writings to date have been to this end. For instance:

Cultivating a Life for God and *Search & Rescue* were written to help reproduce healthy disciples.

Organic Leadership, Raising Leaders for the Harvest (with Bob Logan), and *TruthQuest* were written to develop healthy leaders.

Organic Church and *Beyond Church Planting* (also with Bob Logan) were written to release healthy church reproduction.

Church 3.0 is the first book I have written that is actually focused on the big picture of releasing healthy church movements. Although it addresses healthy churches (you can't have a church movement without them), it presents a bigger picture. The upgrades I am recommending in this book are all dedicated to helping us see a true global church multiplication movement. God designed creation to have its own means of maintaining health. Fertility follows health but is supplanted by the sickness that comes from unhealthy mutations. When that happens, the organism cannot reproduce and thus spreads the illness. This is not simply survival of the fittest; it is God's design for keeping the creation sustainable for generations. I believe this is also true of the organic nature of His church, which is a living thing.

One of the reasons I believe our conventional churches are not multiplying is because God doesn't want to multiply them. Frankly, he doesn't want more of the problems we currently face. We, as God's people, must become better so that when we are multiplied the world will be better. It is time for an upgrade.

Like all upgrades, however, there is a cost. The new system must replace the old. The two systems cannot work simultaneously. This doesn't mean that your church should be closed for good, or that everyone should start doing church exclusively in homes. What I mean is that we need to replace old ways of thinking about God's church with new ones that can release the health, growth, and reproduction meant to be characteristic of the church. The solution is not found in models but in a mindset. The "CP*You*" must be running the right software.

Whatever type of church you are part of, you can change your thinking about these things, discover greater health, and be part of a global movement for a different kind of church. The word in the New Testament for repentance, "*metanoia,*" means to change one's mind. Jesus wrote letters to seven churches in Asia Minor in which he says to "repent" eight times. Apparently churches need to change their mind, and a lot. We must learn to change the way we think about things because we can be easily seduced into lazy patterns of thinking. To repent, we must stop thinking in the old way, and start thinking in the new way. It is not enough to stop thinking wrongly; we must also train our fresh minds to think rightly about things. In each chapter, I not only share what is wrong with some of the old ways in which we think but offer a better solution.

This repentance, or changing the way we think, is not optional for cutting-edge churches to reap the benefits. It is something every church should be willing to do. For this reason, Jesus concludes each letter to the seven churches with the same words: "He who has ears to hear, let him hear what the Spirit says to the churches." We all need to regularly question if we are indeed hearing what the Spirit is saying to the churches. We cannot simply assume that what was will be, and always should be. Unless the Scriptures truly state it clearly, we should expect the Head of the church to be saying something new to us regularly, and we should be listening.

I realize I run the risk of confusing people with a book of this title, after all of my work establishing the idea of an organic church. Let me be clear: the church *is* organic. Organic is not a metaphor about the church. Church is not *like* an organism; it *is* an organism, and like all organisms she should be healthy, be fruitful, and reproduce after her own kind in a natural way.

The idea of an upgrade in the operating system of the church is using a metaphor to make a point. Please understand that I am not moving away from seeing church as organic in any way whatsoever. Using the parable of upgrading the operating system of the church, I want to show that in all the ways in which we are most concerned for church we can do better. We are indebted to do better. To do otherwise would be to lose perhaps the greatest opportunity in human history, all because "we never did it that way before."

At the same time, we are also entering a time when the Web is moving quickly toward being more viral, integrated, forming self-sustaining communities; it is becoming personally adaptable, peer-to-peer, and in a sense . . . well, organic. People are speaking today about Web 2.0 in this manner. Social networking on the Internet is teaching us much about ourselves and connecting us with ourselves. Twitter, Facebook, MySpace, Flickr, and LinkedIn connect us to one another in ways we previously could not do so. Suddenly I am bantering back and forth with friends I haven't seen in thirty years, as if it's been only thirty minutes. In a real sense, the Web is not artificial; it is alive because it is us.

So what comes next? I am not the person to tell you what technology has in store for us, but I can tell you what I am learning about the church that is coming.

This book may appear to be simply answering the questions I am most often asked about organic churches, and to some extent this is true. But the book is much more than that. The questions are simply a place from which to launch an exploration of the shifts that must take place for churches to become healthy enough to reproduce. I answer the questions I am most often asked about organic church, and I use those questions as an excuse to reveal how we need to change our thinking . . . to repent. So before you begin, I want you to ask yourself if you are willing to have ears to hear.

This book is about a return to fertility and function for the church that can make a difference in the world, thereby making the world a different place.

acknowledgments

There are times when I do actually feel like an engineer reimagining a new kind of church. I am not, however, alone in a secluded, sterilized, hermetically sealed basement developing a new version of church; quite the opposite. I have been in the dirt planting seeds and pulling weeds. And I have not been alone. This book is not the product of my own work but the experimentation of many, and there are a few whom I must recognize specifically for their contribution.

Awakening Chapels have been a learning laboratory for more than ten years now, and I am grateful for every one of you who have allowed me the privilege of learning with you.

Church Multiplication Associates and all my Greenhouse friends have been a constant source of blessing. You have been very patient with all the variations of training I have thrown your way. Over the years, your number has become too great for me to now list every name, but know that you are not forgotten or unappreciated.

Paul Kaak, you have refined all my thinking and encouraged my heart as we plowed ground, planted seed, tended to the growth, and together watched the harvest come. Your wisdom is reflected on so many pages of this book that I must thank you for coming along with me on this journey.

Alan Hirsch is a friend and co-conspirator. I have found that I was thinking of him often as I was writing, so I owe him a shout out. Bro, you have inspired me to write with greater thoughtfulness, boldness, and reflection. Thanks.

Thom Wolf has been a mentor to me, and also a deep vein of outstanding ideas. It is hard to find a book I have written that does not demonstrate some of Thom's genius.

You will not need to read very far in this book to realize that my entire family is at the core of all I am about. I must thank my life-love and closest friend, Dana, for walking with me all these years. You have shown such patience with my strange ideas, ever-increasing travel, and the occasional verbal assault against your husband from someone you've never even met.

I also must acknowledge my children, Heather, Erin, and Zachary. I have no greater joy than to watch you all walk in the truth. Keep it up! I am so proud of each of you.

dedication

This book is dedicated to my brother and fellow organic
church gardener, Paul Kaak. Some years ago we dreamed
and schemed together of what could be, and today
it is becoming. What a ride!

I use the word "bro" a lot (especially when I forget a name).
So using it in reference to Paul just feels a little cheap.
But actually he is like a real, flesh-and-blood brother to
me. We have sibling squabbles and yet willingly share
everything. We stay up till all hours of the night talking
about anything and everything. I tease him, and he teases
me right back, but woe to anyone else who would do the
same. I would take on any school-yard bully for him, and
I know he would do the same for me.

church 3.0

what about this book?

shifting from church 2.0 to 3.0

It is impossible for a man to learn what he thinks he already knows.
—Epictetus

DID YOU EVER have a silly song in your head that you wished you could get rid of? It happens to us all. Some songs are so contagious that if one person hums the tune for two minutes, soon everyone in the room will be humming or thinking about the same song.

Chip and Dan Heath tell of an interesting Ph.D. study conducted at Stanford in 1990 based on a simple game of tapping songs.[1] There were two roles for people to play in this experiment: "tappers" and "listeners." The tappers were each given twenty-five well-known songs such as "Happy Birthday to You" and told to tap the melody on a table. Listeners were to guess the name of the song. It sounds simple enough.

In the experiment, a total of 120 songs were tapped out. The listeners guessed right on only 2.5 percent of the songs. The listeners succeeded in guessing the right song 3 tries out of 120. What was remarkable about the study, and what merits repeating

1

the story here, is that the tappers were asked to predict their success prior to tapping. They estimated that the listeners would figure it out 50 percent of the time. How could they be so far off? That is what is so interesting in the study.

The problem is that when the tapper taps, she is hearing the song played in her head. You can't do the exercise without hearing the song; try it. The listeners, however, do not hear the song in their head; all they hear is a collection of random taps as if someone is trying to tell them some encrypted message with Morse Code.

Tappers were amazed how hard it seemed for the listeners to figure out the tune. When they guessed wrong on a well-known song such as "The Star Spangled Banner," they would just look at the listener in a flabbergasted way, as if the listener were stupid.

The Heath brothers concluded: "The problem is that the tappers have been given knowledge (the song title) that makes it impossible for them to imagine what it's like to lack that knowledge. When they're tapping, they can't imagine what it's like for the listeners to hear isolated taps rather than a song. This is the Curse of Knowledge. Once we know something, we find it hard to imagine what it is like to not know it."[2]

In many ways, I believe we evangelical Christians suffer from the curse of knowledge. Not that knowledge is evil or a bad thing to have, but it can prevent us from learning something new. How many times have you tried to explain something new to someone, only to watch his eyes glaze over with inattentiveness and then hear him say repeatedly, "Yeah, I know. I know." You know the person doesn't really know, but try convincing the person of it. This is the curse of knowledge preventing someone from hearing something new. It happens all the time.

When it comes to explaining some of the remarkable changes that are coming with Church 3.0, we simply must address the curse of knowledge before we can go much further. For hundreds of years now, we have all been operating under the knowledge of an old system, and it is all we have known. We have had the same song in our head for centuries. For you to even be somewhat open to the new ideas I am suggesting in this book, we need to address the fact that what you have known is not necessarily the only way to understand things in the Bible or the church.

I am not proposing that we dump the Bible and instead learn from sociologists and trendy pop thinkers. In fact, quite the opposite: I want us to seriously ask ourselves if what we have always assumed to be in the Bible is indeed there. You see, I think we have a song in our head when we read the Scriptures, and the result is that we hear what is playing in our head more than what is written on the page. We are thumping out the tune on our Bibles instead of letting the Scripture teach us a new song. We must set our minds free from the ancient songs that are rattling in our heads and read the New Testament as if for the very first time. Is it really possible? If we are bold enough to try, we can discover some interesting things. I want to challenge you to take that adventure.

The truth is, it will serve you well throughout this book to try to mute the songs in your head, the ones written by our church fathers, and look at the Scriptures with fresh eyes. For far too long, Christian leaders have claimed that an idea is "biblical" because they want it to be. In reality, all they did was simply tag on a few verses, often taken out of context, and put parentheses at the end of *their* idea. Doing this claims unfounded authority for ideas, but it also teaches a song. All of us have done this. We need to stop, so I am asking you for a little grace to listen to what I am saying in this book.

Be noble-minded, like the Berean people in Acts 17:10–15: "Now these were more noble-minded . . . for they received the word with great eagerness, examining the Scriptures daily to see whether these things were so." Having learned the Old Testament and the song of the rabbinical teachers for years, suddenly they were hearing some remarkable truths that countered all they had been taught for centuries. They checked the Scriptures with eagerness to learn and find out what was said. They were not closed-minded; they were noble-minded, and there is a difference—a big one.

You will probably find, at some point in this book, that what I am sharing jars your sensibilities because it may be a radical departure from all you have known about church. It is possible that I am not reading the Scriptures well. Then again, it is possible that the song we have been taught to sing is not really prescribed in the Bible. It may be a good song, but there could be other good songs, perhaps even better ones. Be eager to search the Scriptures with a noble mind, but only if you have the courage to discover that you may not have been dancing to the right tune.

upgrading the operating system

Computer software upgrades can be a blessing and a curse. They come with fanfare and promise. Sometimes they deliver on the promise; at other times, they deliver nothing but headaches.

The software is often updated in secrecy and then released to the public without any true testing of how the changes will interact with third-party products. You may be the one to discover that the upgrade doesn't work with the important systems you rely on every day. System patches and new plug-ins are released to try to mend the problems after the fact. For this reason, many experts suggest that you wait several months to adopt a new upgrade, so that others can be the lab rats that either find the cheese at the end of the maze or become trapped in the process. Once the early adopter rats are happily consuming a wealth of fresh cheddar, then you can safely make the switch.

What would happen if everyone stopped upgrading? The consequence would make a poor upgrade seem like the greatest breakthrough since the light bulb. Why? If we stop upgrading, we stop growing, learning, and becoming better. We need to improve, all the time. Granted, this leaves us with the potential for poor-quality upgrades, but that is better than no upgrades at all.

For some reason, the church is always the slowest to upgrade. Our conservative religious nature, which borders on superstition, tends to make everything sacred (especially things that are not meant to be so) and therefore untouchable. The result is that the church is often left behind, and soon irrelevant. When a ministry is blessed by God, we consider it His endorsement of the method. Long after the method is out of sync with culture and out of step with any good results, we still consider it God's way and keep it going—often for decades or even centuries. Making changes in the church is often considered heretical and blasphemous. The sound of the eight lethal words of church management still echo in the boardrooms of the Western churches: "But we've never done it that way before."

In software, as in the church, some upgrades are routine and minor, aimed at making the system a little better equipped to face the challenges of the day. Usually, a new feature or two, along with necessary patches, are added to the same basic system. In those cases, the upgrade usually bears the same first digit but is a fractionally higher number; the move is from 2.3 to 2.4, or maybe from 2.3 to 2.3.1.

Occasionally an upgrade changes the entire system. When blended technology, lessons learned by experience and testing, and breakthroughs in computer technology itself all demand a new system, patches and added features are not enough. The old system must be scrapped and the new one put in its place. Those upgrades are demarked by a change in the first digit of the software—from 2.7 to 3.0.

Of course, there is a learning curve that comes with this new upgrade, but the new advancements are so valuable that they make the learning worthwhile. A short time after this occurs, an entire industry can step up and make the old systems and hardware that supported them entirely obsolete. Stores discontinue the old technology as the whole industry moves forward. Remember DOS and floppy disks?

A good upgrade does a few things. It makes operation simpler and more intuitive. It also is more powerful in accomplishing all its important tasks. Finally, a good upgrade opens up the software to whole new markets that would never have tried to use the product in the past.

There have been two major upgrades in church formation, since Acts, that have changed the entire system. The first occurred dramatically during the rule of the Emperor Constantine. The church shifted from an underground, grassroots, organic movement to a more institutionalized organization. I believe the second is occurring now.

church 1.0

The first-century church was Church 1.0, with its minor differences. The Jerusalem church would have been the original Church 1.0. Antioch would be Church 1.1. The Galatian churches, started in the first journey of Paul and Barnabas, would represent Church 1.2. Corinth would represent a change to 1.3, as Paul added some patches to how he approached church. The Ephesian church would be Church 1.4. And so the changes went on, through two centuries of church life, kept simple and organic by oppression and persecution from ten Roman emperors. Heresies emerged and were purged. There was the establishment of regional bishops and institutionalization of some of the forms of Christianity during this period, but overall the church remained a grassroots, marginalized movement under the heat of intense persecution.

All that changed in 313 A.D., when Constantine declared that the empire would not only tolerate Christianity but restore to the church all lost property. He was the first "Christian" emperor; Christianity went instantly from the margins to the mainstream, and everything changed. Christianity became the state religion, and the church did not change much from that point on. This was the shift to Church 2.0 and all its eventual variants.

church 2.0

Over the centuries, after Constantine, the Western church evolved in many ways, but none has been a significant systemic change. There was establishment of both the Roman Catholic Church and the Eastern Orthodox Church, and for hundreds of years there were very few changes. The Reformation split the Western church into the Roman Church and the volatile Protestant church, or Church 2.1. In spite of the differences, the institutional system remained mostly unchanged. The Reformation set loose (and persecuted) the Anabaptists, but this was just a change from Church 2.1 to 2.2. Whether the church adapts to reach coal miners in eighteenth-century England or postmodern pilgrims in the twenty-first century, most of the changes have been patches and plug-ins to the Church 2.0 system. Whether you are talking about high church or low, Pentecostal or Reformed, the church has remained in the 2.0 range of upgrades. From Baptist to Brethren, from Mennonite to Methodist, the changes in the system are relatively untouched over the centuries. Music or no music? Pipe organ or electric guitar? Whether seeing tall ceilings with stained-glass windows, or meeting in a box building without windows, the actual system of church has gone relatively unchanged.

You have the priests or pastors, the Sunday service with singing and a sermon, the weekly offering, the pulpit with pews, and the church building. These have been constants since the fourth century. Even if you move the whole show into a house instead of a church building, if the system hasn't changed you have only shrunk the church, not transformed it. Changing the style of music does not upgrade the system. Turning down the lights and turning up the volume is a simple patch to the same old system. Choirs and hymns or praise bands and fog machines, kneeling, or standing are miniscule changes to the system. Sermonizing with topical messages or expositional ones is not changing the system; it's making minor adjustments. Sunday schools or small groups as secondary learning environments are not a systemic change at all, just a variation on the same old operational system.

Although most of the advances to Church 2.0 over the centuries have been plug-ins and patches to the same old system, there have been anomalies along the way. Usually, these anomalies are the result of rampant persecution driving the church back to the old default system. One could say that these are examples of going back to the Church 1.0 system, because their 2.0 system crashed in the face of extreme heat. The radical Anabaptist churches are an example. The Chinese house church phenomenon is also a departure from the expression of the Church 2.0 system. These experiments are really not the norm and have not, to date, influenced the church as a whole in any permanent fashion, except perhaps to say that they are part of the learning that has led to this new operating system—Church 3.0.

church 3.0

I believe that the second major shift is occurring now, in our lifetime. Many people want to go back to the beginning again. As much as I am enamored of what I learned about the church of the first century, we simply cannot go back; we can only go forward. Granted, if we went back it would be a vast improvement on where we have been more recently. I have to ask, though: Could we do even better than Church 1.0? Some may find even such a question as this heretical. It is only a question, but it bears consideration.

Could we actually improve on the first-century church? A careful study of Acts reveals that even in the first decades of the church there was profound improvement as people learned from experience. Why not seek more improvements today, building on the foundation of two thousand years of mistakes? I believe it is possible. I think we can see the awesome impact and rapid spread that the first century saw, but we also can benefit from two thousand years of learning and use today's technological advances.

Imagine if the apostle Paul could buy an airline ticket and be across the world in twelve hours instead of twelve years. Imagine what he would do with the Internet and the ability to see events unfold globally and instantaneously. Our ability to understand culture and translate languages today is built on two thousand years of mistakes along with the successes they produced. Perhaps more than any other benefit we have is looking in hindsight at how easily institutionalization took over the church. It was no longer people in relationship to one another, but an organized system. Armed with that knowledge, we can now move forward. The early church flew blindly into a trap of a religious hierarchical system that kept her in the dark ages for hundreds of years. History can train us for the future, if we listen to it. No, Church 3.0 is not a shift downward in church life or quality. It is an upgrade in every sense of the word, perhaps even rising above the early church. Why would we suspect that God is content with our going backwards? Why wouldn't He want us to grow and develop in better ways?

The best upgrades do a few things. First they allow greater power in what you want to accomplish, and Church 3.0 is a huge boost in raw spiritual power. Every part of the body of Christ can function at a much higher level. A second thing you may look for in an upgrade is to move to a simpler and more intuitive way of using the system. This upgrade to Church 3.0 is certainly that, in many ways. It is built on simplicity and potency bound together to increase speed and power in the influence that the church can and should have. Third, upgrades take advantage of the latest discoveries in technology and help you interact better with all the other electronics you may use. Church 3.0 is far and away better at being fluid, mixing with multiple expressions of church structure, and overcoming the world's obstacles. Fourth, an upgrade should have greater capacity to accommodate much more information, functionality, and storage. Finally, some cool new features in an upgrade should significantly improve the system's performance and make it much more fun to use. Church 3.0 is so enjoyable that it is quite common for those who have made the switch to comment that they could never go back to the old system.

Do not be deceived into thinking that this is just another patch to the same old system; it is a radical change from the core of the church. Church 3.0 has rebuilt the function of the church in every sense, from the smallest to the largest capacity. Figure I.1, developed by Paul Kaak and me, demonstrates that the coming changes are polar shifts that will mean a fundamental change in church, from the core.

	Church 2.0	Church 3.0
Seating when gathered	Rows	Circles
Environment	Anonymous	Intimate
Leadership source	Institutions of higher learning	Harvest fields
Growth	Addition	Multiplication
Results	An audience is attracted	A spiritual army is mobilized
Ministry practitioners	The ordained	The ordinary
Resources	Imported to the harvest	Discovered in the harvest
Primary leadership role	Pastoral teacher	APEST team
Learning lab	Classroom-based education	Trench-based education
Cost	Expensive	Inexpensive
Ministry setting	The meeting place	The marketplace
Success	Full seating capacity	Full sending capacity
Church posture	Passive: "Y'all come!"	Active: "We all go!"
Attraction	Felt need programming	Obvious life transformation
Model of church life	Academic	Family

Figure I.1 Contrasting Church 2.0 with Church 3.0

the change is not just coming;
it is already here

I am not a futurist. I am no prophet. This world has changed in dramatic fashion, right out from under us. God has already called a few brave people to lead the way with the church upgrades of the future. In this book, I list many shifts that must take place for the future of the church because I have seen them already at work. As a habit, I do not write a book until I have experienced what it is I am writing about. Having traveled all over the world, training national leaders on the ground doing the work, I must tell you that these upgrades are already put in place by the Lord for a time such as this. Read this book, not as some guy's wild vision for what could potentially happen, but as a report of what is already taking place. For me, the question is not "Will this happen?" but "Will you and your church be a part of what God is up to in these incredible times?"

All this to say that there is something happening, and it is a shift of global proportions. In the last couple of years, *Time* magazine, the *Los Angeles Times,* and the *Chicago Tribune* have published articles on the rising movement. A Japanese newspaper (with a circulation of 2.5 million) and the *Wall Street Journal* recently interviewed me about our movement. Each journalistic piece examined the large numbers of people leaving the old ways of doing church (Church 2.0) for new, more relational and viral churches less dependent on clergy and programs. Something is going on. We are at the start of a new movement.

what is this book about?

This book is not a defense of organic church, because I do not feel the need to defend something that is natural and fruitful. Even though I am answering questions most often asked about organic church, I am not defending it; I am demonstrating that we can all do church better. Your church, no matter what kind it is, will do well to make some of the shifts mentioned in this book. Even if you must make small and incremental shifts, the ideas expressed here are all about becoming healthier, relating to one another more naturally, and empowering all of God's people on mission together. If you are in a situation where virtually none of these recommendations can be employed, then at least you can be informed of what many believe is coming for the kingdom of God, all over the world.

This is also not a book saying why organic churches are better than the other kind. Anyone who knows me knows that I do not think the organic church is a model of church, but natural principles and processes that can and do work in any model. Organic church is a mind-set, not a model. It is a way of relating more naturally to God, one another, and the world in which we are all planted. When I refer to the organic church movement, understand that this movement is not strictly house churches, but churches of all sizes and structures. The movement has spread through diverse denominations and parachurch organizations. Granted, if you were to use our principles and processes from the start you would end up with a rapidly multiplying network of simple churches, but we are conducting training (every part of it) in established church structures, and it is just as relevant for those settings.

The goal of this book is simple: to look at several ways in which the church can accomplish its mission better in the future than it has in the past. The change to Church 3.0 is a shift from a program-driven and clergy-led institutionalized approach of church to one that is relational, simple, and viral in its spread. Instead of seeing church as something that serves its people, church becomes people who serve—God, one another, and a hurting world. The change is from an organization to an organism that is healthy and reproductive. Church is no longer a place to go to, but a people to belong to. Church is no longer an event to be at, but a family to be a part of. Church is not a program to reach out to the world, but a people that bring the kingdom of God with them into a lost world, with a contagious spirit.

In a sense, I am hoping to encourage us to open our eyes, look at a problem from another angle, and ask: If the Bible does not prescribe our current methods, can we do this better in another way? After doing just that for more than a decade now, and testing the process and ironing out the kinks, I am now putting forward some of what we have discovered. These upgrades have been tested and proven to be useful improvements for any and all churches, not just house churches. This book will be helpful for any church to apply; in fact, I believe we are at a point where we must make these changes. It is time to upgrade or die.

In Part One I lay out some profound changes that are taking place in our world today, presenting unprecedented opportunities for the church if we can make changes that capitalize on them.

The rest of the book is designed to answer the questions of those who are curious about what is happening but cannot seem to envision another way of doing church. I am asked the same familiar questions about organic church everywhere I go. What do you do with kids? What do you do to keep rampant heresy from overtaking organic churches when there are no trained leaders? Do you ever meet in larger venues? This book will address these questions, and many more.

This is not, however, simply a book to answer these questions. I want to show not only that we have thought through the issues but that we can actually improve on what has been done in the past. If our goal is simply to do church the same way but in a smaller setting, we have done nothing. Frankly speaking, I would rather be in a dysfunctional megachurch than a dysfunctional house church, because there I can at least hide in the crowd. If this new movement isn't an upgrade, then all of us should quit. We are long overdue for an upgrade on how church is experienced.

Welcome to Church 3.0.

global changes demand a better church

1

what about the world we live in?

from a village church to a global village

The future has a way of arriving unannounced.
—GEORGE WILL

NOT SINCE THE GREAT FLOOD of Noah's day has the world changed so rapidly as in the past twenty years. Population has increased at an exponential rate. Advances in technology have changed the very way we relate to one another. During the student revolt in Tiananmen Square, footage of a single man stopping a line of tanks symbolized the resistance. During the demonstrations in Freedom Square in Tehran in 2009, there was not one photo but thousands of posts on Twitter, Facebook pictures, and cell phone camera footage instantly sent all over the world. The entire world mourned as it watched a young woman, Neda Agha-Soltan, dying in the streets from a bullet wound. The world has become a smaller place, with immediate connection to anybody at anytime.

What would you think if someone told you only fifteen years ago that your car would speak to you and tell you when and where to turn? What would you have said five years ago if I told you that I'd just "tweeted" you? I wonder what development will come next year that will alter our vocabulary and our way of relating to one another.

Perhaps the institution most notoriously slow to change is the church. We are famous for resisting change, but we cannot afford to resist any longer. Our core belief in the Gospel itself and the consequent sanctification of believers is all about change, so we should be more welcoming of it. In the light of our Gospel truth and the constantly changing world, we simply must choose to make changes to take advantage of current global opportunities. We have not seen the same opportunities for the Gospel since perhaps the first century.

My mentor, Thom Wolf, often points out that the twenty-first century is quickly becoming the sister century to the first century.[1] There are remarkable similarities between them. In this chapter, I list six corresponding characteristics tying the first century to the current one that create opportunities and challenges for the church.

a single and dominant superpower

For two hundred years, there was a type of peace on the planet, not because of the good nature of the people but because of the dominance of a world power that had no rivals: the Roman Empire. Historians have called that period Pax Romana, Latin for the peace of Rome. It was during this time that God stepped into the human world in the person of Jesus of Nazareth.

This Roman superpower actually benefited the spread of the Gospel in many ways. The first overseas missionaries were able to use their privilege of Roman citizenship to fulfill their missionary enterprise. Paul's Roman citizenship allowed him to be taken to Rome (at the government's expense) to proclaim his testimony to kings and ultimately the emperor himself. The Gospel was further advanced while Paul was under house arrest in Rome. There he was able to evangelize, train leaders, write letters, and fully accomplish his calling to bring God's word to the Gentiles. Finally, the persecution of Christians by the Roman Empire helped spread the flame of Christianity across the world.

Today, for the first time in quite a while, we are experiencing another time when a single government is the dominant power in the world: the United States. Pax Americana has come, for better or worse. It has been anything but a peaceful time, but since the fall of Soviet Communism the United States has stood alone as the dominant force on the planet. The United States is not ruling over the rest of the nations, but it certainly plays a central role in important disputes. Wherever there is conflict, the United States tries to help settle the issue. Both the Israelis and the Palestinians call for the United States to do something when conflicts arise in the Middle East. Whether the United Nations sanctions it or not, the United States will police nations such as Iraq, the Balkans, and Afghanistan. We often do not carry this responsibility well, and "ugly American" is sometimes an earned sentiment, but our influence is definitely real even if it is not positive.

Today, having U.S. citizenship has some advantages as well. Being from the world's only superpower does not make one popular, but it may open doors for advancement of the Gospel, and it will certainly afford some privilege.

a single, global trade language

In the first century, there was a single language that became the common language of trade for the whole world. It was not often the first language of any people, but they learned to be proficient in it for the convenience of trade and communications around the known world. It was Koine Greek.

The first-century Christian leaders, notably Peter and Paul, took advantage of this linguistic opportunity to write letters that could be circulated globally and spread the Good News around the world in a language all could understand.

Today, English has become the common trade language of the world. Everywhere you go and in every nation of the world, English is spoken. A person who speaks English can find immediate opportunities for spreading the Gospel into a growing number of nations and people groups that are learning English in increasing numbers. Many nations will actually pay you a salary to go overseas and teach English, and a growing number of missionaries are taking advantage of this and using the Bible as their textbook.

technological advances create a global community

In the first century, there was a new technology that made the world a smaller place. It brought together cultures, languages, and trade from various places in the world. This advance was so revolutionary that it has remained the bedrock of civilization throughout the rest of history. Chances are that you have relied on this technology even today without giving it a second thought: it is the road. The Roman roads were more than a series of verses in a book of the Bible describing how to receive salvation. They were an expanding network of highways linking all parts of the world to Rome. Remember the saying, "All roads lead to Rome"? There is truth to that, because it was from Rome that all roads found their beginning.

Paul, Barnabas, Peter, and John all traveled on these roads. The Gospel came at a time when the word could spread more quickly and further than ever before because roads existed and enabled global evangelization to occur.

Today the incredible technological advances of the computer chip, telecommunications, satellites, and jet travel have shrunk the world. Because we are taking life one day at a time, the changes may seem to creep up on us unnoticed, but all our lives have changed in radical ways in just a decade. I will never forget watching the World Trade Center collapse, live on TV, on the morning of September 11, 2001. Because of Facebook, I am exchanging jokes with high school friends I haven't seen in thirty years as if it were only thirty minutes ago that we parted. Today you can get a sales call in Massachusetts from an Indian woman in Delhi, selling a product made in Singapore for a company headquartered in London, on a telephone manufactured by a company in Japan that is financed by a sheikh in the United Arab Emirates. It is indeed a smaller world today.

The world is not just smaller; as Thomas Friedman pointed out, it is flatter.[2] Calling this new era (starting in the year 2000) Globalization 3.0,[3] he says: "[This new Globalization] is going to be more and more driven not only by individuals but also by a much more diverse—non-Western, non-white—group of individuals. Individuals from every corner of the flat world are being empowered. Globalization 3.0 makes it possible for so many more people to plug in and play, and you are going to see every color of the human rainbow take part."[4]

The rise in technology has created a world where we are all connected, but it also levels the playing field so that any one of us can have a voice. In a real sense, with blogs, YouTube, self-publishing capabilities, social network sites such as Facebook and Twitter, everyone now can publish thoughts and publicize them to a mass market without the help of a large company. There is potential for anyone with a good idea to make a difference.

Nations that once were closed to the Gospel are losing the struggle to keep the Internet at bay with their citizens. Radio broadcasts pass over walls that people cannot. We can board a jet and be on the other side of the world in less than a day. The opportunities for the spread of the Gospel have never been so remarkable.

relativistic philosophy

When the world becomes smaller and people are more exposed to other religions, cultures, and philosophies of life, it is not uncommon for there to be a rise in relativism—a belief that truth is not absolute, but relative. This view is articulated as, "What is true for you may not be true for me." This philosophical view grew during the first century, which was best summarized in the statement made by Pontius Pilate when he asked Jesus, "What is truth?"

Relativism ultimately leads to a corruption in morals and ideals. Like rust, it eats away at anything solid and eventually hope and reason are lost. Most people have a yearning inside for something substantial that relativism ultimately cannot satisfy. The New Testament Church was able to take advantage of this prevalent philosophy by offering the stability of real truth to a world of increasing despair.

Today, the philosophy of relativism is increasing at an alarming rate. It takes only a short time under such a framework for life to lose all meaning and darkness and despair to pervade all of one's thoughts. The longer people live under such a philosophy of life, the more they hunger for solid ground beneath their feet.

This is what we have to offer. Most of us feel threatened by the doctrine of relativism, but we should not be afraid of it. Most people find it a convenient belief, but not a practical one. The despair it brings creates a ripe climate for the Good News of the kingdom of God.

pagan and occult activity

The first century was rampant with the practice of paganism and superstitious worship of a plethora of gods. Paul ran into much of this on his journeys. It was evident in Athens, where he saw many idols erected to gods, and even one to the unknown god just to cover all bases (Acts 17:22–23). He ran into it again in Ephesus, where an angry mob rioted in the streets because their livelihoods were threatened by the number of people destroying their instruments of occult worship as they converted to Christ. He encountered many false idols in Athens and was provoked to anger and grief. Paul and Barnabas were worshipped as cult gods one moment and stoned the next in Lystra—from stardom to stoning in one afternoon.

Today the practice of Wicca, witchcraft, occult worship, and paganism is rapidly increasing among young people. They long to experience the spiritual world that they know exists. They have a deep yearning to worship and have unfortunately turned to the creation rather than the creator. The occult promises power, spiritual influence, and hidden knowledge, but it delivers enslavement to superstition and fear.

Vampires, Goths, magicians, and even Dungeons and Dragons are no longer found only in fiction but becoming a subculture of our society. They are becoming a part of people's lives. As when Paul traveled through the empire, today people are worshiping a multitude of gods and seeking spiritual enlightenment and power.

Paul took advantage of this religious curiosity. On Mars Hill, or the Areopagus, he presented the true creator to the epicurean and stoic philosophers of the day. We too can make the power and experience of the true kingdom of God attractive to people, just as it was in Ephesus when Paul brought the kingdom there.

sexual promiscuity, perversion, and chemical addictions

Rome is well known for its drunken orgies. The combinations of wealth, power, relativistic philosophy, and pagan worship practices all lead to the spread of sexual immorality and perversions. It is commonly believed that the dissolving moral foundation contributed to unraveling the Roman Empire.

Today sexual perversion is rampant. There are multiple side effects of this ugly increase in sexual activity. Sexually transmitted disease is increasing in pandemic proportions. In our lifetime we are dangerously close to losing a great part of the population of the world's largest continent to AIDS. Unwanted pregnancy and abortion are abundant. There is still a trafficking of young women, who are held captive as sex slaves in parts of our world. Many fatherless children grow up to have little or no respect for authority and wreak great havoc on our urban neighborhoods.

The New Testament believers found the bondage of sexual immorality a difficult challenge, too. Sexual perversion always leaves broken and used lives. A life of sexual bondage and "throw-away" sexual partners will consume souls with darkness, sickness, and eventual lunacy, demonizing, and death.

Although these are all painful realities and harsh challenges, they also present us with opportunity. People who are victims of such ugliness can be responsive to the hope of freedom and forgiveness. Broken people are most receptive to the Gospel. The kingdom of God has hope of freedom, and forgiveness for such people.

aslan is on the move

In the C. S. Lewis story of *The Lion, the Witch and the Wardrobe*, the world of Narnia was enslaved to a cold and harsh hundred-year winter without Christmas. Just when things were at their worst, hope was born, through four young visitors who found their way to Narnia by way of a closet that was for a moment a portal between two worlds.

Change did not come easily. There was an epic battle between good and evil, with betrayal, loss of life, imprisonment, slavery, and ultimately redemption. As things started to shift, there was a moment when good news started to spread. Winter started to melt away. Christmas returned. Green once again began to spring forth with blossoms and running streams and rivers set free from their icy imprisonment. The word spread: *Aslan has returned and is on the move.*

The long reign of darkness and bitter cold broke up in unprecedented ways. No one could even remember how it was before the White Witch cast her spell on Narnia. Buried deep in their souls, locked in a primal and intuitive sense, the inhabitants of Narnia knew there was something better. In their forbidden legends, they knew of a free Narnia and their creator Aslan, but none could dare hope in his return . . . that is, until the nearly forgotten prophecies started to come true and the rumor of his coming started to spread.

I believe we are seeing something tantamount to that same awakening in this day.

Throughout history we have seen glimpses of revival and awakening in specific regions and nations. We have seen God's people arise with renewal and a rebirth of the church, but it has always been localized. Today we are seeing something new that has not occurred since the first century. I travel around the world and meet people of many races, nationalities, and cultures, and I see something that is changing all at once and everywhere in God's kingdom. On a global scale, God is speaking simultaneously to His people and calling them to a new and fresh expression of His kingdom here on earth. It is a wonderful time to be alive.

In all of human history, there was no time that saw the kingdom of God spread as rapidly and as globally as the first century. Every Christian longs for the experience of kingdom life as described in the book of Acts. I am suggesting that we now live in a new century that has equal, if not more, opportunity for the spread of the kingdom. These are dark days, and darkness is when the light shines brightest. We must make changes ourselves if that light is to shine in this world.

We must realize that the church of the past is not equipped for the opportunities of the future. We must shift in our systemic core so that we can take advantage of the global opportunities we face. We must upgrade the church for this new age. It is time for Church 3.0 to rise and spread.

2

what about our changing culture?

from ministry in a modern world to postmodern

In times of change, learners inherit the Earth, while the learned find themselves beautifully equipped to deal with a world that no longer exists.
—ERIC HOFFER

IN THE PREVIOUS CHAPTER, I shared some of the global changes that have mirrored the first century. But the changes are not just happening in external or environmental ways; they are in the hearts and minds of people. There is a shift from a modernistic worldview to a postmodern worldview. The church must recognize this change and adapt how it presents its message, or the Gospel will largely go unheard by a disinterested society. In this chapter, I articulate some of the shifts that have occurred culturally from modernism to postmodernism. I want to demonstrate that such changes that have already occurred can actually present tremendous opportunity for the Gospel, without threatening the veracity of the message itself.

what is postmodernism?

Postmodernism is like a worn bar of soap in dirty bath water; as soon as you think you have a good grasp it slips out of your hand and is lost in the murky water, leaving you blindly groping once again.

Perhaps it is so hard to get hold of because it isn't really born out of a linear, cognitive thought process—that would be too modern. It is really more of an emotional reaction to modernism than a philosophical choice. I find it almost humorous to read how people analyze postmodernism from the viewpoint of a linear philosophical process, as though it were all thought out in advance and we all agree on a chosen philosophy of life.

Postmodernism is not a logical choice so much as an emotional and even cultural reaction. Although there are a few who are more philosophical about their postmodern worldview, I suspect the vast majority of people today are more a product of their environment and the reality of a failed modern approach to life. Their postmodernism is born out of frustration with the unfulfilled promise of modernism. There is collective resistance to modernistic values that appear to have resulted in a "methodical" approach to life in general, which appears to lack spontaneity among emerging generations. The linear rules and resulting logical solutions of the modern approach are not valued highly; rather, there is a desire to have relationships with many diverse people and see something poetic about things that cannot fit into the logical flow of a method. For most, this is a gut reaction, not a full-orbed and classified philosophical approach.

There really shouldn't be a postmodern manifesto, as though someone sat down and wrote out what our collective thoughts are and where we are heading. As soon as someone does, it will be offensive to everyone else. The collective response will be, "You can't put a label on us!" The gut reaction against modernistic classification is a strong and instantaneous distaste, emotional but real and not to be underestimated. It is not illogical, just not bound by a linear and logical taxonomy. Postmodernism colors outside the lines, because the lines are too restrictive and represent an old system that didn't work. The results may not be clean or consistent, but they can be quite beautiful.

Even the name *postmodern* lacks logic. How can we be post what is now? Does that make us futurists? The term really is fitting in many ways, though, because postmodernism is a reaction against something that is logically defined. Postmodernism isn't supposed to "make sense," in a classroom or a scientific textbook. It is more about what it isn't than what it is. Postmodernism's starting place is defined by what it is against rather than for; its end, though, may be very much in favor of people in all their creative and diverse expressions.

Modernism, born in the enlightenment, lied to us. It told us that the human mind could solve all our problems. It is a basic humanistic approach that puts human beings at the center of its worldview. President Lyndon B. Johnson declared that poverty would be done away with in his generation. Johnson is gone, and poverty remains. Science promised we could eliminate all disease, as it did with smallpox. Today we have more disease than ever, new diseases running rampant . . . and smallpox threatening a comeback. Modernism has failed. Welcome to a world after modernism. The emerging postmodern world lacks some definition because it is more a reaction against the old worldview than a proactive solution. This reaction has some startlingly helpful analysis, however, and it has some inherent values that present great opportunity for the Good News of God's kingdom.

neither a modern nor a postmodern church

The church in the West appears to be quite threatened by the shift to postmodernity. Even though many see this time as dark and not valuing truth, I see some values undergirding the relativism that are actually encouraging. Perhaps another reason the church in the West may be threatened by the postmodern shift is because in many ways it is really a product of modernism. We have valued a linear and logical approach to truth, which is quite modern. We have tended to think education is our salvation and the more we teach people the better the world will be, which is also a modern assumption. In typical modernistic fashion, the Western church approaches spirituality with programs and new models of ministry, thinking that we can manufacture spirituality; it tries to solve problems with a three-step method that will produce a logical and linear solution.

As I unpack some of the shifting values, you will be able to see how the church of the past was at its core modernistic. Postmodernism has some valuable insights for the church, even if we don't buy all of its thinking. Perhaps more important, we need to honestly examine our modern assumptions, which have no more spiritual veracity than do the postmodern.

I do not want to do away with truth and replace it with a hodgepodge of ideas that do not fit together, but at the same time I do not want to be content with forcing God's truth into my logical and linear systems. I want not only a propositional truth; I want truth incarnate in a person with eyes that weep for the world and hands that reach out and touch it.

Propositional truth is truth presented in a verbal statement, like a statement of faith, a creed, or *proposition*. Truth can be presented in this way, but it is often seen as lifeless and out of touch to a postmodern viewpoint. Incarnate truth is lived out, in the flesh. If your truth remains a proposition and never becomes incarnate, it is just a statement of fact, not of faith. Jesus didn't say, "I *know* the way, the truth, and the life." He said, "I am the way, the truth, and the life." Truth is not just a proclamation but also a person. It is a "who," not just a "what." When we see that truth does not have only teeth but eyes to see, ears to listen, and hands to reach out and touch a leper, we can relate to it on a whole new level. Truth is personal and lives where I live.

Awakening Chapels, which I have been a part of starting, have been called a "postmodern church," and I am always uncomfortable with the designation. It is a church planted in a postmodern culture, but it is not postmodern. Awakening reaches postmodern people and may reflect some of their cultural values, but the church is not postmodern.

God's kingdom is not modern; nor is it postmodern. At the same time, it can flourish in both. Within every person and each culture as a whole are two conflicting realities: the image of God and the ugliness of sin. Culture is a collective assent of people living within the boundaries of their shared values. God's kingdom is always countercultural, standing in contrast to the sinful values found in all of us. At the same time, the kingdom of God redeems the image of God found in each person and in a culture as a collective of people who share similar values.

The essence of the Gospel of the kingdom does not conform to a culture; it transcends the culture and at the same time transforms it from within. Our mission is not to make the kingdom or its core message bend to the culture, but to position it in a way that is both appealing and unappealing at the same time. It must be appealing to people by calling out to the latent image of God felt deep within all of us. At the same time, it must be unappealing to the dark values of sin found within every person and culture. The Gospel does not need to be made relevant; it is relevant and always will be. The issue is not relevance but influence. Our goal should be to tap into the image of God found within a people and then offer the powerful alternative to being enslaved to sin.

We will discover that recognizing the good found in people is a far more productive start to a conversation than immediately shining a spotlight on the darker, but still valued, parts of their soul. By acknowledging the God image, we are not endorsing all the ugly parts of a culture; we are simply being good news for people designed to hear it and ultimately to bear it. Some will awaken to this primal connection within, and others will reject it in favor of the darker values. The church that grows from the soil of the culture will hopefully well represent the God-image values found within that culture but also stand in contrast to the evil values found there—and thereby be both appealing and unappealing.

shifting values of an emerging world

Because postmodernism is largely an emotional reaction, it can best be understood with values. Values express how people feel about things and what is important to them. Because values are an expression of what you want, they also cast a shadow against what you are not choosing. In other words, you choose to value one thing at the expense of another. To me, a list of values stated simply in the positive and isolated from choices lacks potency. Void of a contrast, values leave all the options of other values as equally unchosen. This can be deceptive because in reality any true value is chosen instead of another one. You must value one thing over another, or it isn't a value. It is simply a prefer-ence, which can reflect a deeper value, but not the whole of it. A value should represent a deeper conviction, one that is consis-tently demonstrated in choices, actions, and statements. A value reflects something of who you are. A preference can change with the climate, and when it is not available then another preference will do just fine. It may be easy to change your preferences, but it usually takes a radical transformation to change your values.

I have found that values are best explained in contrasts, and since postmodernism is a study in contrast with modernity we can understand its values when we place them in contrast to modern values. If we look at the shift from a modern worldview to a more postmodern, we can better understand what is happening in the people of this world, the people we are called to reach with the Good News. You do not have to subscribe to either modernism or postmodernism, but you do need to see how God is shifting the world for us to be more effective than we have been in the past.

what postmodern culture values

relationship over mission

The modern mind was all about the importance of the mission at hand. Every business proudly proclaimed a mission statement on a plaque by the cash register to let us know that it exists for us, not our money (yeah, right). Every leader had a personal mission statement. People were valued by how helpful they were to the mission. People didn't hide their agenda but viewed all of life through the lens of their own task at hand. If you helped me with my agenda, then you were a friend, but if not you were unashamedly forgotten because the mission came first and was of utmost importance.

The postmodern values relationship more than mission. Even if you have nothing to do with the fulfillment of my mission statement, knowing you and spending time with you is of value.

This is the strongest of values in a postmodern context, and it dictates the other values. For example, truth is relative to postmodern people, most often because they value relationships with all kinds of people and don't want to exclude any. Because relationships are so important, lying about who you really are is the greatest sin because it leaves the entire relationship built on deception. Authenticity is therefore highly valued. Postmodern people want to know and be known.

Mission is still important to the postmodern, but it is secondary to relationship. Mission to the postmodern is more about a sense of doing good things than about promoting a specific market niche or corporate cause.

The message of the kingdom of God has always flown best on the wings of relationships. From the beginning, this has always been God's plan. I often take an informal survey when speaking to a group about the importance of spreading the good news through relationships. I ask people to raise their hand if they first received the Gospel in an anonymous fashion, devoid of any relational witness. For example, you were flipping through the channels on TV and heard an evangelist preach and got saved all by yourself. Or you heard a lot of noise in the local stadium and went in, thinking it was a Cubs game, only to find out it was a Billy Graham crusade and you accepted Jesus. Very few usually raise their hand.

Then I ask them to raise their hand if a close friend, relative, coworker, or classmate showed them the difference Christ can make in a life and explained the Gospel to them. Usually 95 percent of the room will raise a hand at this point.

I then ask an important question: *Why is it that when we consider ways to reach out to the lost we always plan events rather than using the natural relationships God has already given to us?*

After considerable research, Ed Stetzer, Richie Stanley, and Jason Hayes discovered some interesting obstacles as well as opportunities for the church that, until now, have gone mostly unseen. In their book *Lost and Found,* they tell us that "more [younger unchurched people] would prefer to read an inspirational book than seek inspirational help from a church. Remarkably, only one in six would go to church if seeking spiritual guidance."[1] At the same time, the study tells us that nine out of ten young adults have at least one Christian among their close friends.[2] I am not a brilliant researcher, but it seems to me that these two ideas are telling us something, and we should pay attention.

Postmoderns do not view "organized church" as a place to find spiritual guidance, yet 91 percent have a close relationship with a Christian. The question I have is, Why don't we switch our strategy from attractional church programming to something that empowers and releases those close Christian friends to have the real influence? Instead of reaching the 17 percent who would look for guidance at an organized church,[3] why not go after the 91 percent that have a relational connection with a Christian?

What's more, the research showed that about nine out of ten young adults surveyed who are not affiliated with church said they would be willing to listen to someone share his or her beliefs, and three out of five would be willing to study the Bible if a friend asked them to.[4] Almost half of the young adults surveyed also said they would be willing to attend a small group of people to learn more about the Bible and Jesus.[5] What are we waiting for? It seems to me we have an open invitation! All we need to do is shift our understanding of church from an institution to a relational community. But we have not made that shift yet. Almost eight out of ten young adults in the same research agreed that "Christianity today is more about organized religion than about loving God and loving people."[6] We can no longer afford to keep the church as the front door to God's kingdom; it was never meant to play such a role. Relationships have always been the pathway to Christ. Today, nine out of ten young adults believe they can have a good relationship with God without being involved in a church. One in ten believes church is the only place to learn what it means to truly be a Christian.[7]

A serious problem the church has faced in the recent past was that her people were separate from the world, in their own subculture, and had a difficult time finding any unbelievers they knew personally. We would go to Christian Schools, work for Christian organizations, and shop exclusively at Christian stores. We knew what a non-Christian looked like only from watching Jerry Springer on TV. No wonder our idea of reaching the world with the Gospel was often nothing more than sending the church choir to the mall at Christmastime to sing songs that are already playing over the loudspeakers.

This is all changing as younger people, born within a post-modern culture, emerge in the kingdom. They already have a relational bent that will help in the advancement of the kingdom, way beyond cold-turkey door knocking and passing out tracts to strangers on the subway.

authenticity over excellence

A short time ago, it seemed as though every book on the nonfiction bestseller list had the word "excellence" in it. We all wanted to separate ourselves from the rest of the pack by our standards of excellence. A simple search of Amazon.com for books with the word excellence in it resulted in 153,744 options.

Today things have changed. Authenticity is more valued than excellence. People have found that it is possible to have excellence and yet not be real. They have seen too many who have a façade of quality but in truth are shallow and lack substance. This is why authenticity is so important. Postmodern people can smell a lack of authenticity immediately.

One day, on a short puddle-jumper flight from Bloomington, Indiana, to Chicago, a student and I were the only passengers. Because of so few passengers the attendants asked us to sit in the back next to each other for balance (as if she and I weighed anything at all alike). We began talking and continued for the next hour. She was about to graduate and was on her way to an important job interview at a big corporation headquartered in Chicago.

I wanted to ask her about her goals and dreams. I expected her to say something about starting her own business, making partner in a law firm, writing books, teaching, or starting a family. I asked her with a smile, "So you're starting your new life; what do you want to be when you grow up?" I was speaking jokingly, but her answer was very serious. She said, "I want to be respected."

This is a good example of the values of people who are postmodern. She didn't really care what she did; she cared that those who know her best respected her for being authentic.

This desire for authenticity has even affected the not-so-real world of advertising. "Get Real" is a slogan for a popular soft drink that is on the same shelf next to one that claims "It's the Real Thing." Graphic images are not so crisp and clean with sharp edges, as they once were. Broken letters, off-kilter lines, shaky camera angles all are more desired than the perfect graphic images of the past because these images reflect the reality of being made by people with all the foibles of reality. Logos that look as though they were typed on an old pre-electric typewriter are popular. When such images are seen as mainstream rather than real, they lose prestige and pass from the scene.

Reality shows have taken over many of the time slots on TV. They began on MTV with shows such as "Real World." Although they may be anything but similar to our real lives, they are unscripted and have a sense of "anything can happen" that keeps audiences watching. There is no moral to the story and no hidden subplot, but the shows have a sense of intrigue with their unpredictable twists and turns. Audiences may also identify more with the people on the shows, even in surreal circumstances, than they do with actors speaking lines that were written by committee in a third-floor room at the network's offices.

Of course, all of this is just a corrupted expression. Real authenticity will always shine in the sea of the pseudoreal that is pumped at us through the media. There is nothing real at all about "Real World." The popularity of these shows indicates that people want something that is authentic, but they are being left unsatisfied with what the world is offering.

The highest compliment, for a postmodern, is to hear you are real. The greatest offense is to try to be something you are not. Hypocrisy is a crime of high treason. In fact, there is hardly another sin that is worse. Whereas heresy was the worst thing for the modern person, hypocrisy is the unforgivable sin to the postmodern. Hypocrisy is the new heresy of the postmodern world.

Even though they value authenticity over excellence, don't be mistaken: the postmodern may still perform with excellence, but only if it is all about authenticity first and never at the expense of being real.

This is a chance for the kingdom of God to shine brightly among the darkness of fake real. We can show people a new reality that is more real than the superficial lies being thrust on us all. I commend people for their value of authenticity because it is close to the heart of God. Satan is a father of lies; Jesus is truth incarnate. He is real. We don't need a postmodern advertising campaign to show the world how real He is; we just need to let people encounter Him themselves.

experience over proposition

Because modernism was built on the rational mind, all solutions were found by discovering the right formula, ordering the right set of propositions so they added up logically. Your proposition was evaluated by how it stood up to the scrutiny of reasoned thought, so knowing and saying things that are correct was valued.

Today, people are looking to experience what is important, not just hear about it. This is becoming an experiential culture. The occult and witchcraft are on the rise because they offer a spiritual experience beyond sitting in a pew and hearing about the spiritual world. The pattern of the modern church used to be: believe, behave, and belong. Today we must see a new pattern where people first belong, then behave, and finally believe. Intellectual assent to a set of propositions is no longer what people want or expect from the collective. They want to associate, belong, and experience the church before any set of propositions is agreed on. We can know something far more holistically than simply cognitive agreement. Common experience can be powerful glue to a group of people. Delineating the group's beliefs can be much easier and even enjoyable if people have first fought through a real and formative experience together. An environment where propositions are tasted and tested against real life results in stronger conviction in a sound belief system. The beliefs that are the byproduct of such an experience will also have a far more tangible sense of realism. A set of beliefs without such experience, naked in a sterile list void of real-life testing, appears lifeless to people.

The postmodern says, "If I can't see it, taste it, feel it, smell it, touch it, it isn't real." Drug abuse is not declining, even though our best modern minds have explained all the ill effects—because people want to experience something more than they desire health. Similarly, people are experimenting with all kinds of sexual experiences. There are many people turning to cults, the occult, and Eastern religion, seeking a true spiritual encounter.

Extreme sports are growing in popularity because they taste a more real experience of life. To feel the heart beat faster, the adrenaline pumping through your body, to hear the air fill your lungs and feel the wind in your face: this is experiencing life to its fullest.

There was a time when many churches condemned people for seeking a spiritual experience. Imbedded in modernism, Christianity had become mostly a rational belief system where personal feelings were not to be trusted. A search for experience was seen as abandonment of the stability of truth in favor of pacifying one's own feelings. This is unfortunate because it has left many churches lacking any real encounter with the spiritual life that Jesus died to give them. Although we don't base our faith on experience alone, God questions a faith that lacks experience (James 1:21–27).

We need to take the Christian life out of the library and back into the streets, where the Spirit of God can demonstrate His fruitfulness and allow people to encounter real spiritual life. Jesus didn't die so that we can win philosophical arguments and remain stuck in the pastor's study or the Sunday pulpit. Our lives should be experienced in the crucible of the real world. If our spiritual life is not real, then it is not worth keeping; if it is real it should shine brightly for the world in darkness to see.

When we started our churches in Long Beach, we discovered some pretty dark and twisted scenarios that were forged to draw people deeper into the bondage of occultism. It was like a spiritual chain of events going deeper and deeper into evil. At first the coven and witches would simply meet people at the local coffee house. Every day the entire coven, vampires, and Satanists hung out, drank coffee, socialized, and invited people to a party on the last Friday of the month. People came to the party at the bar wearing costumes—black leather, chains, and lots of gothic makeup. After everyone had a few too many drinks and danced a lot, those in the coven came in and invited people to the next experience.

The last link in the chain that we found was an underground club called Vampiricus. A couple of our team visited the club and witnessed things that they still wish they hadn't. Almost everything about the club was illegal. After our brief visit, one leader felt that he needed to shower for an hour to get rid of the evil.

An exceptional evangelist, Rob, was on our team. At the coffee house he had befriended Jack, a witch and one of the leaders looking to recruit people. One evening, Jack confided in Rob that the lighter magic of Wicca was not powerful enough for him. He was seriously considering going deeper into the black magic that promised to be more powerful. Jack was hungry for a spiritual experience that could affect the world around him, and as he put it, the "tree-hugging witchcraft of the white magic" was boring him. Not only a recruiter, Jack himself was being drawn more deeply into the occult. When we pieced together what was happening, we decided that we would address this whole system head on. Some would say that there was not any mastermind behind this "conspiracy," but whether or not a human was engineering this system there was certainly a mastermind behind it, and we could not sit back and let it continue.

We agreed that the most powerful thing we could do was pray. Rob, Josh, and I went to the party on the last Friday of the month. Others on our team remained at home praying, and a small band took their positions outside the bar in prayer while we ventured inside. We stayed only a few minutes and were there with specific work in mind. We talked to no one but God. We went to all four corners of the large room, watching people, and praying for them. As we started to walk out of the bar, Jack was coming in. When he saw us, his eyes widened in shock. He asked incredulously, "What are you doing here?" Rob said, "We came here to pray." Jack took us by the arm and escorted us out of his party. On the curb outside, he squared off with us, looked us right in the eye, and asked, "What did you pray for?" I answered, "We prayed that the people would lose their desire for these things." I never felt such strong tension between two people looking eye to eye as that moment. I could literally feel the fear in Jack's eyes. When I answered him, a wave of disappointment and insecurity washed across his face. Looking disgusted, Jack grunted some obscenity and turned to go back to his party. We turned to go back to our homes. I learned that night that Satan believes in our prayers more than we do. We prayed for Jack, and I wrote his name on a card in my Bible and prayed for him daily.

He is like so many people, wanting to have a true spiritual encounter but not even considering Christianity because that religion appears impotent stuck behind stained-glass windows, not out in the real world. When such people get caught up in the spiritually disappointing bondage that the occult gives them, they either settle or struggle on in their quest, still never even considering that going to church will satisfy them. When the church comes to them and displays true power, they are shocked.

At the coffee house one night, I walked in and noticed a small crowd gathered around a young man named John. He was talking animatedly to the group, sitting up on the back of his chair. Curious, I walked over, leaned against the wall next to him, and listened in. He was evangelizing—for witchcraft. As I listened to him espouse the benefits of casting spells to shape events and move people to do things, I began to pray. I asked God to give me an opportunity to at least present an alternative. God loves it when we pray for opportunities such as that, so He answered me immediately. John slowed down in his talking, turned to look at me, and asked, "What do you believe?"

I answered John with calm but bold assurance, "I believe that there is nothing more powerful than Jesus Christ . . ." But before I could even finish the sentence, John interrupted me with mockery. He said, "Oh, when are you Christians ever going to learn! Yours is a dead religion, with no life, no power, and no relevance. Christianity has been dead for centuries, and yet still you continue. Why don't you try something that really has power and actually works?"

At that point I felt a little offended, not for myself but for my God. I was more than glad to step up to the challenge, with a challenge of my own. I said, "Really, you think that?" "Yes, absolutely!" he said. "Well then, let's put it to the test," I countered. "What do you mean?" he replied. I began to sense fear in him, so I continued. "Well, here in front of all these people, why don't you and I agree on something that we would like to see changed in some way. I will let you go first, and you can cast spells all you want for as long as you want and we'll all watch. When you have had enough time, I will pray, and I will only pray one time, and we will see which god is more powerful. Game?"

I have never seen someone back-pedal so quickly, and everyone else saw it too. He would not have any part of my little challenge and instead "had to go somewhere" in a hurry. The small crowd disbanded, and I left, disappointed that I wasn't going to be able to call fire down out of heaven to destroy the prophets of Baal.

The next hill to take was Vampiricus. We went there with a team remaining home in prayer for us. This time, we did not go inside but felt comfortable remaining outside. Jack was again there. We stood outside and prayed simple prayers, asking God to put something healthier in the hearts and desires of these people and to do something to turn their affections away from this evil. We then went home.

We focused the rest of our spiritual ventures for the next year or so on the coffee house. Many people came to Christ there; in fact, it is there that Josh surrendered to Christ. We had several radical salvations, exciting baptisms, and a few organic churches started out of this good soil. In a relatively short time, the entire spiritual environment changed there.

About half a year later, Jack came up to Rob at the coffee house and said, "I don't know what you guys did, but no one wants to come to our Friday night parties anymore." Rob replied, "Yes, you know exactly what we did." Jack confessed, "I know, but I still can't believe it!"

A short time later, I was sitting out on the patio of the coffee house with a couple who were being trained prior to relocating to Portland to start organic churches. We were sharing a conversation with a guy simply named TJ, who was being groomed for high-level leadership in the occult. In our discussion, for some unknown reason he casually made a strange comment that I know he came to regret. He said, "By the way, we all decided together that this café is now neutral territory and none of us are allowed to cast spells here anymore." Realizing that perhaps he shouldn't have divulged such information, he tried to change the subject. I was laughing too hard to let it slide by. He asked me what was so funny; my friends were equally curious. I said, "You didn't decide this was neutral territory. You just found that none of your curses worked here anymore so you had to make up some excuse." Obviously insecure, TJ tried to defend his comment, saying, "No, it's true, we did decide this." I then said to him, "Well, over a year ago this stopped being a place where your curses were effective. This is not neutral territory. This is now God's territory, and your spells and curses are meaningless here."

While he was still trying to object to this last comment, God spoke up in an obvious manner. One of our newer disciples, Scott, walked right up to our small conversation. Another young man was with him. Scott interrupted us and announced, "Uh, this is Sergio, and he just told me that he would like to become a Christian right now." I looked up at Scott and said, "Well, bro, you know how to pray; show him how to surrender his life to Jesus." Right there, in front of this insecure occultist, a brand-new disciple led another to Christ. God was stating clearly: This is where My kingdom has come, this is now territory of the King. To this day, the coffee house has a whole different feel to it than when we first came. One of our church planters even works there now, serving coffee.

About a year after that encounter, when I was attending meetings in Hawaii, I received a call from Rob. It was just a brief call because he was preparing to move to Salt Lake City to start churches. He said, "You'll never guess who just became a Christian." Rob is such a good evangelist that I knew I couldn't possibly guess; it could be anyone, so I just waved the white flag and said, "Who?" With a chuckle, he said one word: "Jack."

I learned that people want to experience something spiritual in nature, but when they go to church they hear a sermon and sing some songs and it isn't enough for them. We all believe that we have spiritual power, but so few of us actually take that power out to the streets and boldly let people experience it. Like Jack, there are millions of people longing to encounter true spiritual power. Our spiritual enemy is out there, baiting them with the false promise of spiritual power, and unless we go out there ourselves many will never know the real and powerful experience that living with Christ can be.

Two years after my challenge with John, he gave his life to Christ on Good Friday at the same coffee house. Jesus promised that those who seek spiritual truth will find it. We can be the ones who bring the true spiritual encounter to them, but we will have to get out of our buildings and meet them where they live.

mystery over solution

The modern mind loves answers, preferably the right answer for every question or problem. It breaks down every question or problem into smaller parts in a grand search to discover what makes it tick. We have discovered a lot in doing so. For one thing, although we found many answers, we also discovered that we can't always come up with a solution. Even the answers that we think we find have often created a whole new series of problems. The public grows weary of safe drugs being approved only to find out two years later that they are not so safe and are being removed from the shelves. It used to be that a physician was the height of the trusted professional in our society, but today that trust has been eroded.

We have reached the limits of this rational, scientific method of discovering the world, and we trust it and the institutions and professions promoting it less than we used to. We are discovering that scientific and technical organizations have their own selfish agenda and are not above corruption. Today, it is not just politics and religion that are suspect; it is business, education, law, and medicine as well.

We have tried to define life in a linear timeline and are waking up to the fact that life is more mosaic than linear and anything but formulaic, despite what the great modernist institutions still tell us.

The postmodern is not obsessed with solutions. In fact, mystery is more attractive than answers. The journey is better than the destination.

Life simply seems more poetic in a postmodern world than the sterile scientific world created in a modern classroom. Postmodernism fits better in a life of chaos and confusion, where things don't occur in an orderly fashion as they would in an artificial laboratory environment. The church planters of the future won't follow the corporate formula passed down from their fathers. They will be artists and musicians, unafraid of trying new things and failing. They will be unmoved by the façade of success dictated by desired results and measurable milestones. They are not in pursuit of the end as much as the path of discovery itself.

Rather than a formulaic approach to reaching this world that offers a four-step solution to all of life's woes, new forms of church will offer the adventure of following Christ in a lifelong pursuit through hell and high water. Rather than a simplistic solution to life difficulties that no longer rings true, the kingdom of God offers a real relationship with a God who has suffered injustice Himself and suffers alongside us as we walk through life together. Gone are the days of "Ten Rules to Success in Your Life." Now the message is of the kingdom that has mystery, paradox, and poetry. This is a message that finds meaning in relationship and in experience. The Gospel has always had those characteristics, but our modern mind-set could not see or appreciate them as we can now.

One of Paul's favorite terms in speaking of church life was "mystery." We have spent too long in our modern mind-set trying to explain all mystery, and we have lost sight of the mystery in faith. When people come to the door with religions that have all the answers, I am skeptical. If you can explain everything about your God, then your God is pretty small. I love the Triune Godhead because it is beyond my full grasp. I don't apologize for that; I revel in it. I am frankly bored with theologians who have nothing but answers. I am more intrigued with a question and the quest it can initiate.

diversity over uniformity

The days of wearing uniforms in church are gone—and I'm not picking on the Salvation Army here. At one time, when you went to church everybody wore clothing of the same color and style as they led worship in a service. Today, not only will the styles of clothing differ; so will the kinds of people.

Postmodernism was born in cities amid growing diversity. It acknowledges and values the diversity of a world that gets smaller every day thanks to technology, trade, and people migration. The modern mind-set valued tolerance, but tolerance is not enough for the postmodern who needs diversity.

For postmoderns, a meeting that is all Caucasian or all African American is suspect and not inviting. They want more than tolerance of others; they seek an embrace of differences, valuing the beauty in difference.

The kingdom of God is probably the best place to see the diversity of God's creation, but that's not necessarily true of our churches. Martin Luther King Jr. used to say that 11:00 on Sunday morning is the most segregated time in the United States. But the kingdom *can* be different. I often find my eyes tearing when I read in Revelation the description of the kingdom being made up of people from every tribe, nation, and tongue (Rev. 7:9–10).

In my little church, over the last few years you would meet people who are Mexican, Romanian, African American, Caucasian, Samoan, Chilean, Palestinian, Egyptian, Native American, and Cambodian. We have poor unemployed people, college students (often these first two groups mentioned here are the same), wealthy business owners, homeless people, and hard-working middle-class people struggling from paycheck to paycheck. We have people in their late sixties and some toddlers wobbling from lap to lap hoping for a second cookie from a friendly church member. We used to have two wheelchairs present every night. This church has sent missionaries to relocate overseas, starting similar churches in France, Spain, North Africa, Cyprus, and Japan.

Though probably not impressive for many large urban churches, this is a church of between twelve and fifteen people meeting in a living room!

Such a church is attractive to someone who wants intimate relationships with real people in an experiential context and is looking for expressions of diversity. This is what I believe the church of the future will look like.

journey over destination

In modernist thinking, the finished product itself was the reason for putting in the work creating it. Today this is changing. The creative process itself is now as important as the product or destination.

Traditionally, the kingdom of God has been packaged as a one-time gift that, once received, is done. But the Bible describes a process. We are all in a journey from glory to glory. Our salvation is past, present, and future. We begin a life-changing process that has no ceiling to our growth potential in this life. Our graduation is not complete until there is a flat line on the monitor next to our bed.

Even the presentation of our Gospel should be more journey-oriented than destination-oriented. The Good News of Jesus is not just fire insurance for the future, or a get-out-of-hell-free card. Our invitation to the world is not just to go to heaven, but to live in His kingdom here on earth.

The problem is that when you are more concerned with the end product, expectations are vastly different from those coming from a process orientation. The bottom line is not as important as the journey to the finish line. I believe our churches will be much healthier once we are no longer concerned only with decisions to accept Christ but rather with the process of becoming like Him. I do celebrate new life, and we throw a party whenever we have a baptism. Personally, however, I have greater joy when I see steps of faithfulness on the part of new disciples that assure me these brothers and sisters are making progress on the journey.

When it comes to selecting leaders, having a process orientation can be far healthier than the way we simply look for already matured Christians. When we consider a checklist of qualities necessary to qualify as a leader, the problem is that we select people who are not necessarily still in a growth mode. I am far more encouraged by people who are moving forward than those who have reached a certain plateau of maturity.

conclusion

One of the most successful cinematic ventures of all time was the movie *Titanic*. Its story about the failure of a modern and "unsinkable" technological machine and the importance of real relationships, however short-lived, touched a nerve in an emerging postmodern culture.

In my view, the Western church is like the *Titanic*. We have bought into modernistic values and are heading in a linear and methodical path, full steam ahead, straight for an iceberg. The iceberg up ahead is the cold, hard fact that the world has changed and we are unprepared for it. In brevity and much summation, I have tried to expand our understanding of these changes. We face global opportunities, unlike at any time in history. If we can see what is coming and make some changes, I do believe that history will tell a story of incredible kingdom expansion and healing of nations in our day. The changes that are needed are fully consistent with the kingdom of God and the Good News of Jesus Christ, but different than what we have done in the past. There are several changes, or upgrades, we can make that will better enable us to be a transformative presence in this changing world.

In the rest of this book, I discuss the questions I am most often asked when talking about the organic nature of God's church. I have divided the rest of the book into two more sections. Part Two deals with structural upgrades that the church can adopt to make a much broader and more profound difference in the changing world. Part Three explores the pragmatic concerns arising when people consider a shift to a more organic expression of the church, such as how we manage ordinances, children, heresy, and finances.

part two

structural issues

3

what about the church's mission?

from coming to going

*The reasonable man adapts himself to the world;
the unreasonable one persists in trying to adapt the
world to himself. Therefore, all progress depends on
the unreasonable man.*
—GEORGE BERNARD SHAW

A LAKE AND A RIVER are very different things. In broad strokes: a
river is constantly changing, adapting, and moving. A river can forge
into rough ground and smooth it out over time. A river can
carve out great canyons and transport goods to those who are in
need downstream. A river can create energy; it is a power source.
A lake is constant and mostly unchanging. We can walk into the
lake and walk out in exactly the same place with no change. With
a river, however, when we enter into it we are moved and cannot
possibly exit in the same place in which we first encountered it. All
who enter into the river are moved to another place, taken into
the flow and thrust into deeper waters. A lake is safe; we can wade
in at our own pace and go as deep as we want to go. A river is dangerous and will sweep us into its momentum and perhaps take us
to places we may not want to go. A river seems to have a will of its
own. We can flow with it, but it will not bend to our will; all we can
hope for is to tap into its will and let it take us for a ride.

The kingdom of God is meant to be more like a river: a movement, an untamed surge of energy that can change a landscape and take people for the ride of their lives.[1]

The kingdom of God is not static but a movement. It has a flow, a direction in which its energy moves. It cannot go in two directions at the same time; one current will submit to the other and when the white water settles the two will have merged into one flow.

There is a current that we must all surrender to, and that is the mission of God on earth. The flow of the mission and the life of God's kingdom move outward, cutting through the terrain and bringing the cool water of God's kingdom to thirsty souls. Mission is not an option for the church; it is the *cause* of the church, and we must always keep this in mind. The church is at her best when she is on mission, for this is where she was meant to be—born to be. If you want strong relationships and healing within the church, getting on God's mission together can and will bring this about better than almost anything else. When we focus only on ourselves—teaching, healing, building up—mission will be lost in the busy schedule of self-interest. Life flows from the flow of God's mission. The mission takes us out, not the other way around.

I was tempted to entitle this chapter "A River Runs Through It," referring to the church and her mission. The truth is, however, that the church is found in the river, because the mission of Christ's kingdom is in fact bigger than the church. We are asked to join in the mission, not to simply add the mission as one of our things to do.

In this chapter I will define what I mean by church and being missional. We will look at the contrast between an attractional church mind-set and one that is going out on mission. We will also look at how we are meant to measure the success of a church on mission. Some material in this chapter will be reminiscent of my earlier work *Organic Church* because it is necessary to understand what I mean by organic church as we progress through the rest of this book. I assure you that a lot of new insights and information will make this chapter a worthy read even if you have read my earlier works.

what is the missional church?

The church is not sent on a mission by God; rather, God is on a mission and the church is called to join Him. The mission is not the church's; it is the *Missio Dei*, or "mission of God," that we are called to be part of. Andrew Jones of *TallSkinnyKiwi* blog fame points out: "*Missio Dei* stems from the Triune God: the Father sends the Son, the Father and the Son send the Spirit, the Father and the Son and the Spirit send the church into the world."[2]

Missional activist Alan Hirsch points out what being missional is *not*.[3] First, the missional church is not synonymous with the emergent church, which is primarily a renewal movement to contextualize Christianity for a postmodern generation. Missional is also not the same as evangelistic or seeker-sensitive, terms that generally apply to a more attractional church. Missional is not a new term from church growth; it has a bigger agenda. Finally, missional is not just social justice. We should engage the needs of the world, which is part of the mission but certainly not the whole of it.

Hirsch goes on to say: "A missional theology is not content with mission being a church-based work. Rather, it applies to the whole of life of every believer. Every disciple is to be an agent of the kingdom of God, and every disciple is to carry the mission of God into every sphere of life. We are all missionaries sent into a non-Christian culture."[4]

attractional versus missional

There is a vast difference between an attractional and a missional posture of church. The difference is not in the organization but in the release and flow of God's kingdom. With the attractional form, the flow is always coming into the church, which is rooted and bound to a geographical location. In a sense, the attractional expression of church is like a lake, waiting to receive from other tributaries. The missional church, like a river, is always flowing outward. One is centrifugal, the other centripetal.

The attractional mode of church sets up its base and stays there, hoping that others will come to it. The missional expression of church is on the move, probing the culture, prodding the people groups looking for those who are in need and responsive to the Good News.

The church is not meant to be sedentary but sent—"one holy, catholic (universal), apostolic (sent) church."[5]

a true-seeker service

In the Bible, God is always the Seeker (John 4:23) going after those who are lost, wherever they are to be found. He pursued Adam in a garden and Moses in a desert. He pulled Jonah off the bottom of the sea and Peter off the top of it. Jesus found Matthew in his office and Paul out on the road.

God became a man and squeezed into the world through a slimy, narrow birth canal, just like the rest of us. He chose to come to us on our turf, rather than expecting us to rise to His. Jesus preached everywhere that "the kingdom of God has come near." He came to seek and to save the lost (Luke 19:10), and He now invites us to join Him. He invites us to go to the lost— rather than, as is so often the case, expecting them to come to us. But, as I have said before, if you want to reach this world for Christ, you are going to have to learn to sit in the smoking section, because that is where the lost are found.

Many ask, "How can we make the church more attractive to the lost?" If we start down this path we unintentionally leave our true path: Letting people see how attractive Jesus is! It's all about Jesus, the true seeker of all who are lost . . . *not about us.* In a sense, for every step we take toward impressing people with our own strengths we move further from letting them become impressed with His.

With our current forms of church, it is possible to conclude that the more attractive the people are, the more capable we are of growing God's church. Our culture leads us to follow its assumption that the more skilled and beautiful the people are, the more useful they can be to God and the more capable of spiritual work. This is hogwash. In fact, the Bible seems clear that the opposite is true.

God always prefers to reveal Himself in the weak rather than in the strong. It is the simple vessels that often reveal God's glory more than having to find Him amid laser lights and fog machines. The curiosity of a child's question, the embrace of a loving grandmother, the accepting handshake of a good friend, the smile of a proud father, the warmth of a soft shoulder to cry on: these are the things that reveal God's character more than any sermon or worship song.

Love for one another is a powerful ingredient in transforming the world, but sitting in an auditorium listening to a preacher talk about it is not as powerful as being able to see it and taste it firsthand. A "neighbor nudge" for two minutes on Sunday morning is not enough.

When we teach about organic church, it is not the kind of church (organic, seeker sensitive, purpose-driven, whatever) that is attractive to lost people; it is Christ, and Christ alone. When we make it about church—what kind of church, what is done at church, how it is done, who the preacher or singer is—we miss the point. Unless we realize that it is Christ in us that makes church anything better than the Kiwanis club, we miss the plot. Lost people do not spend their hours trying to figure out how to get to church, or what kind of church they would like. The typical lost person sees only two things that church is good for: marrying and burying, and most are trying to avoid both.

Lost people *are* curious about Christ. It is not accidental that three of the best-selling books in recent years are about Jesus Christ: *The Purpose-Driven Life, The Shack,* and *The Da Vinci Code.* Jesus is on people's minds and in their curiosity. They want to be part of something that is significant. They also want to be a part of a close-knit family that cares for one another. I believe that an organic, relational, and missional expression of church offers a better opportunity for people to experience those things. Being another spectator on Sunday morning is not enough for most people who have not yet found Christ, and it shouldn't be enough for those who have found Him.

Coming into a living room and finding a close-knit spiritual family where everyone is involved, each praying and singing and sharing his or her inner life, is quite amazing for someone who has not learned to trust yet. Sensing the power of Christ working in and through such people can break open any heart.

I have seen toughened street kids weep in the presence of Christ among His people and just pour out their confession because of the conviction of Christ. I have seen Palestinian Muslims surrender everything to Christ in the midst of a spiritual family that prays to the living God. I have witnessed tough gang assassins surrender to Christ in prayer. Just recently, four fraternity students gave their life to Christ in a meeting at the frat house in front of their peers. Christ in us is powerful; it is the hope of glory. Simply being another anonymous person in a pew is not so powerful, no matter how expressive the music, how professional the drama, or how moving the sermon.

the cost is too high

The missional and relational church is also far more cost-effective. Relationships and spiritual connection become the valued currency rather than expensive buildings, technology, and promotional advertisements. Without any overhead of salaries, mortgages, or upkeep of equipment and facilities, money can be released to actually meet people's needs and bless people beyond another service on Sunday morning.

I often ask myself what non-Christians think of Jesus solely on the basis of how Christians spend their money. If indeed how we spend God's money reflects what is most important to our God, then the conclusions the world makes about the Christian God will be important. If you look just at that, the Christian God must be concerned with our Sunday rituals, more so than anything else. It would appear that God is also interested in the idea that we know certain facts about the Bible and that He grants more spiritual empowerment to those who know the most. How could non-Christians think otherwise, considering the great deal of time, effort, and funding going toward an hour-and-a-half experience once a week in which teaching is the primary focus? We could show the world the love of Jesus in so many more tangible ways, but instead we continue to invest billions of dollars in a once-a-week event hoping to impress people into becoming church members. Perhaps we think they will also give us money to put on next week's event. I am confident that our spending habits as a people reveal that we spend more on ourselves than anything else.

The typical attractional church model costs too much to multiply effectively. Buildings, budgets, and big shots are the roadblocks to reproducing churches. So are the salaries, rent or mortgage, equipment, and advertising that add to the long list of expenses. In today's turbulent times, many in church are feeling the resources drying up. Last week, I was in a pastor's meeting where many were wondering how their churches would continue. Some were selling off their facilities just for survival. I believe we will see more of this in the coming years.

Survival is one thing, but bringing the Gospel to a city proactively is another entirely. I have seen a research report that outlines what it would take to share the Good News with the people throughout the United States. The report lists the financial costs needed to reach particular cities for Christ using the traditional attractional model of church. The results are alarming. Reaching just one city alone would be astronomical. Atlanta would cost more than $63 billion.[6] New York City would cost more than $418 billion.[7] Where would we expect to get such amounts of money? I guarantee you that the government is not going to bail us out on this one.

Giving USA, a nonprofit foundation that studies philanthropy in the United States, in its 2009 report found $106.89 billion went to houses of worship and denominational organizations in 2008.[8] That entire amount could reach only the greater Washington, D.C., area and would leave the rest of our country lost. Of course, if it did go to that cause, it would not cover any of the costs of all our current churches and ministries, and they would all go out of business. This says nothing of missions to the rest of the world.

If you compare the attractional model to the organic or missional model of church, I think you will find the cost alone makes it clear which is a more reasonable approach.

This is just not a good way to reach a city for Christ, let alone a world. There are better ways. We could reach cities faster and for a fraction of the cost with a simpler approach to church.

it isn't working

The attractional model of church costs too much; in the end, one must ask, "Is it working?" Thirty years ago, the number of attractional megachurches in the United States was only a handful. Today every *city* in the country has a handful of megachurches; some have two hands full and still cannot contain them all. According to the Hartford Institute for Religion Research, today there are more than twelve hundred megachurches, which they define as having a weekly attendance larger than two thousand.[9] This is a momentous change. You would think that this is good news, yet the truth is that at the same time the percentage of Christians in America has not grown, but diminished.[10] In 1990 evangelicals were 86 percent of American Christians, but they dropped to 76 percent in 2008.[11] What's worse is that we as a people in America are not better for it. Our culture and the values of our population have not improved; they have worsened in that time.

One must ask, "Why would we pay so much money to reach only a few people and lessen our impact on the world?" It is as if we are paying an exorbitant amount of money for a supposed cure that all data reveal is actually causing the illness in the first place. This is foolishness. We are so easily duped into thinking that because lots of people come to our services, and in turn supply enough money to continue offering the services, that we are actually successful. Others see this supposed success and launch out to try the same thing, and soon we have lots of megachurches all deluded into thinking they are the truly successful churches, when in reality we are losing the battle.

These churches, offering many wonderful programs and music to attract people, by and large draw Christians from other churches. The "Wal-Mart effect" is at work here. A large full-service, big-box church opens up and the smaller family-style congregations close their doors, unable to compete with the productions and programs of the bigger church. I cannot celebrate that as success.

I am not saying that every attractional megachurch is reaching only Christians. There are always some exceptions to the rule. For the most part, however, I do believe that the megachurches are attracting people who find Christian worship music and preaching attractive, which would adequately describe only a small segment of our society today: Christians. Most who do not follow Christ are not attracted by these things; sorry, but it is pretty obvious to them. It is time *we* realize it. Granted, conversions are not all that being missional is about, but it is the core of what it means to be missional.

We need to be about reproducing healthy disciples, leaders, churches, and movements, in that order. We cannot focus on reproducing complex and expensive systems if we do not first reproduce the simpler and more basic entities. We do not start churches to make disciples. We must make disciples, and then start churches. It doesn't cost a dime to make a disciple; it only costs one's life.

empowered versus entertained people

For me, however, the greatest advantage of organic church is that regular Christians are empowered to do the work of the kingdom and are not waiting for the professionals to do it for them. My hope and dream is to unleash an army of ordinary Christians empowered with Christ on a sleeping world. Organic church can do that. It makes all of us priests, and everything is sacred. To the pure, all things are pure. All of us are called to ministry. All are ordained. A job at Hewlett-Packard is a holy calling into ministry. The workplace becomes a sacred calling for the ordinary believer to bring the kingdom of God into a place yearning for light.

In organic church thinking, Christian leaders are no longer to do the work of the ministry, but to equip the Christians to do the work. Evangelists are not called to reach the lost, but to equip the saints to do so. Teachers are not just called to teach, but to equip Christians to teach. We could see ordinary Christians fulfill the great commission by "teaching them to observe all that (Christ has) commanded (us)" (Matt. 28:20). This is a revolution that will turn church as we know it upside down, and in the process all the passive Christians will be poured out into the world like salt out of a saltshaker. Wow—now, that will change the world!

People find a mission that is larger than themselves compelling. They want to change the world. They do not respond in the same way to a church that is sedentary and waiting for the world to come to it.

In most forms of church, we ask for volunteers all the time. We offer spiritual-gift assessments to see where people fit best into our program, but we never really offer challenging experiences. Handing out bulletins, directing traffic wearing a bright orange vest, chaperoning a youth function, or changing a diaper in the nursery may be helpful for the church program, but none of them is a task worth giving your life to. Many who struggle to do these things have a nagging unspoken question: "Did Jesus come so I can do *this*?"

We must transition from seeing church as a once-a-week worship event to an ongoing spiritual family on mission together. Then people will see church as something worth giving their lives for. Honestly, people need one another more than they need another inspiring message. You would be surprised what people will do for Jesus, or for a brother or sister, that they will not do for a vision statement and a capital giving campaign.

I have seen young people go to an unknown city at their own expense to spend a week there without any money, family, or friends waiting for them. With no reservations at a hotel and no reservations in their heart, they were willing to seek ways to bring God's kingdom to lost people, trusting completely in God to provide for them. Sleeping on park benches or in first-class hotels depending on what doors God opens up for them, these young people rise to the occasion with guts and conviction. These same radicals would probably not want to hand out bulletins on Sunday morning or take a turn in the nursery. Why would they volunteer for something so radical? They want their lives to count for something. I firmly believe that we have so few volunteers because we ask so little of them.

extractional versus incarnational

One of the reasons our spiritual enemy likes for us to stay with an attractional mode of church is that it also extracts people from their place in the world to join the ranks of the church. Instead of connecting to the world, it isolates people inside the church community.

I have met countless Christians who have spent so much time in the Christian ghetto that they no longer even know any non-Christians. In *The Shaping of Things to Come,* Alan Hirsch and Michael Frost refer to this as extraction.[12] Why is this bad? There are four reasons extraction is derailing the church from her mission.

First, *the new Christian loses the opportunity to grow into maturity.* In an attempt to protect and nourish a new believer, we often fall into a trap that actually does the new follower more harm than good. We protect the follower from stepping into an environment where she must choose to exercise the very faith she is purported to have. This opportunity to choose between what is of faith and what is not should be a crucial first step for a new follower of Christ. It allows the person to start exhibiting real faith in an environment that solidifies all that she has begun to believe. Instead, we make Christian life a safe, unchallenging, and anemic exercise in assenting to a Christian culture and beliefs and avoiding trouble. Overprotective parents can have a detrimental result in the lives of their children, natural and spiritual. I am not suggesting that we leave new Christians alone in a hostile world, but simply that we let them step out in faith and show their family and friends that they have chosen a new path for their life.

Second, *the contacts of the new Christian are left unaffected by the Gospel.* When an adult comes to faith in Christ, a special opportunity is presented. New Christians have a relational web of contacts who do not know Jesus. These people are probably at least curious about their friend's new choice. Even if at first they have a hostile reaction, it is an opportunity to reveal some true acts of faith. Once a Christian has become acculturated into Christendom and begins to associate primarily with other believers, these once-hot relational contacts cool and eventually die off.

Third, *the church is removed from relevance in the marketplace.* As a people who avoid the world at almost any cost, the church has seemingly lost any sort of positive influence in our society. Lobbying in Washington, D.C., for a more conservative political agenda exerts far less influence than Christ's sacrifice deserves. An occasional single hit from a Christian cross-over artist and a mention of Jesus in an acceptance speech at the Grammys is not all Jesus died for. We are always tempted to believe that a more famous stand for Christ before the masses will be the most strategic impact we can have. This is a grave mistake. The fact is, if we can have more impact with the people we actually know personally, our personal impact will be deeper and farther-reaching than three minutes of media attention on Fox News.

Fourth, *the community at large is robbed of God's kingdom influence.* When we cut off the natural relational ties of new followers in favor of building only safe Christian relationships, we move our impact even further from our world. The influence we sac-rifice by cutting off these God-ordained relational ties is in fact the most significant kind of influence the kingdom can have. In fact, this is the impact the kingdom was established for: a changed life. The church is considered by the outside world as a group that is judgmental and fearful of the world and wants to have its own subculture, and it is entitled to not have to pay taxes for it. We are amazed when we read stories of community gov-ernments that are hostile to churches having any stake in a com-munity, but I have to ask why they would really be motivated to want us there. From their point of view, what do we do to make our culture better? In fact, our usual stance is to want to rob the community of some of its people and cut them off so they can join our own subculture. Somehow, I do not see this as the way our King desires having His kingdom viewed. When Jesus was on earth He was always bringing goodness to the community. He fed them, He healed them, and He stood up to the establishment on their behalf. He came to bring justice and compassion, not a separated, self-important sense of entitlement, and He even paid taxes when He didn't have to.

what is a church?

Unfortunately, as the world looks at our churches, particularly in the West, it sees only what people have done or what programs they are doing. The world is not impressed. In response, we scheme and plot and plan: "What can we do to make our church more appealing to the people in our community?" This is, once again, the wrong question. It's as if we we're trying to boost God's approval ratings. It is God's name that is at risk, not ours, and we are not responsible for protecting His reputation. He can handle that, by Himself, just fine.

A better question is, "Where is Jesus seen at work in our midst?" Where do we see lives changing, and communities transforming simply by the power of the Gospel? Where do we see fathers restored to a life of holiness and responsibility? Where do we see daughters reconciling with mothers? Where do we see addicts who no longer live under the bondage of chemical dependency? Where are wealthy businessmen making restitution for past crimes that went unnoticed? These are the questions that lead people to recognize the living presence of Jesus, loving and governing people's lives as their King. When people encounter Jesus, alive and present as King, they get a taste of God's kingdom on earth as it is in heaven.

I have come to understand church as this: the presence of Jesus among His people called out as a spiritual family to pursue His mission on this planet.[13] Granted, this is quite broad, but I like a broad definition of church. The Scriptures don't give a precise definition, so I'm not going to do what God has not done. I want something that captures what the Scriptures say about the body of Christ. In one of only two places where Jesus mentions church in the Gospels, He says, "For where two or three have gathered together in My name, there I am in their midst" (Matt. 18:20). His presence then must be an important element of church.

To a church that has lost sight of its true love, Jesus says these harsh words: "The One who walks among the lampstands, says this . . . remember from where you have fallen, and repent and do the deeds you did at first; or else I am coming to you and will remove your lampstand out of its place—unless you repent" (Rev. 2:1, 5). To a disobedient and unhealthy church, Jesus threatens to remove the lampstand (representing the church) from His presence. The presence of Jesus is crucial to what church is. His presence is life; His absence is death. He is the most essential portion of who and what we are. He should be the most important thing about us, and the most recognizable aspect of us that the world sees.

In most of the definitions of church found in theological treatises a list of necessary ingredients is given including things such as qualified elders, regular meetings of believers, practice of the ordinances, and a doctrinal foundation. A noticeable absence is the inclusion of Jesus on the lists. If Jesus is missing in our understanding of church, He will likely be missing in our expression of church as well. Therein lies a huge problem in our churches. We have defined church by what we are and do, rather than by Jesus' presence at work among us.

In many of the churches in the West, ministry is done *for* Jesus, but not *by* Jesus—and therein lies a big difference. If we evaluated our churches not by attendance or buildings but by

how recognizable Jesus is in our midst, our influence would
be more far-reaching and our strategies far more dynamic.
Unfortunately, it's possible to "do church" but fail to demonstrate
anything of the person or work of Christ in a neighborhood. If
we start our entire understanding of church with Christ's presence among and working within us, then we will expect to see
much more radical change, starting with us and extending to the
neighborhood and the nations.

Alan Hirsch has challenged how we typically order our thinking about Jesus and the church. We generally place missiology as
a subheading of ecclesiology. With this pattern, mission becomes
just a part of all that the church is about. I believe Hirsch rightly
orders the thinking process in another way:[14]

Christology—determines ➤ **Missiology**— determines ➤ **Ecclesiology**

Christ comes first. He then commands us into His mission.
The byproduct of our mission is spreading His kingdom on earth
via the building of His church. As much as I value church planting, I have come to realize that we should stop planting churches.
We should plant Jesus, and let Jesus build His church.

Because we have been confused on the order of things, we
have propagated less-than-fertile works around the world. We have
planted religious organizations rather than planting the powerful presence of Christ. Those organizations often have Western
structures and values foreign to the indigenous soil in which they
are planted. The result is a misplaced priority in a new emerging
church. If only we would simply plant Jesus in these cultures and
let His church emerge indigenously from the soil. A self-sustaining
and reproducing church movement will grow that is not dependent
on the West and is more integrated in the culture from which it
grows. Rather than a group that strives to be separate and removed
from its culture, the church will be engaged and transformative of
that culture.

It dawned on me one day that the Bible never commands us
to plant a church. When the disciples were sent out, they were to
bring the kingdom (or reign) of God to the places where people
lived life. When Paul and Barnabas went out, they didn't think of
their task as starting churches but instead making new disciples

of the King. Our command is to connect people to Jesus as their King. We are to extend the reign of Christ on earth. The byproduct of this work is church. We often think backwards about these things. We think that if we start a church the kingdom will come and Jesus will be glorified. The truth is the opposite of this. If we glorify Christ by bringing His reign to a new place, the church will emerge in that place. It will not stay there but will be a church on mission to bring Christ to the next town and the next territory.

Church is not meant to be the agent of change; Jesus is. The Bible doesn't say, "For God so loved the world that He sent his only begotten *Church*." Church is the result of the Gospel, not the cause. In a sense we are confusing the fruit with the seed. We must plant the seed of the Gospel of the kingdom, and the fruit will be the changed lives living out their faith together, which is church. Hirsch comments, "We frequently say 'the church has a mission,' a more correct statement would be 'the mission has a church.'"[15]

While doing some organic church training in Asia, I noticed the impact of planting churches rather than the Gospel. We were in a church building that looked as if it could be found in middle-class America. I spoke on a stage behind a large wooden pulpit in front of an audience seated in pews. Behind me were four empty chairs that were heavy and also carved out of wood, and a large cross hanging on the wall. A pipe organ was to my left. The people even had red hymnals with the same songs in them that I remember from my first church experience. You have seen all of this before, because it is the way church has been done here in the West for a couple of centuries. The only hint of the indigenous culture on the stage was the carvings found on the chairs and pulpit, of native design. The missionaries, with the greatest of hearts, came to this island off the coast of China and planted a church as best they knew how. Fifty years later, it still looks like a "church," and the neighborhood around it has remained unchanged.

Dr. D. T. Niles of Sri Lanka had this to say about planting the seed of the Gospel rather than planting church expressions:

> The gospel is like a seed, and you have to sow it. When you sow the seed of the gospel in Palestine, a plant that can be called Palestinian Christianity grows. When you sow it in Rome, a plant of Roman Christianity grows. You sow the gospel in Great Britain and you

get British Christianity. The seed of the gospel is later brought to America, and a plant grows of American Christianity. Now, when missionaries come to our lands they brought not only the seed of the gospel, but their own plant of Christianity, flowerpot included! So, what we have to do is to break the flowerpot, take out the seed of the gospel, sow it in our own cultural soil, and let our own version of Christianity grow.[16]

I have taken to telling people: Don't plant churches. Plant Jesus! Plant the Gospel of the kingdom. Church will grow naturally from that, and reproduce organically.

The core importance of God's church is not how the followers are organized, discipled, or helped. The core reality of God's church is Jesus Christ being followed, loved, and obeyed. All else is consequence rather than cause. It all starts with a relationship with Jesus, and since Jesus is on mission to seek and save the lost so are his followers.

Christ alive, forming spiritual families and working with them to fulfill His mission, is the living reality of Church 3.0. The church really is an embodiment of the risen Jesus. No wonder the Bible refers to the church as the body of Christ.

When we lose sight of our true mission we can no longer determine if we are a success or a disaster. The mission determines the success or failure.

how do we measure success for the church?

Fruit is always about reproduction. The true fruit of an apple tree is not an apple, but more apple trees. Within the fruit is found the seed of the next generation. We are the fruit of God's kingdom. Christ in us is the seed of the next generation. We all carry within us the seed of future generations of the church, and we are to take that seed and plant it wherever the King leads us.

The difference this can leave in the soil of a people group is significant. Our backward approach of the past would leave behind churches that govern God's people. Perhaps if we put Christ and His kingdom first we would leave behind agents under submission to the reign of their King. The body of Christ would then be under submission to the Head, as it always should have been.

Our mission is to find and develop Christ followers rather than church members. There is a big difference in these two outcomes. The difference is seen in transformed lives that bring change to neighborhoods and nations. Simply gathering a group of people who subscribe to a common set of beliefs is not worthy of Jesus and the sacrifice He made for us.

We must shift from an *institutional* manner of measuring to an *influential* manner. Instead of the number question, we must look for the personal influence of the real church—the people. Many ask for benchmarks to measure success of the organization, as if *that* is measuring the church. It is not. The church is not the building, the organization, the programs, or the event. You can measure all those things and still not measure the success or failure of the church, because the church is something else entirely. Church is not a "what" but a "who." The church is disciples in relation together on a mission, following Jesus into influence in the world. Once you factor that simple shift into the mix, the entire equation changes. How do you measure the influence of a person in relation to other people? This is a far better barometer of how we are doing as a church or a movement. As I said in *Organic Church*:

> Church attendance is not the barometer of how Christianity is doing. Ultimately, transformation is the product of the Gospel. It is not enough to fill our churches; we must transform our world. Society and culture should change if the church has been truly effective. Is the church reaching out and seeing lives changed by the Good News of the Kingdom of God? Surely the numbers of Christians will increase once this happens, but filling seats one day a week is not what the Kingdom is all about. We do Jesus an injustice by reducing His life and ministry to such a sad story as church attendance and membership roles. The measure of the church's influence is found in society—on the streets, not in the pews.[17]

transitioning from institutional success to influential success as seen in acts

I like the transition that occurs in Acts. In the early chapters, success was measured in precise numbers that were added to the growing local church (Acts 2:41; 5:41). Later, the success was measured by how "the word of the Lord was being spread through the whole region" (Acts 13:49). Once the church transitioned to become a more organic decentralized movement, success was measured by how many churches were growing stronger in faith and being added to the movement daily (Acts 16:5). Eventually, success was measured by the fact that "all who were in Asia heard the word of the Lord, both Jews and Greeks" (Acts 19:20). Did you catch that? It doesn't just say that the word could be found in every place of Asia, as if the Gideons were there and left a free Bible in the nightstand—as incredible as that would be. It says that every person who was in Asia, Jew or Greek, had heard God's message! Talk about reaching a people group.

What happens when we celebrate things that don't matter and ignore the ones that do? I asked that very question on my Facebook page recently and received a ton of interesting responses. Perhaps the saddest was the simple reply, "You get church." Ouch.

We fuel what we celebrate. When we turn inward and hide in our own selfish bubble, we lose a grasp of reality. We become deluded into a place of selfish consumerism and passive opinions that count for little more than the whining of a spoiled child. Our true north is lost and we spiral into a deeper and deeper level of deception as we invest more in what we think is success. We think we are doing well when in fact long ago we took the off-ramp from God's true missional agenda and are now lost in a maze of new programs for ourselves, for our organizational prosperity.

Ten years ago some of us started going to a coffee house in Long Beach to make disciples. As I described earlier, the coffee house was full of people steeped in evil of many sorts. Within the first few nights we met witches, warlocks, Satanists, vampires, drug dealers, and gang members.

One of the first people to give his life to Christ was a young man named Josh. He grew up on the streets and was involved with a gang. He lived a life addicted to drugs, promiscuous sexuality, and anything else that kept him numb to the pain in his life. We baptized Josh in the ocean with three others. After their testimony, another jumped into the water in surrender to Christ and was also baptized. A few minutes later, two of Josh's friends also gave their lives to Christ and were baptized. This was indeed a premonition of the sort of kingdom impact that was to come, but not immediately. Josh's early growth was up and down, two steps forward and three backward.

Josh went through several years of failed attempts at sobriety, including recovery groups, rehab, and strong accountability. He could never keep a job, and though bright he could not finish a single semester of college. Then something happened that changed everything. One evening he watched his father and older brother fistfighting on the front lawn of their home. His father collapsed to the ground and died from a major heart attack. His brother hit his head and was in a coma for several weeks, suffered some permanent damage, and never fully recovered.

This event triggered a need in Josh to clean things up on a deeper level. He came to me one day and confessed many damaging things that he had kept secret for a long time. After he came clean, he started to grow like a weed. First he stopped doing drugs and alcohol. Then he got a job at a coffee house that he still holds to this day. He also started college and is about to graduate with certification as a respiratory care technician. Recently he even quit smoking. Although admirable, those successes are not the most important.

Josh became a real change agent. For more than a year, he led the church I started while I sat in the back of the living room, watching and listening. He led others to Christ and is making disciples who are also change agents. Juan is one such disciple who is starting many churches at Cal State Long Beach. Josh himself started three churches this past year. Both Juan and Josh are graduating from our TruthQuest theological training system. He has become one of our Greenhouse trainers and has helped lead the training in Chicago and in New Delhi, India.

Josh is what the church is supposed to be all about: finding people trapped in darkness, bringing them light, and letting them loose. A changed life and the changed world around them are the measure of our success. The Gospel deserves as much.

the world measures our success

For far too long, we have been afraid of the world and how it will affect us. Missional-minded people choose to have an effect on the world, not the other way around. In a real sense, it is not our testimonials, year-end reports, and newsletters that tell of our success; it is the voice of those who are not even in the church. Look at how Luke describes Paul and his band of missional disciples through the eyes of those steeped in the world system:

> And when they had brought them to the chief magistrates,
> they said, "These men are throwing our city into confusion"
> [Acts 16:20].

> They began dragging Jason and some brethren before the city
> authorities, shouting, "These men who have upset the world have
> come here also; and Jason has welcomed them, and they all act
> contrary to the decrees of Caesar, saying that there is another king,
> Jesus" [Acts 17:6–7].

> You see and hear that not only in Ephesus, but in almost all of
> Asia, this Paul has persuaded and turned away a considerable
> number of people, saying that gods made with hands are no gods
> at all [Acts 19:26].

"I get it!" came a remark from a pastor in one of Reggie McNeal's D.Min. classes. "I have been thinking all along about changing the *church*. You are talking about changing the *world!*" Reggie concludes, "He did get it!"[18]

We have got to set our sights on something much bigger than a church with thousands in weekly attendance. Contrary to what you thought, changing the church is not the idea of this book. That is a small goal not worth fulfilling. The only reason to shift from Church 2.0 to 3.0 is to change the world. Anything less is demeaning of Christ's sacrifice.

this scares the devil into hell

One side effect of pursuing excellence in church production is that common Christians become spectators who can contribute a percentage of their income to keep things going, though little more. We have raised the bar so high on how church is done that few believe they could ever do it themselves. The dark side of this endeavor is that we have lowered the bar of what it means to be a Christian, such that simply showing up to the weekly one-hour event with some regularity and a checkbook is all it takes.

My goal in life is to reverse this practice. As I first said in *Organic Church*, I want to lower the bar of how church is done so that anyone *can* do it, and raise the bar of what it means to be a disciple so that they *will* do it.

A few years ago, I had a lengthy and frank discussion of the difference between missional and attractional church with a famous pastor of a large multisite, video-venue, attractional church. We were going to speak on the same platform about church multiplication the next day, so we went to dinner and decided to put everything out on the table. It was refreshing and fascinating, and I know it was probably a whole lot more interesting than our talks the next day. The dinner was awesome too!

In the end, the pastor summed up the difference between us. He astutely pointed out that I view every Christian as an influencer, and he does not. He sees some Christians as not being made to take on influential roles in the church and needing others to simply feed them. This is a keen observation. How we view the follower of Christ can make all the difference in how we go about doing church. In the end, we left with different views in our understanding of church but, I hope, with a renewed level of respect for one another.

I will never forget meeting with an organic church made up of high school students. As we were all singing praises to the Lord, I felt His pleasure. I asked the students to share the size of the biggest church they had ever attended. Southern California has many megachurches. Several were mentioned, ranging from two thousand to twenty thousand attendees.

"I think Satan is more intimidated by this little church of fifteen kids than by any of those Godzilla-sized churches," I said. They all snickered and looked around the room at one another with smiles, thinking that the old man had finally lost his mind.

I then showed them why I thought this way. "How many of you think you could start a church like one of those megachurches?" No one raised a hand. I then asked, "How many of you think you could start a church like this one?" All raised their hand. The snickering stopped. It was one of those holy moments in life that are hard to forget. I asked them to look around the room at all the raised hands, and I said, "I assure you, Satan is terrified by this. And he should be!"

4

what about church growth?

from incremental to exponential

Every time we eat, we eat the fruit of God's
tremendous reproduction power given to plants
and animals. Look around out of doors; it's
everywhere—grass, trees, birds, bees, babies and
flowers. All creation is shouting it! This is the way
God works! . . . We ourselves don't make the church
grow or reproduce, any more than pulling on a stalk
of corn would make it grow.
—GEORGE PATTERSON

I HAVE GIVEN MY ENTIRE ADULT LIFE to trying to discover the secret
to starting spontaneous church multiplication movements. It was
an obsessive curiosity that has become a life calling. Unhappy with
anything less, I have abandoned much in its pursuit. One of the
things I figured out through many failures along the way is that
the potent DNA of a movement is not found in books, in seminars, or with elite scholars or specially gifted personalities. The
true ingredient necessary for a movement is not just in China,
India, and certain developing countries. No, the potent mix necessary to release a real, spontaneous multiplication movement of

God's kingdom is found in the most obvious but least expected place of all. All along, the secret has been under our nose—literally! The ingredient most necessary to start a spontaneous movement of God's expanding kingdom is found in the heart of every follower of Christ. It is inside of you. It is inside of me. It has been in us all along, every one of us who follows Christ and is indwelt by His Spirit. The "mystery" is "Christ in you," which is the true "hope of glory" (Col. 1:27). Refusing to see the potent seed within us, we have actually prevented it from spreading, and without even realizing it. That's an amazing thought when you let it sink in.

My friend Alan Hirsch likes to use an example to make the point. If all the Christians in the world were suddenly killed off or abducted by aliens, and only one little Christian girl was left behind, she would have all that is necessary for God to start the entire Christian movement from her alone.[1] The power of the kingdom of God is in Christ present within us. It is that simple and yet that profound. We mess things up by making it all complex. I am not discounting that certain people have gifts that are valuable in starting movements (in fact, I am working on another book on the very subject). In every case, though, it is Christ who builds His church, and if He is in each of us then the seed of a massive and spontaneous expansion of His kingdom is within us all. It is Christ who gives those very gifts to His church (Eph. 4:9–11). We must never lose sight of this.

The impulse of a movement is inherent in the kingdom of God itself. It does not need to be manipulated or added to for a movement to happen, but simply released to be what it was made to be. We must get back our confidence in the kingdom itself rather than in our strategies and mechanisms. How many times did Jesus shake His head and comment with a sigh of disappointment, "Oh ye of little strategy"? It is not more strategy, but more faith in the King and His reign, that we need.

If this is true, then there is a simple idea we need to grasp if we want to turn things around. If the movement of Christ's kingdom is already present in each of us, it is not so much that we need to figure out how to make it happen, but instead stop doing whatever is preventing it from happening. In other words, it isn't that we lack models, funding, strategy, leadership, or doctrine. We are investing too much in the things that are choking the movement and not simply releasing what Christ has already put in us. Could it be that we are holding back a real movement while all the time searching for one? I have come to believe this is true and it is slowly killing us. It might sound strange when you read this, but I believe stopping the mission of expanding God's kingdom with multiplication movements is actually harder work than the mission itself. I also believe that the mission is much less expensive than all our efforts that end up preventing it from happening in the first place. We could save money and effort and see much more effective results if we shift to a new way of seeing the mission accomplished.

Imagine a man pushing a heavy car up a hill, near the top. He wants to see it roll far and fast, so with all his might he pushes the car up the hill. As he fights against the weight and gravity, he struggles under the load, but he is determined to start this movement. In fact, all he has to do is step out of the way and it will do all he wants and more. He is the one preventing what he wants from happening. Every square pound of pressure he invests in this exercise prevents him from accomplishing his goal. He doesn't need to do more work to make it happen; on the contrary, he needs less—much less. Ironically, the harder he works the further from his goal he actually ends up. This is how I see the church preventing the kingdom from being the movement it is intended to be. We are often like the man pushing the car, not realizing that we are already near the top. God has already placed us at the top of the hill, poised to release a movement, but we are investing all our might trying to make it happen as if we were at the bottom, when all we really have to do is step out of the way and let nature do what it is designed to do.

I believe that a profound reason movements occur more easily in places and times of severe persecution is because the church is then prevented from doing things that hold back the kingdom, such as hiring professionals, buying and maintaining facilities, creating programs, and writing curriculum. Without these distractions, rapid and spontaneous movements can emerge. In a persecuted church stripped of any other resource or object of devotion and faith, Christ becomes more real. The Gospel is all the people have left, and a movement results.

All the movement inhibitors and impediments are removed; the church is free to move unchecked and with great power. Can we see this happen in the nonpersecuted Western world as well? Of course we can.

We can learn much by comparing the results of the Communist revolution in Russia with those in China. Both were bloody revolutions that attempted militarily to snuff out all opposition, close down all churches, remove all missionaries, and incarcerate all of the church leaders. Prior to the revolution, the church in Russia was centered on cathedrals led by priests and was distant from the everyday lives of the people. When Soviet Communism seized the church and all her assets, the people had nothing to turn to spiritually, and there was no movement. In China, leaders such as Watchman Nee had already made strides to empower ordinary Christians with the Gospel and let indigenous churches form in homes and places of business. As a result, when the revolution occurred the true church was still intact even after her buildings and leaders were taken away. In fact, the Cultural Revolution of Mao Zedong sought to eliminate all religion from society in China but instead mobilized the church; it grew from about two million Christians in 1949 to more than sixty million.[2] It is estimated today that there may be upward of eighty million Christians in China.[3]

Why did the church thrive in China and not in Russia? The foundation of empowering the common Christian in China set the stage for what happened there. The Little Flock movement and others were already in place, so that when the heat of persecution hit the church she exploded with growth. There was no such preparation prior to the Soviets' rise to power in Russia.

All the core ingredients necessary for a movement are already inherently given to us. In this chapter, I address ten factors necessary to keep a movement from stopping dead in its tracks. These ten factors are the difference from being a movement or a monument. I share these factors so that we can see how important it is to step out of the way and let the momentum of Christ's incarnational kingdom start to roll. Before we do that, we must first know what a movement is: how it looks, and what it is and is not.

what is a movement?

David Garrison does an outstanding job of describing church planting movements in his excellent book by the same name: *Church Planting Movements* (CPM). He defines a *CPM* as a rapid multiplication of indigenous churches planting churches that sweeps through a people group or population segment.[4] According to Garrison, there are ten essential ingredients in a church planting movement[5]:

1. *Extraordinary prayer.* Wherever the church spawns a movement, prayer is at the center and is pervasive and continuous. There was prayer ongoing in Hernhutt during the Moravian movement twenty-four hours a day, seven days a week for more than a hundred years.
2. *Abundant evangelism.* The Bible says, "If you sow sparingly you will reap sparingly. If you sow abundantly, you will reap abundantly."
3. *Intentional planting of reproducing churches.* Wherever CPMs are found, the people are intentionally setting out to start churches among people, and do so without even needing to be persuaded to.
4. *The authority of God's Word.* In Acts, the language Luke consistently uses for movement is "The Word spread."
5. *Local leadership.* To have churches starting other churches, the leadership must emerge, grow, and be deployed indigenously, and not be dependent on influence from outside.
6. *Lay leadership.* When a movement is spreading, there is neither time nor resources to educate, train, and ordain professional leaders. The truth is, whenever a movement starts to require educated leadership, it comes to a grinding halt.
7. *House churches.* It is universally true that wherever CPMs occur the church is found in homes rather than expensive buildings; the church is found where people live.
8. *Churches planting churches.* The natural manner of reproducing is after one's own kind. Churches are meant to plant churches that plant churches. We are to be fruitful and multiply and fill the earth. A mission agency or denominational board are not the means to start churches and were never meant to be.

9. *Rapid reproduction.* Wherever there is a CPM, the reproduction rate is shortened so that the multiplication rate accelerates.
10. *Healthy churches.* As with any living thing, healthy ones reproduce naturally and sickness can cause infertility.

"Movements" can be a technical term for any type of sweeping social change.[6] The Protestant Reformation was a movement; some may even say it still is. The term is applied to the American Civil Rights Movement, the Polish Solidarity Movement, and the Indian Independence Movement.

Simplified to its bare minimum, I guess the most obvious requisite to being called a movement is that you are moving, spreading a message of change or renewal. It is true that the term is thrown out a little too easily. Calling a denomination with declining attendance and number of churches a movement would be a misnomer at the very least, unless you can count momentum in the wrong direction as a movement. We run the risk of losing the meaning of the word if it is thrown out too liberally.

CMA is definitely a movement in the broad sense of the idea. We have spread from a handful in 2000 to tens of thousands across forty-plus states and thirty-five nations in nine years. There is definitely some momentum, and it is in the positive direction.

Church Multiplication Associates is not an easy thing to get your mind around. In a sense, we are a network of like-minded networks with varying models and cultures. We are not regional, national, or denominational. We are decentralized and do not ask for allegiance, loyalty, or dues for our organization. In fact, "organization" is a little too strong a word for us; we're not that organized. I have found the best word to describe us is, quite simply, as a movement. We work hard to create catalytic ways of releasing the power of multiplication in followers of Jesus, leadership, churches, and ultimately movements. We design simple ways for ordinary Christians to carry the virus of the kingdom to others. From there, we let it all go and grow on its own. Because we are so decentralized and do not have the usual handles of a top-down structure, it is difficult to grasp who or what we are. We are a movement, regardless of how other people perceive us or define the term.

In CMA, our training mechanism is what we call the Greenhouse. We use it to stir up the soil of people's hearts, scatter the seed, and douse the potential crops with water, all in a weekend intensive experience. We did fifty-two Greenhouse trainings in 2008, about one a week. In the early days of doing Greenhouse, about 20 percent of those who attended one started a church. If this is still true (studies are only now beginning to be conducted), and actually we have far greater receptivity today than we did back then, then we are starting more than a church a day just through our training events. We are undoubtedly starting more than that because this doesn't take into account daughter, granddaughter, and great-granddaughter churches. We could easily be seeing two to four churches starting per day this year.

Our very first Greenhouse training was in the year 2000. Since then more than twenty-one thousand people have been trained in organic church through our Greenhouses.

In 2007, Leadership Network sponsored a "House Church Report" conducted by Ed Stetzer's ministry that surveyed some of our leaders who attended the annual conference.[7] One-quarter of the leaders who attended the conference responded. There were ninety-seven leaders representing fifty-three organic churches contributing to the study.

The results indicated that 82 percent of the leaders were being mentored or coached by other individuals as one of their primary means of training, which is important in a multiplication movement. Discipleship in organic churches was significantly occurring in 79 percent of those in the survey group. These numbers are probably much higher than conventional Christian leadership would claim, but in my opinion they are not high enough.

The fifty-three organic churches represented in the survey started fifty-two new churches in 2006 alone—almost a 100 percent rate of reproduction. Over the past five years, 30 percent of our daughter churches have started granddaughter churches. That is a pretty high level of missional fertility for a Western context. CMA is also seeing a high percentage of conversion growth among our churches in the United States, with slightly higher than 25 percent of our growth through people coming to Christ for the first time. A quarter of those coming into the movement are turning from the darkness into the light. We hope and pray that this increases in the near future.

Some would point to our rate of conversions and compare it to the much higher rates in other places of the world such as China and India, and conclude that we are not a church planting movement. CMA has much higher conversion rates in other parts of the world as well, and if we counted the few who responded to the survey and represented works overseas, our conversion rate would jump to over 100 percent. I feel this is an unfair comparison because we are in a nation where Christianity is the majority religion. It would be irresponsible for us to turn people away who have a belief in Christ but want to be involved in this grassroots movement, even though this does decrease our conversion rate somewhat.

Our goal, however, is not to be a church planting movement. As I mentioned in Chapter Three, we don't even want to plant churches. We want to plant the Gospel, and the result will be a band of followers on mission together . . . a church. What I really want to see happen is best described as a Church Multiplication Movement. A CMM reflects the results more than the means. I know it is nitpicking a little. Semantic differences aside, I believe that what truly distinguishes a multiplication movement from a planting movement is that there are multiple generations of reproduction found in all levels of church life, rather than simply the addition of a large number of churches.

a basic lesson in math

I am no mathematician. My high school math teacher would chuckle at the thought that I would have anything good to contribute to a conversation about mathematics. Maybe it takes a simple-minded, mathematically challenged individual to help us see the obvious.

Basic math is made up of four processes involving numbers: addition, subtraction, multiplication, and division. In the sequence of positive numbers addition and multiplication gain in numerical sum, while subtraction and division reduce. When it comes to the kingdom of God we want to increase, not decrease, so addition and multiplication are preferable.

Multiplication is a popular topic in missions and church today. Unfortunately, when you look more closely you see that much of what people call multiplying is really just addition. A church adds a small group, and it is called multiplying. Another worship service is added on Sunday morning, and it is called church multiplication—but it is addition. Adding a venue for worship in your church or a satellite campus is not multiplying a church; it is merely adding. I am not against addition, but let's not call addition multiplication.

The thing about basic math is it is a world of absolutes; there is one right answer and an infinite number of wrong answers to every equation. If the processes are mixed up, the solutions are way off. In Christendom today we have poor math skills, and because of it our bottom line is wrong in the end.

Imagine what would happen if you got the two processes mixed up in other areas of life. What would happen if NASA engineers added when they should have multiplied? What if Wall Street mixed things up and multiplied when they should have only added? The results would be problematic at best, disastrous at worst. So why do we confuse the two when it comes to something as important as reaching the world for Christ?

Even if you add an additional church to your denomination, you are still not multiplying, at least not yet. Two plus two equals four and two times two equals four as well. In the early stage of multiplication, addition plays a part. The difference starts to happen with succeeding generations. If you merely add another two to four, the sum is six, so on. But if you multiply by two you get to eight, then sixteen, and now you know you are multiplying.

the momentum of multiplication

Addition is good, but multiplication is better. Addition produces incremental growth, but multiplication produces exponential growth. Paul gets to the heart of multiplication in his second letter to Timothy when he says, "The things which you have heard from me in the presence of many witnesses, entrust these to faithful men who will be able to teach others also" (2 Tim. 2:2). This is the key verse in the Bible about what it means to multiply disciples. There are four generations in the verse: Paul, Timothy, "faithful men," and "others also." Of late, I have taken to counseling people to not use the multiplication language before the fourth generation. Until we get to "others also," we have not succeeded in multiplication. It is possible for a strong leader to attract other leaders who, because they are leaders, will have followers. You can have three "generations" of influence without really multiplying. To get to the fourth generation of disciples, leaders, or churches, everyone must give everything away to the next generation. *Then* we are multiplying. This is truly the test of a movement in my understanding.

Multiplication begins more slowly than addition. This may seem to contradict Garrison's definition of a CPM as "rapid multiplication," but it doesn't. In fact, you cannot have a multiplication movement that is not rapid. This doesn't mean it begins rapidly; indeed, multiplication starts slowly. It gains velocity at an exponential rate as it goes—that is, velocity increases with every generation. Like the car starting to roll from the top of a steep hill, it builds in momentum as it goes. Every foot it passes in descent increases the speed and momentum, which becomes increasingly harder to slow or stop.

To illustrate this dynamic, Christian Schwarz and Christoph Schalk, in their *Implementation Guide to Natural Church Development,* give an example:

> Imagine a water lily growing on a pond with a surface of 14,000 square feet. The leaf of this species of water lily has a surface of 15.5 square inches. At the beginning of the year the water lily has exactly one leaf. After one week there are two leaves, a week later, four. After sixteen weeks half of the water surface is covered with leaves.[8]

The authors then ask, "How long will it take until the second half of the pond will also be covered? Another sixteen weeks? No. It will take just a single week and the pond will be completely covered."[9]

the seduction of addition

Multiplication may move slower than addition in the initial stages, but in the long run it is the only way to fulfill the Great

Commission in our generation. The population of the world is rapidly multiplying. If all we do is add disciples and churches, we will not even scratch the surface of what we have been commanded to do. Nor can we simply add multiplication to our current addition strategies, because each one has completely different requirements. We must stop adding if we want to start multiplying. Could it be that our commitment to strategies that cannot multiply is in fact what is keeping us from seeing a movement here in the West?

Because addition is faster in the beginning and multiplication takes time, we are often content with growth through addition. We are easily seduced by the more immediate success and instant gratification of addition instead of waiting for the momentum that can build with multiplying. As I said in my book *Search & Rescue*, "Don't be content with addition! Stop applauding the pathetic success we see in addition and start longing again for the incredible power of multiplication."[10]

In our current context, however, the success promised by addition is hard to turn down. It is so rare to have a church ministry grow at all that one growing fast with addition is desirable enough. It is hard to turn away from the glamour of potentially being labeled the fastest-growing church. It is difficult as well for leaders to turn away from the crowds and invest in the few, but Jesus Himself did exactly that.

Jesus knew the power of multiplication, and He was willing to wait for it. He rejected the pressure of the crowds and chose instead to spend His life with the few that would multiply. We need leaders who are willing to do the same.

the true test of multiplicative ministry

In *Search & Rescue*,[11] I mention some questions that have haunted my life over the last couple of decades. They have led me to a simpler way of living for Christ and of being church together. I share them here because they help us see the difference between addition and multiplicative strategies.

Here is the first question: What would your church do if one hundred people came to Christ tomorrow? You would probably rejoice and find some new seats for your church auditorium.

What would your church do if a thousand people came to Christ this week? You would probably have to start adding many more services and hiring new staff. What would your church do if ten thousand came to Christ this month? Now you are stretched beyond imagination, but it is feasible to hire a venue to handle that size of group for church. What would your church do if one million people came to Christ this year? You are surely beyond the limits of your idea of church. But the real question is not "what if?" but "how?" How can our churches be prepared for rapid expansion? In a sense, by starting with the sums at the end of the calculation we can see what we need to change to get the longed-for results.

Now, let's get more personal with these ideas. Take your current goals for your ministry and multiply them by a million. If you hope to reach one hundred people this next year and you multiply that sum by one million, you come up with one hundred million people who will come to Christ in a year. Does that sound farfetched to you? Of course it does; it is far from any reality we have ever experienced. Humor me: What if it *could* happen—would your current ministry methods be able to handle that amount of growth? The answer is more than likely no. Your buildings could not hold such numbers. Your staff could not accommodate the needs of that many people, and you couldn't hire enough staff to do so. You couldn't add enough worship services to your weekend or even your week to satisfy that populace. Everything about the way you see and do church would have to be altered radically.

The truth is, if you do not have the ministry structure or systems to reach that astonishing new goal in your lifetime, then you do not have the systems that will multiply. If accommodating this growth isn't possible, your ministry strategy is based on an addition model. The fact is that multiplication growth can reach exponential results and a momentum that is far beyond anything we can imagine based on an addition mind-set. The test of which mathematical process you are using is found in the capacity of the solutions. In the end, the capacity for exponential growth and that for incremental growth are worlds apart. We can talk about multiplication all we want, but if the only key on our calculator has a plus sign we will never see multiplication happen.

You cannot use an addition strategy to produce a multiplicative result. This is just reality. We can't start with addition and end with multiplication. We cannot pretend that the methods of incremental growth we employ will result in exponential impact. Otherwise we're fooling ourselves. In a sense, you must stop hitting the plus sign and start hitting the × key if you want to change the results from incremental to exponential. Hitting the addition key harder and more frequently will not result in multiplication, only more addition.

If you are tempted to think that the difference between a multiplication movement and addition is not that important, then you have not read far in the Bible. The first thing God ever said to man had nothing to do with a garden or a tree, but was a command to multiply: "Be fruitful and multiply and fill the earth" (not the garden). I am struck by the fact that even the vilest and most evil of men have obeyed God's first command, while the average church in the West has not!

The last word Jesus gave to His disciples was to also multiply. The Great Commission in Matthew 28 contains implicitly within it the imperative to multiply. It is a command to make disciples by teaching them to obey His commands, which include the command to make disciples. Everyone is to teach one to reach another one. This is the way a multiplication movement starts. It never really gets more complicated than this, even though it could mean a movement that connects hundreds of thousands, even millions or billions of lives.

Like the car that is just starting to roll, a movement is most vulnerable to being stopped early on, when the slope is not steep and the momentum is weak or nonexistent. As it gets rolling faster and faster and the hill becomes steeper, it's harder and harder to stop the car. If the same man tried to stop the car halfway down the hill, he would be just a grease spot on the road and the car would not even pause as it rolled over him.

In the same way, we determine the success of any movement by how we begin it. If we start out with addition, we never let the intrinsic power of a multiplication movement emerge as it naturally should.

In many ways, our church organizations, addition-oriented goals, need for control, and desire for dynamic and irreplaceable personalities in leadership all tend to interrupt the outflow of the movement before it ever gets started.

what church multiplication is not

In my attempt to help you understand what a multiplication movement looks like, it may be useful to start with what it isn't. This is one way of debunking the assumption that you can multiply by just fidding with addition strategies you may already be using. Multiplication is a complete and radical departure, as you'll see later on when we get to the two absolutely necessary properties of a Church Multiplication Movement, or CMM.

First of all, church planting without multigenerational reproduction is not and never will be a CMM. I do not mean that every generation from young to old must be present in organic churches, though it is a nice thing when they are. What I mean is simple: mother churches have daughter churches, and then granddaughter and great-granddaughter churches. Simply having a lot of daughter churches does not make a CMM. Unless each generation is capable of giving birth to a new one, you are not multiplying, but simply adding (Figure 4.1).

A great many church models today start satellite branches and call it multiplying. A recent study done of the rapidly spreading trend toward multisite churches reveals that this is truly an addition strategy, not multiplication. In their book *A Multi-site Church Road Trip: Exploring the New Normal,* Geoff Surratt, Greg Ligon, and Warren Bird take their readers on a trip across the United States to show us what is going on in this trend. According to their book, on a typical Sunday in 2009 some five million people—almost 10 percent of Protestant worshippers—attend a multisite church in the United States or Canada.[12] Leaders at some forty-five thousand churches are seriously considering the multisite approach according to a recent survey by LifeWay Research.[13]

Surratt, Ligon, and Bird point out in their book about six or so "grandchildren" campuses of the multisite "revolution" across the country.[14] To date there is no evidence of a fourth-generation church plant or campus, which I believe to be the true evidence of multiplication. The authors cite three thousand multisite churches of two or more campuses. This would account for probably tens

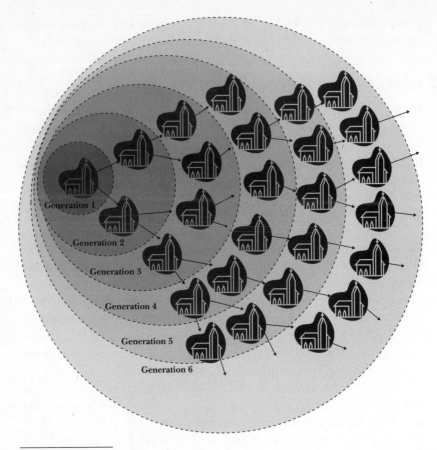

Figure 4.1 Multigenerational Growth

of thousands of services on thousands of campuses, and of that large number less than ten grandchildren can be identified in the United States, and no fourth-generation churches can be found to date. Addition is better than subtraction or division, but it is not multiplication.

Second, gathering and assimilating Christians from other churches to form new ones is not a CMM and never will be, no matter how many times you do it. We simply must stop celebrating such foolishness. "Sheep stealing" is not only not a church multiplication movement; it isn't even addition. It is subtracting from other churches to form new ones. Simply reshuffling the deck doesn't add a single thing to the kingdom of God. I guess certain denominations think they are growing even at the expense of others, but if they believe this is success then we have already failed.

Third, big revival meetings and evangelistic crusades are not CMM, because everything reproduces after its own kind. Crusades can reach people with the Gospel, but they do not start churches or become movements. They never can. The reason is that a multiplicative movement must have units multiplying after their own kind. Just as dogs birth dogs and cats beget cats, churches must birth churches. If we rely on crusades to do it, then we are starting immediately with a strategy that not only cannot produce a multiplication movement but actually prevents it from happening, because it begins with a dependency on something else to give birth.

Fourth, a centralized leadership development institution that sends out many church planters cannot produce a CMM. In a similar vein, no centralized leadership development institution, whether it be a seminary or a church planter boot camp or anything else, can produce a CMM. A single institution that sends out many church planters, as Figure 4.2 demonstrates, produces only incremental growth.

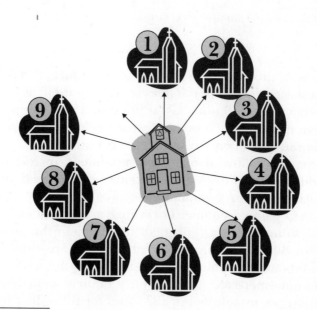

Figure 4.2 Incremental Growth

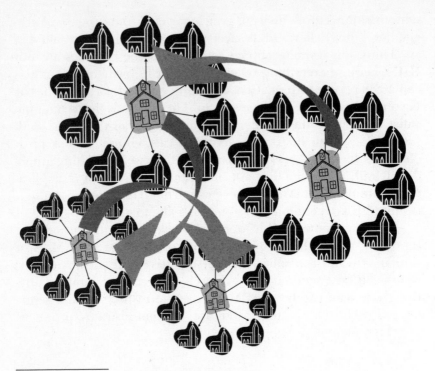

Figure 4.3 Institutional Multiplication Growth

Unless the institution itself starts to reproduce, this is only an addition strategy. Yet even if it does reproduce itself, as Figure 4.3 demonstrates, it is still not a CMM but only a leadership training institution movement. Granted, if we actually saw such a thing it would be cause to celebrate, even if it were not a CMM.

I have only heard of one such movement, in Indonesia. It is the Evangelical Theological Seminary, pioneered by Chris Marantika. This unique seminary requires its students to plant a church in order to graduate. Their goal, articulated as "1:1:1," is to have a church in every village of Indonesia in this generation (by 2015). Successful and qualified students are then encouraged to also start a seminary extension using the same curriculum. They have started around thirty branch seminaries since the first one was established in 1978, and thirty-two hundred new churches have been started by the students.

As admirable as this is, it is still not a CMM. The problem is that the church is not seen as sufficient to reproduce itself, so it never does. If the church did reproduce with leadership grown from within, then the institution would not be needed.

To have a multiplication movement, all the units must be capable of reproducing themselves. There are two properties that must be found in the churches themselves if we are to see a CMM.

what a cmm church is

In order to be a CMM, a church must be:

1. Self-perpetuating: she is healthy, enduring, and will continue to live without needing any outside props or infusion of resources.
2. Self-propagating: she reproduces and will naturally start self-perpetuating groups that will in turn do the same.

When you set out to start a church, if the church is dependent from the beginning on outside resources and organizations, it is likely that it will never reproduce spontaneously and will not start self-perpetuating groups. If this is the case, you have begun with a strategy that requires dependency; you have set up churches that cannot reproduce spontaneously.

A church may still possibly reproduce at a slower rate, but the likelihood that it will spawn a movement this way is nil. This is the main reason we advocate simple churches; they reproduce quickly from the start. Slower church planting models may work as long as they are reproducing, but we strongly urge people to consider the methodology that will reproduce more rapidly and spontaneously in order to see a true multiplication movement.

ten essential principles of a spontaneous multiplication movement

After many years of trial and error as well as studying movements overseas and in history, Paul Kaak and I created a list of qualities necessary for a Church Multiplication Movement. This list is in our Greenhouse materials.

A truly spontaneously reproducing church movement:

- Is decentralized; no central control center must approve all decisions. Everyone is empowered with the work so that the movement spreads to the outskirts spontaneously without needing permission or support.
- Is composed of self-replicating units of people at every level of development—disciples, leaders, churches, and even movements themselves. Every unit of church life must be capable of reproducing itself without needing persuasion, manipulation, or programs from the outside.
- Has minimal organizational structure that is dictated by the life of the church, not the other way around. We say, "Don't organize it until you have an it to organize . . . and even then, go slow."
- Does not depend on outside resources. All resources for the harvest are found in the harvest. Part of what a CMM does is redeem what was stolen from God by the Enemy. All that is necessary for a harvest can be found in the harvest.
- Is driven by ordinary Christians who have been transformed by God and who cannot help but share the Good News. Absolutely essential, this is the fuel of the spreading movement.
- Is relationally linked rather than corporately or organizationally bound. It is not an accepted application and dues that hold these churches together, but relationships. They are not bound in dependence on one another; nor are they independent—they are interdependent.
- Is characterized by reproduction at all levels simultaneously. This reproduction develops first in the smallest unit of church life and then spreads throughout, ultimately reaching the global scope of a movement.
- Begins its momentum with the spiritual, before the strategic. Personal transformation precedes community transformation.
- Moves evangelism from individual conversions to group conversions. Entire households, social webs, and tribes come to Christ rather than individuals.
- Is dedicated to having kingdom life touch the domains of society and culture, not just individual lives. The people of such a movement represent Christ's kingdom incarnationally throughout all parts of society.

developing organically from the micro to the macro

One reason it is important to pay attention to how we start a church is that the kingdom of God builds on a foundation of a changed life. Too often we shoot high, aiming at the more complex levels of church life and skipping over the impact of a changed life. The advancement of God's kingdom is not brought about by clever plans or dynamic leaders; it is carried on the backs of ordinary people who have met Christ, who have fallen in love with Him, and who will live and die for Him as their King. We need to recognize that all reproduction occurs at the cellular level and never really goes beyond it. Therefore, to get to the complex we must first multiply the simple.

In essence, if we can't reproduce healthy disciples, then we will never reproduce healthy leaders. If we can't reproduce healthy leaders, then healthy reproduction of churches is impossible. Without reproducing healthy churches, we will never have a CMM. If we invest our energies and resources at the larger and more complex organizational levels and skip the simpler and smaller levels, we cut the legs off any future movement. Jesus never commanded us to start or multiply churches. His command was to make disciples that can multiply. Figure 4.4 helps to show the natural flow of reproduction of life in God's organic kingdom.

roadblocks to reproduction

In today's Western church culture, there are three consistent roadblocks to church multiplication and reproduction: buildings, budgets, and big shots.

Buildings are not bad or wrong; they are simply not alive and therefore cannot reproduce. Buildings usually cost an exorbitant amount of money to purchase and even more to maintain. Perhaps the worst part about buildings is that they capture our emotional infatuation and ultimately our devotion. They anchor us in one place and become a missional black hole. This has been the status quo for so long that our buildings have actually become synonymous with church in our minds, and in the minds of the people we are trying to reach.

If it costs a lot to start a church, then it stands to reason that fewer will be initiated because the newer church will not have

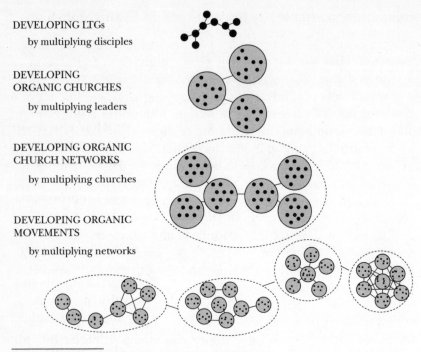

DEVELOPING LTGs
   by multiplying disciples

DEVELOPING
ORGANIC CHURCHES
   by multiplying leaders

DEVELOPING ORGANIC
CHURCH NETWORKS
   by multiplying churches

DEVELOPING ORGANIC
MOVEMENTS
   by multiplying networks

Figure 4.4 Reproduction of Life at Every Level

the budget, the financial wherewithal to repeat the pattern established by the mother church.

If key leaders who carry the weight of all the leadership are seen as needed for the church, this cuts off reproduction. Dependence on big shots—big names or prominent clergy—does two sinister things: (1) it dulls the regular Christians and (2) it exalts a few to higher status and importance in the church. Both of these outcomes curtail all reproduction from the start. This is not to say that dynamic leadership is not useful in a movement. Rather, the formation and reproduction of the church cannot be carried by the personality of one person; there will never be multiplication, just addition. Leadership in a movement is more about influencing influencers than it is about being the one who is the "face" of the church. For instance, if the vision comes from one person and is carried out by others, then there is a dependency that curtails true reproduction. Sound leadership in a movement is not coming up with the vision and then casting it to others, but instead helping others find a vision for themselves and releasing it to the ends of the earth.

beware the institutional trap

When you think of it, you could argue that every denomination was at one point a church planting movement. How else would you reach the condition where you have enough churches spread out around the world to be called a denomination? But in most cases a healthy movement has been replaced with an institution that eats up people, money, and time and doesn't reproduce. It seems almost certain. One can only hope to delay this inevitable outcome for as long as possible.

As I stated earlier in this chapter, the multiplication movement is actually latent in every one of us and ready for an explosive outburst if we allow it. No matter how we start, unfortunately we almost always end up with the same institutional stop mechanisms that have kept the kingdom from being unleashed all along. Even where the kingdom is unleashed, it doesn't seem to take long before the hardening of the categories occurs and soon we are in yet another institution. This doesn't have to be inevitable, if you keep ten basic operating principles in mind:

1. *Keep the focus on biblical priorities.* When we start valuing methods and traditions as sacred as Scriptures, we have become a religious institution. It is even possible to elevate biblical practices to a place where they were never meant to be and find ourselves institutionalized. The Jewish leaders that Jesus faced did so with holy days, dietary restrictions, and circumcision. It is not so much the biblical commands that are the problem but the priority they take in our spiritual lives. If we start to value our own religious efforts above the Lord's grace, we run straight into the trap of religious institutionalization. The methods themselves are not wrong or unbiblical; they simply represent a misplaced priority. Perhaps the most obvious example today is the priority we place on a Sunday morning worship service. This is not a bad thing from a biblical point of view, but it is not as valued in the Scriptures as we have inflated it to be.

2. *Lead, don't manage.* Once the people expect to be managed and leaders fulfill that expectation, the organization has become an institution. If programs become sacred to the people in a church, leadership is reduced to simply keeping things going, and going as well as can be expected. Management, by definition, keeps things the same, while leadership can bring change and progress.

3. *Make it about volunteers, not employees.* Increased staff creates pressure to maintain a level of income for the organization, and soon it is run more like a business than a spontaneous movement. It is hard for an institution to call for volunteers because the heart of the movement has been forfeited for sustaining the institution, and who wants to give their life for that? The result is that the organization hires its laborers and supervises them. That's a business, not a movement.

4. *Be proactive, not protective.* Establishment of programs and policies to protect the organization and or its leadership causes the organization to stop being proactive in the world and culture by turning the focus of its energies inward rather than outward. The world becomes a threat and the church retreats from where it was meant to shine as a light. At that point, decisions are all made to protect the institution rather than proactively engaging the risky mission it was originally called to. Defense is never the best offense, but sometimes a good offense can be the best defense.

5. *Focus on mission, not money.* As assets rise over time, risk taking declines. Managers of the church find themselves making decisions weighted toward protecting their resources rather than investing them in mission. Mission is sacrificed on the altar of wealth, under the banner of "good stewardship."

6. *Remember that leaders are servants.* In a typical institution, those in power are motivated to protect their positions. They shift from actually being a servant to simply being called one. People don't mind being called a servant; they just don't like being treated like one. It doesn't take long for leaders to begin to have an attitude of entitlement. It can progress to the point where these leaders wear special hats and robes, and people must bow down before them even though they are called minister or servant. They are seen by the people as being more

spiritual and special to God in calling and giftedness (that is, ordained) and thus are separated (consecrated) for holy ser- . vice (ministry). At the end of the day, however, a truly humble servant simply does what is expected of him or her. Nothing more. There is no entitlement. Our privilege is to serve the living Christ, and that is enough. All of us are called equally to serve the Lamb of God who sacrificed His life so that we can.

7. *It's all about the presence of Christ, not programs, policies, and precedence.* "That's the way we've always done it before" too easily becomes the mantra of the church. In an institution, getting anything done means following a policy and procedural manual. As the church institutionalizes, it eventually becomes a program that can be plugged in and operated with or without the Holy Spirit. My friend Wolfgang Simson often says that programs are what the church does when it no longer relies on the Holy Spirit. This is unfortunately too often the truth.

8. *Stay at the margins, not the mainstream.* Once a movement takes on a sense of prominence and recognition, it starts to value respect, and acceptance begins to move from the margins to the mainstream. It is hard not to see this as a good thing when it is happening. In the end, however, we are to be hated by the world and fruitful on the margins of life, not in the mainstream. Christianity has always done better in the shadows than in the limelight.

9. *Remember that it's about multiplication, not addition.* As the Christian movement shifts into an institution, growth shifts from multiplication at the grass roots to addition of programs, buildings, and staff. Eventually, bigger is viewed as better, and we are deceived into thinking that success means adding more people and dollars to an already fat church institution. More is never enough. We get seduced into addition strategy and never see true multiplication again. We believe that a bigger institution is the only picture of success that we can hope for.

10. *Keep structure flat and lean.* As the institution grows, it builds layers of hierarchical offices to manage, run, and support the organization. Each layer of fat creates hunger for more. It is a vicious cycle. Each new department that invests energy in programs to meet specific needs creates its own need for further funding and management, such that the entire institution is

a movement
of God for people

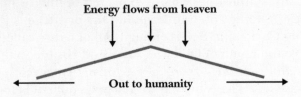

Energy flows from heaven

↓   ↓   ↓

Out to humanity

Figure 4.5 Flat Structures in Movements: A Movement of God for People

a monument
of people for God

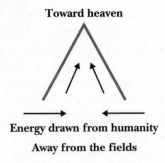

Toward heaven

Energy drawn from humanity

Away from the fields

Figure 4.6 Fat Structures in Institutions: A Monument of People for God

constantly growing. Each new staff member elevates another person to supervisor and increases his or her responsibility and need to be employed. Because those at the top of the pyramid feel pressured to keep everyone below comfortably employed, so they believe they need to grow more to do so. Growth requires more programs and staff, and thus the cycle continues to feed itself. The institution gets lost in this maze of "need and feed" and becomes more about self-preservation rather than a leaner missional movement. The further down the road of self-preservation the organization travels, the further away it moves from the original purpose and grassroots orientation. Figures 4.5 and 4.6 illustrate the contrast between a movement of God for people and a monument of people for God.

It is possible to organize a church around more organic and reproductive principles and processes without necessarily killing off what we have. We must take steps to transform disciples and empower them from the start to reach their friends, family, and coworkers. We can no longer afford to be content with addition strategies. We must be careful not to take steps early on that establish an addition methodology rather than multiplication. We must focus smaller and let the kingdom expand in influence via relationships rather than events. We must simplify everything at every level. Most of all, we need to believe in the kingdom, more than in our own plans and strategies. We need to get out of the way.

5

what about church models? part one

from congregations to networks

Every church that multiplies, measures
[success or failure] outside its walls.
—Bob Roberts

ONE OF THE MOST FRUSTRATING QUESTIONS I get is when people
ask me how we "do" church. Don't get me wrong, I appreciate the
desire to learn and always answer graciously. Behind this question,
however, is a desire to have a plan that explains how to do what
we do so that the person or church can deploy the same procedure. As Joseph Myers points out in his book *Organic Community*,[1]
this is a paint-by-numbers approach to ministry and always results
in a lifeless copy rather than the Master's piece.

The frustrating thing about this question is that people seem
to think changing a church procedure or structure will make
all the difference. It doesn't. This is why my answer is usually as
frustrating to the person asking as the question is to me. I typically say: "In a spontaneous church multiplication movement it is
important that we not dictate how things run, or we will inadver-
tently stifle the creativity and autonomy of each church. We can
suggest multiple solutions to problems that we have learned by

our experience. If you discover a new way to solve the problem, please let us know and we will add it to the list of suggested ways. What is most important is that you listen to the Lord in your own missional context and follow His lead. You will not be disappointed if you do that."

A new model of church is not the solution to all our ecclesiological problems. Any discussion of models should remain descriptive, rather than prescriptive in nature. In this spirit, I unpack what church networks can look like and how churches are transitioning to be more organic, and then I examine a variety of models of churches laid out for us in the New Testament. You will see that there is more than one way to do church.

The dramatic shift from Church 2.0 to 3.0 will undoubtedly change the very way church is experienced. For so long, a church and a congregation were virtually synonymous. This is so imbedded in our mind-set that we assume that a congregational approach is the only biblical way. The word *congregation* does appear in the New Testament in reference to the church, but it occurs only in reference to the Jerusalem church and once for the Antioch church (Acts 4:32; 6:2, 5; 15:30). Is a congregational model the only one presented in the New Testament? Is it the only way to be the church?

networks

Today one of the rising trends in the Western church is a move toward networks rather than single congregations or denominations. Many church-associated networks that are not denominations but cross-denominational lines have sprung up over the last decade: CMA, Acts 29, the Association of Related Churches (ARC), the New Thing Network, Stadia, GlocalNet, Vision 360, Mosaix Global Network, and the Orchard Group, as well as numerous others.

There is a fast-rising field of science known as complexity theory, which includes the study of networks. In his book *Six Degrees: The Science of a Connected Age,* Duncan Watts says, "In a way, nothing could be simpler than a network. Stripped to its bare bones, a network is nothing more than a collection of objects connected to each other in some fashion."[2] Of course, this broad definition can be applied to almost anything, from people in a network of friendships (as in a church) to routers supporting the Internet, or neurons firing in the brain.

Rapid technological advances have led to the necessity and growth of this discipline. Network theory crosses many disciplines from its parent—mathematics—to chemistry, biology and physics, sociology and marketing, and today even ecclesiology. Mark Buchanan, author of *Nexus: Small Worlds and the Groundbreaking Science of Networks,* mentions that "for the first time in history, scientists are beginning to learn how to talk meaningfully about the architecture of networks of all kinds, and to perceive important patterns and regularities where they could see none before."[3]

In a recent meeting of the Exponential Network, a network of networks, the churches that were represented varied greatly, from simple organic churches to mega multisite models. I asked many of the church leaders what the glue was that holds their churches together in a network. There were many answers, but a common element in all was "relationships." Some churches had everyone go through the same training. To become a member, others had people submit an application. Some churches were based on assent to a certain ideology. Others paid dues to a central office, and still others did not. Of those I talked to, each network included churches of a variety of denominations, rather than a single church tradition. One other thing that these networks all had in common: they are all less then ten years old.

the formation of organic church networks

My book *Organic Church* describes the formation of organic churches and the DNA that is the glue that holds them together, but it does not go into any detail about the formation of organic church networks. There are many types of networks. Some are more centralized than others.

William M. Evan presented four types[4] of interactive configurations of networking in his research published in 1972.[5] No one has really added to this observation in more than thirty years of scholarship. In an article about the variety of terrorist cells and swarm tactics employed in decentralized warfare, John Arquilla and David Ronfeldt expand on the three primary types of network (the dyad is eliminated)[6]: the chain network, the hub network (also called star network), and the all-channel network (Alan Hirsch's work *The Forgotten Ways* also cites them).[7] Arquilla and Ronfeldt point out that all can be without hierarchy, or even maintain a hierarchy within the various nodes or groups and yet still constitute a decentralized network environment without a hierarchy as a whole (Figure 5.1).

The chain network is the most decentralized, with each link further removed from the start than the previous one, and each unit is only connected to the one before and after it. The hub network is more centralized, though not necessarily hierarchical, because there is a connecting of all the units to a central unit. These authors claim that the all-channel network, in which all units connect with every other, is the hardest to initiate and maintain, but it is growing because technological innovation makes connection more possible even in a decentralized network. It is essential that in the all-channel network there be something (a cause, a common belief or idea, a shared passion) that ties every group to the network as a whole and to every other group. This can be the most fragile form of network to establish, and yet once formed it can also be the most resistant to outside attack. As the all-channel network grows, it resembles what is called a "Bucky Ball" (Figure 5.2), which is a carbon molecule called a *fullerene* that looks sort of like a soccer ball but is expandable. Named after R. Buckminster "Bucky" Fuller, this type of molecule resembles the geodesic domes he designed.

Within the all-channel network, it is possible to have a variety of the other two forms of network (hub and chain) occurring simultaneously. This all-channel network depends "on the existence of shared principles, interests, and goals—perhaps overarching doctrine or ideology—which spans all nodes and to which the members subscribe in a deep way."[8] In fact, as the churches and networks reproduce, all of them eventually resemble the same Bucky Ball diagram, which looks much like a molecule.

I have never seen an all-channel network actually functioning in CMA, where each group is linked and communicating as well as exchanging resources and ideas. CMA as a whole is the closest thing to an all-channel network, with the DNA as the glue

A CHAIN NETWORK

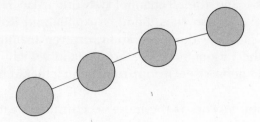

A HUB NETWORK

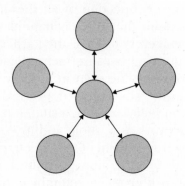

ALL-CHANNEL NETWORK

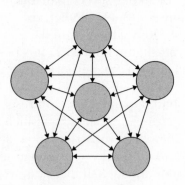

Figure 5.1 Chain, Hub, and All-Channel Networks

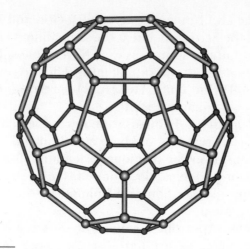

Figure 5.2 A "Bucky Ball"

that connects us all to one another and to the global movement. CMA may be the first global Bucky Ball organic church network. However, we cannot possibly engineer the communication process to maintain such a network with so many nodes born so quickly and others dying off just as fast. So within this all-channel network are a variety of networks that are chains, hubs, or a hybrid of all three.

I believe Jesus is ultimately building a type of all-channel network that represents His body on earth. CMA is therefore in the process of becoming an all-channel network. It will not be humanly engineered connections, but a more mystical presence of Christ in us that is the spiritual link. We cannot possibly keep track of each group and the people in them, but Christ can and does so intimately.

The only way for an all-channel network to be built is to reproduce churches with common DNA. In our movement, the DNA is clearly defined and accepted by all. It is the ideology of our network:

Divine Truth. Truth comes from God. It is the revelation of God to humankind. It is best seen in the person of Jesus and the Scriptures. In both cases, there is a mysterious connection of the Divine and human. Jesus is both God and human. God authored the Scripture, but at the same time there were more than forty human authors as well. Nevertheless, Jesus and the Scriptures are both without blemish. The indwelling Spirit of God is also Divine Truth. He brings the revelation of God and the frailty of humanity together.

Nurturing relationships. Humans were never created to be alone. We are social creatures and have a natural and intrinsic need for relationships. Our relational orientation is a reflection of the image of God in us. God Himself is relational and exists in a community: Father, Son, and Holy Spirit. God is love because God is relational.

Apostolic mission. Apostolic means to be sent as a representative with a message. We are here for a purpose. We have been given a prime directive to fulfill: to make disciples of all the nations. This part of us also comes from who our God is. Jesus is an Apostle. He is the Chief Cornerstone of the apostolic foundation. Before He left this planet, He spoke to His disciples and said, "As the Father has sent me, so send I you" (John 20:21).[9]

The DNA at the core of every disciple, church, network, and global movement is the important glue linking us together and connecting us to Jesus, the Head, directly (D) to one another as family members (N) and to the world where we are all on mission (A).

At CMA, the initial team of leaders starting out with a global movement in mind made conscious decisions all along our path not to centralize or create an artificial glue to keep us together as an organization. We decided that if the divine truth of Jesus and His word, the nurturing relationships of being in His family, and the apostolic mission He has given to each of us are not enough to bind us together, then we will not be together. We purposely chose not to resort to what we saw as lesser forms of organizational glue, such as a single name or brand, organizational dues or covenants, or some mandated methodology. We determined that Christ as Head and the resulting consequence of our being a family together on His mission was enough, and to substitute something less would eventually kill the movement. With this decision, we lost all sense of control, tracking, and centralized support structure. We often explain to people that we could not possibly count all the churches in CMA, which is true. We do prefer it this way as well. With this movement we will be able to see if Jesus really is enough, and that is worth it to us. We are still in the midst of this grand experiment, and so far we are not disappointed in Jesus.

There is a real, but mystical, glue that connects us all in the one body of Christ: "There is one body and one Spirit, just as also you were called in one hope of your calling; one Lord, one faith, one baptism, one God and Father of all who is over all and through all and in all" (Eph. 4:4–6). We are all connected. Part of our problem in our churches is that we believe less in this mystical reality than in our own organizations that we can see, touch, and manipulate.

We at CMA have chosen to let the presence of God among us be the only glue that binds us together as a movement. Though we do pass on simple reproducible systems that tend to catalyze the formation of disciples, leaders, churches, and movements, the heart of each system is this same DNA and demands nothing else from each disciple, church, or network. None of our systems are mandatory; they are presented as a way of doing the work, a productive and simple way, but an optional way nonetheless. We understand mandated methods are not compatible with a decentralized grassroots movement that continuously reproduces. Those out in the field simply must maintain a level of autonomy that allows them to hear from God and decide what to do in their specific context.

new testament church models

For many, the early church is the height of church health and desirability. Everyone seems to want to go back to the first-century model of church in hopes that doing so will birth similar results. Most especially want to be like the early church mentioned in the first few chapters of Acts, the church in Jerusalem. Many long to experience what they did. The truth is there are many models of church in the book of Acts, so to classify them all as one form of church would be naïve. The Jerusalem church is one example; Antioch is another. One can learn from the Thessalonica church or the Ephesian church. Each one presents a variation of Church 1.0 and each is different from the others. As I unpack the variety of models in the New Testament, we may find that we are actually not so far removed from the early church as we originally thought.

the jerusalem model: a homogeneous, local megacongregation

The first church is the Jerusalem church. This model would be Church 1.0. She was a wondrous church in her first days: bold, supernatural in power, joined together of one mind, extremely generous with its own (Acts 2:45; 4:32–37). This church grew quickly by addition, from 120 (Acts 1:15) to 3,000 (Acts 2:41) to 8,000 (Acts 4:4) in the first year alone. One could speculate that the counting of numbers was more important, or at the very least more feasible, in this model of church because with later models Luke does not record any specific numbers. This was an attractional-model church, with the vibrant spiritual life of the followers, the miraculous signs performed, and the bold preaching of its leaders as the attraction.

Although other ethnic groups were mentioned in this church, the core leadership and vast majority of the congregation were Jewish. Even these other ethnic groups had to surrender to the Jewish culture for acceptance. Indeed, the church started a separate leadership team to minister to the other ethnic congregants, in spite of the fact that the other groups were proselytes to Judaism, demonstrating further the lack of integration (Acts 6:1–6). Perhaps one can sum up the subterranean fault line that led to the fracture and demise of the Jerusalem church in the simple idea that they had no love for those outside their own people. They were inwardly focused and could not develop a love or compassion for the rest of the world.

The Jerusalem church started as a congregational model (Acts 4:32; 6:2, 5) with the church meeting in homes throughout the week (Acts 2:46). Once persecution hit, it is doubtful that they met for long as a large congregation under the apostle's teaching. Not that they didn't teach; I am sure they did, but I would imagine meeting as a whole congregation became ever more impossible. With twelve full-time apostles,[10] I am sure they could find ways to teach the people throughout the city without needing a large hall for everyone to gather in. We do know that by chapter 8 of Acts the congregation was scattered.

Of all the churches in the book of Acts, I personally believe the Jerusalem church to be the poorest model and one we should be cautious about following. Of course, there is much to learn in the opening chapters, and I would not discount the beauty and power that was evident there. The success of the church in Jerusalem is legendary, and I will not take anything away from it. I would add that it was short-lived and localized. Within just a few years, the church plateaued and began its decline; soon it descended into a cesspool of ugly bigotry, gossip, slander, and legalism (Acts 21:20).

What went wrong? One could argue that they quickly centralized and established a hierarchical leadership chain (Acts 6:1–6). They also welcomed in new "converts" from among the priests (Acts 6:7), which of course is not a bad thing (even Paul was one), but something else occurred. They allowed a Judaistic legalism to saturate the church and choke out all health (Acts 21:20).

The lack of true acceptance of other ethnic groups, even among those who had converted to Judaism, indicates a problem that eventually overcame the entire church. As Acts progresses, it takes great oration and persuasion on the part of Peter and James to prevent this legalism from killing the entire new movement that was born among the Gentiles (Acts 15:1–35). By the time you reach the end of Acts, you see the church so corrupted by legalism that many of its members would even desire to have Paul, the writer of almost half the New Testament, imprisoned or killed. Paul is forced to compromise all that he had learned and fought for, only to still be mobbed and arrested. Even in jail he is targeted for death (Acts 23:12–22). Granted, one cannot say that the church is responsible for all of this; Luke attributes these deeds to "the Jews," but by this time the Jerusalem church had become mainstream and was really viewed as just another conservative sect of Judaism. I am not discounting that there were true believers in their midst, such as James, but the elders warn Paul of this very sort of reaction from those who have believed that they are among the Jews (Acts 21:20). What is most alarming is that there is some indication that Paul was actually delivering a care package to the church from some Gentile churches abroad (Rom. 15:25–27). They accepted the money, just not the messenger. This is not a healthy church or a great example to us all. Within only forty years (by 70 A.D.), the church was dead and gone forever.

I personally do not believe that the demise of the church was strictly because of structural issues or hierarchical development. The issue is much more basic. It is a matter of that church's DNA. The church was not obedient to the Head. In the beginning Jesus laid out, strongly and clearly, that His plan for the church was to receive an explosive power within that would spread out to the ends of the earth. He said: "You will receive power when the Holy Spirit has come upon you; and you shall be My witnesses both in Jerusalem, and in all Judea and Samaria, and even to the remotest part of the earth" (Acts 1:8).

The Jerusalem church, and especially the apostles, were given very clear instructions. God held up His end by providing the power, but the disciples never left Jerusalem. By Acts 8:1 the book says: "On that day a great persecution began against the church in Jerusalem, and they were all scattered throughout the regions of Judea and Samaria, except the apostles."

After a short time of great blessings in Jerusalem but without any mission beyond those borders, God had to force them out. In what may be the most ironic words in the Bible, it says that everyone spread out in Judea and Samaria *except the sent ones* (the apostles)! Because our translations do not translate *apostolos* but simply use the transliteration of apostle, and because we have come to think of apostles as a formal title, we tend to miss the obvious humor, even sarcasm, found in the verse. But it is there. Any first-century person that read the original language would pick it up immediately.

The plan was originally given: Jerusalem, Judea, Samaria, and the outermost parts of the earth. Only persecution moved the people to reach Judea, which is a broader region but culturally and ethnically the same. Samaria, however, is crossing huge cultural boundaries in the eyes of the first-century Jews. The original plan Jesus presented was clear but then quickly, even conveniently, forgotten by the apostles.

When the Gospel finally broke out among the Samaritans, the apostles had to be called in to sanction this new venture

(Acts 8:4–24). It is interesting that the Gospel got there before the "sent ones," but it seems as if the Lord is waiting for them to catch up because the Holy Spirit does not fall on the new believers until Peter and John pray for them. It feels as though the Lord is slowly egging on the sent ones to do what He told them to, but they just don't seem to understand.

God had to overtly interrupt Peter's meal plans with three incredible visions to get him to be even open to the idea of allowing "the way" to spread to the Gentiles. Nevertheless, he was always a little reticent and incapable of committing to the Gentiles for most of his life, preferring to be the apostle to the Jews (Gal. 2:7). Once he was even sharply rebuked in public by Paul for compromising on his own convictions (Gal. 2:11–21). Again, it appears as though God is pushing the sent ones in a not-so-subtle way and always meeting resistance.

God gave to the apostles the opportunity to take the lead on a rapid movement that would ultimately spread around the world and even do what no nation had been able to do in a thousand years: overcome the great Roman Empire. Instead, God had to use accidental church plants, ordinary nameless heroes, and radically turn a violent Pharisee into the sent one who would reach the Gentiles.

We know that eventually the twelve apostles took to going to the world, but it took far too long for the sent ones to actually get going. Others had to lead the way first, which I cannot help but think was not Plan A for apostolic mission.

One does not have to look far to find churches today that follow this model. It is by far the most prolific example across Western Christendom. There are some twelve hundred megachurches (those with more than two thousand in weekly attendance) in the United States and tens of thousands more churches that wish they were megachurches. We cannot lump them all into the same model, but by far the vast majority are homogeneous attractional congregations that are not sending out church planting missionaries to other people groups, extended regions, or the ends of the earth. Although we would be hard pressed to find one that doesn't send dollars to missions work, the church that raises up missionaries from the harvest and sends them out to the harvest is rare. There are definitely some, and I talk about them in the next section when I look at a different congregational model.

Perhaps the best-known examples that fit mostly with the Jerusalem model would be Saddleback Church and Willow Creek. Willow Creek has never had church planting as part of its goals. Much like the Jerusalem church, it is interested in reaching its Jerusalem, but not the ends of the earth. Saddleback has "sponsored" many missionaries, but it doesn't really raise them up from within and send them out. Both churches formed alliances of like-minded churches that are following their model, but these are really adopted churches much like the relationship the Jerusalem church had with the Samaritans (Acts 8) and the Antioch church (Acts 11). I have learned much from Rick Warren and Bill Hybels and have the utmost respect for both. Their churches, like the Jerusalem church, are beacons of light in cities that need them, and neither reflects the ugliness of the Jerusalem church found in the later part of Acts. Both are influencing the nation and the world. My own in-laws (and several good friends) love going to Saddleback, and I'm the one who suggested they go there in the first place. I do, however, believe that we need to shift to another expression of church that is more apostolically missional in its core and reproduces spontaneously if we want to reach the wider world.

Why do so many people point to the Jerusalem church as the model they are following? Of course there is much beauty in the way the church as a whole was born. Luke writes:

> They were continually devoting themselves to the apostles' teaching and to fellowship, to the breaking of bread and to prayer. Everyone kept feeling a sense of awe; and many wonders and signs were taking place through the apostles. And all those who had believed were together and had all things in common; and they began selling their property and possessions and were sharing them with all, as anyone might have need. Day by day continuing with one mind in the temple, and breaking bread from house to house, they were taking their meals together with gladness and sincerity of heart, praising God and having favor with all the people. And the Lord was adding to their number day by day those who were being saved [Acts 2:42–47].

We can and should learn much from this church, but we should learn from her mistakes as well. Many preachers today like to point to the Jerusalem church as their primary model because it is the only one that even vaguely resembles what they are doing. It is the only church that has a regular public preaching to a large audience mentioned in Acts (Acts 2:42). I believe that this type of teaching was short-lived; it did not take long for persecution to push them out of the Portico of Solomon and into the homes scattered throughout Jerusalem.

The Jerusalem church deserves much favor and recognition from us for being the mother church of all churches, even if her church planting was purely "accidental" (Rom. 15:25–27). But there are other churches in the book of Acts that have much to tell us.

the antioch model: a multiethnic, missional congregation

The next church model presented in the Bible is the Antioch church—Church 1.2. It is much like the original church in form. It was congregational (Acts 15:30) and had a larger number of congregants (Acts 11:21). The people were of one mind, and there was regular teaching going on by gifted leaders (Acts 11:26). The people were also generous with all their possessions, giving to those who had need, like the original church (Acts 11:29–30). It was here that the disciples were first called "Christians" (Acts 11:26). The following upgrades in church from the original are very significant, though.

This new church was focused outside of its own needs. While the Jerusalem church gave of its own possessions to help its own, the Antioch church did so for people hundreds of miles away (Acts 11:28–30). It is interesting that the famine is to be worldwide in scope; nevertheless the Gentile churches around the world keep sending relief to Jerusalem (Rom. 15:25–28; 1 Cor. 16:1–3). It seems the mother church has taken on a greater sense of importance so that all other churches feel the need to keep her going. The famine in Jerusalem is of course legendary in its harshness, and I would never criticize the good hearts of these people wanting to help their brethren. I simply want to point out that these second-, third-, and fourth-generation churches actually have a view outside of themselves that results in a healthier church than the actual mother church.

The church in Antioch is the first multiethnic church with intentional missions and church planting as its model. We do not know exactly who started this church, though we do have a list of its leaders (Acts 13:1). Some of the names on the list are Jewish and others are Greek, so we know that it is not just a church that had outreach programs for other ethnic groups, but inherently multiethnic and multicultural, even at the level of leadership. Some "men of Cyprus and Cyrene" had the courage to reach out to the Gentiles, and a large missional and congregational church was born. There was a team of prophets and teachers in Antioch equipping the church (Acts 13:1). They were concerned for the welfare of other churches and sent a care package to others for famine relief (Acts 11:28–30). Although there is no Scriptural evidence that the church met in homes, it would be an unbelievable stretch to say they didn't. Seemingly every church presented in the New Testament had groups meeting in homes (Acts 2:42; Rom. 16:5–15; 1 Cor. 16:19; Col. 4:15; Phil. 1:2). Even though I cannot definitively say that they met in smaller groupings in homes, I am fairly confident they did.

The Antioch church ultimately changed the shape of church for the future and turned the world upside down by being the first to intentionally send out missionaries to reach the nations. Antioch was in touch with the Lord and hearing His word (Acts 13:1). Unlike the Jerusalem church, she had the courage to follow His direction by sending two of her very best leaders, Barnabas and Paul, out into completely uncharted fields. In this case, the sent ones indeed were sent. I could argue that this church is much the same as its predecessor in structure, but her DNA from the start resulted in greater influence on its region, and the world.

There are some good examples of churches today that would fit well in this model. Perhaps the best is Antioch Community Church in Waco, Texas. Jimmy Seibert and his team of leaders have developed a highly missional and congregational church that reaches out to a variety of ethnic groups, raises leaders, and sends missionaries all over the world.

Some other churches that seem to fit in the Antioch mode would be Northwood Church in Keller, Texas, started and led by my friend Bob Roberts. This church has influence all over the world and has started many churches even in its own town. Redeemer Presbyterian Church in New York City, started and led by Tim Keller, is another great example. Hope Chapel, first in Manhattan Beach, California, and now also in Koneohe, Hawaii, was started and led by Ralph Moore and has been a great example of this for decades now. There are virtually hundreds of Hope Chapels all over the world. Mars Hill in Seattle, led by Mark Driscoll, also fits this model, with Acts 29 being birthed out of the ministry and starting hundreds of churches. These examples, like the Antioch church, are congregational and have a strong church-planting focus. Some are more multiethnic than others.

The Antioch church indeed should rate highly as a healthy model for us all, particularly for those looking to be a centralized, attractional church that is both missional and congregational.

the thessalonica model: a multiethnic and missional regional network

The Thessalonica church is another great example of a church that is missional. They received the word eagerly from Paul, Silas, and Timothy (1 Thess. 1:5, 9–10), though perhaps not as responsibly as the Bereans did (Acts 17:11). In the midst of much persecution and hardship, a multicultural church was born made up of a few Jews, many Gentiles, and some of the leading women of the city (Acts 17:5–9). This church, in spite its cultural differences and facing hatred from so many, became world renowned for their love for one another (2 Thess. 1:3–4). They took the message that turned their lives around and spread it widely, specifically by starting works in Macedonia and Achaia. Paul says of this church:

> You also became imitators of us and of the Lord, having received the word in much tribulation with the joy of the Holy Spirit, so that you became an example to all the believers in Macedonia and in Achaia. For the word of the Lord has sounded forth from you, not only in Macedonia and Achaia, but also in every place your faith toward God has gone forth, so that we have no need to say anything [1 Thess. 1:6–8].

Because of harsh persecution from the beginning, this church was never able to be a congregational model. Persecution always forces the church to go underground and remain decentralized. The result is a more organic expression, meeting in homes and spreading more quickly than the other models. This church, like the previous two, was also generous, in fact way beyond its means (2 Cor. 8:1–5). If you can find anything that is less than positive, it would be that their love for one another crossed too far into enabling irresponsible people who were lazy and undisciplined (2 Thess. 3:7–15); they also were confused a bit on their theology of end times (1 Thess. 4:13–5:11; 2 Thess. 2:1–12).

Today you would be hard pressed to find contemporary examples of this model in the West where persecution is not a factor in a church's formation. China and India have many examples of such regional impact of a network of organic churches thriving under the pressure of persecution.

It is interesting that the first church in Acts has all male and Jewish leadership. The next church, Antioch, has all male but multiethnic leadership. Thessalonica then goes further, and Luke mentions that this church had not only a mix of ethnicity but also women leaders. The Roman church, which we will examine next, also had multiethnic leaders and women included among the leaders (Rom. 16:3, 6–7). One can sense progress from the Jerusalem church and the inherent bigotry that eventually killed it to a more open unity found in later models.

the roman model: an urban network of organic churches in a major city

Paul did not start the church in Rome (Rom. 1:10–17). He wrote to the church and personally knew many there (Rom. 16:1–16), and apparently many there were acquainted with Paul's associates as well (Rom. 16:21–23). Paul, however, was not there himself at the time he wrote the letter. Later, of course, he would come to Rome and have a fruitful ministry with global impact. Rome would be the place where he ended his earthly life (2 Tim. 4:6–8).

So how did the church start? From the letter and its content, it seems that disciples of Paul's, some of whom were once in the fierce battles of frontline ministry with him (Rom. 16:3), and some who were the first fruits of his evangelistic efforts in other places (Rom. 16:5), relocated there and started churches following his pattern. There are also some apostolic church planters who had moved to Rome but were not disciples of his (Rom. 16:7). Whether they were intentionally sent there to start churches or moved there for other reasons is not clear, nor relevant. In either case God sent them, they were trained, and a network of organic house churches was born.

In Rome you have a network of organic churches meeting across the sprawling city in various houses with leaders that were a part of each community. It is possible that Paul greeted up to fifteen churches, each with specific leaders. There is no indication of a centralized office or headquarters.

These churches, daughters of Paul's previous efforts, have a missional bent that is spreading throughout the world (Rom. 1:8). As a second-generation church plant, this church is very dear to Paul, who probably feels a little like a spiritual grandpa who can't wait to hold them and bounce them on his knee (Rom. 1:9–17).

Paul writes primarily to make sure the purity of the Gospel withstands the onslaught of the legalists, who are always trying to seduce churches into bondage to a spirituality based on external behavior modification. He also addresses the need to be submissive to governing authorities, which ironically is a common problem among more independent house churches even today, which can often seem angry at the world and bent toward resisting anything that smells of an institution.

Paul appears to be writing his epistle to the Romans at the end of his third missionary journey. He is about to head to Jerusalem, where he anticipates some trouble (Rom. 15:25–32) and ends up imprisoned (Acts 21:27–40). Ironically, he wants to go to Rome from there (Acts 19:21), and it is his arrest in Jerusalem that ultimately does bring him to Rome for the first time (Acts 28:11–31). Some of the missional disciples Paul loved and greeted in Rome had come from Asia. He wrote the letter at the end of his three years in Asia, and already churches had been started as far away as Rome. This would mean that the Epaenetus may be a mere two and a half to three years old in the Lord and not just starting churches but doing so in another people group overseas. There is something we can learn from these Asian churches, and it begins with their mother church, Ephesus.

the ephesian model: decentralized networks of missional organic churches

In my own opinion, the Ephesian church is perhaps the best model of church that we have in the New Testament. Why? For one thing, Paul came there and stayed for three years and never left the city, but in that time all of Asia heard the word of the Lord (Acts 19:10). This is remarkable and unprecedented growth.

Paul established a church in a world-class city that was the center for commerce, political influence, and culture for the entire region. There he won some to Christ and taught them how to go out and do the same. As people went out all over Asia, they carried the infectious message throughout the region. As we have seen, this church even sent people as far away as Rome, where other networks of churches sprang up quickly as well.

This is a much more rapid, reproductive form of church that can saturate a region in a short time, and even start similar works in other nations. Because it is not dependent on a centralized leader, ordinary people spread the movement, even new converts (Rom. 16:5). The churches were simple churches that could meet in homes or even public businesses (Acts 19:9; 20:20). They had to be simple; it is the only way to explain rapid multiplication by these new disciples. In fact, we see a relatively new believer by the name of Epaphras sent out from Ephesus to start churches back in his home town of Colossae (Col. 1:7) and the two adjoining towns as well (Laodicea and Hieropolis), all within the three years of Paul's journey there (Col. 4:11–13). It is hard to tell from the Scripture in what order these churches were born, but it does represent at least four generations of reproduction in a short period of time initiated by a relatively new believer.

A huge part of this rapid reproduction is that the churches are birthed without dependency on the mother church or the original church planter. This is a huge upgrade! Paul is able to say to the elders in Ephesus, "I know that all of you, among whom I went about preaching the kingdom, will no longer see my face" (Acts 20:25). Rather than seeing Paul as their leader and being dependent on him, they hear Paul state, "And now I commend you to God and to the word of His grace, which is able to build you up and to give you the inheritance among all those who are sanctified" (Acts 20:32).

To the Colossians, he writes a letter as the apostle of this expanding Asian network, but he also mentions that they, along with the Laodicean church, have never seen his face (Col. 2:1). Paul doesn't have to start them, run them, or keep them going. He is not the focal point of what brings people into the church or keeps them from departing. These churches were born sufficient in Christ and fully capable of starting the same kind of church.

Paul learned how to start churches that were able to flourish without needing him. To the Philippians he wrote: "So then, my beloved, just as you have always obeyed, not as in my presence only, but now much more in my absence" (Phil. 2:12). He even likens this nondependency on human leadership as an expression of being worthy of the Gospel. He writes to the Philippians that they can stand together against the enemy, unstoppable, whether or not he is there to watch over them because of their direct connection to God:

> Only conduct yourselves in a manner worthy of the gospel of
> Christ, so that *whether I come and see you or remain absent,* I will hear
> of you that you are standing firm in one spirit, with one mind
> striving together for the faith of the gospel; in no way alarmed
> by your opponents—which is a sign of destruction for them, but
> of salvation for you, and that too, from God [Phil. 1:27–28;
> emphasis mine].

In this day of high-profile personalities in pulpits drawing out large numbers of Christians to a weekly service, we could actually learn something from these churches about the Gospel and what it means to be a church. None of us would dare compare ourselves to Paul as a church leader, yet in so many cases we develop a greater dependency on ourselves than he did on himself. Could it be because we have made church about something that is less than the Gospel itself and more about how the particular speaker makes us feel on Sunday morning?

Unlike any other churches, Luke not only tells the story of how the Ephesian church was started (Acts 19) but then elaborates, in a narrative within the narrative, what Paul did there to start the church. Like a Hollywood flashback, he recounts how Paul comes back to talk with the elders from all over the city of Ephesus (Acts 20) and reminds them of exactly what he did. Luke, in his masterful prose, manages to address a question that he anticipates we would ask—How did all who are in Asia hear the message while Paul never left Ephesus?—without even departing from his overall narrative style. It is as though the Holy Spirit is telling us to pay attention to this church.

In fact, one can argue that there is more Scriptural revelation concerning this church than any other. Luke devotes two chapters to telling how it started, as opposed to the few verses given to most of the other churches Paul began. Paul wrote two letters to Timothy as he was stationed in Ephesus. The Apostle John perhaps wrote a letter to the Ephesian church (2 John), if the chosen lady and her children are the Ephesian church (where John spent much time and is said to this day to be buried) and the churches of Asia Minor, as many believe. The letter of 3 John may also be sent to Ephesus, as Gaius does have a history there. Last, but certainly not least, Jesus Himself writes a letter to the Ephesian church (Rev. 2:1–7) and to all the daughter churches born from her (Rev. 2:8–3:22). I do not think it coincidental that we have so much information about what happened in, from, and to the Ephesians' church.

There are some noticeable struggles with this church. Timothy is instructed to keep false teaching at bay. Jesus tells us that after many years the church, although still active, came to lose its first love. No model is perfect, and as I said earlier it is not the model that is most important but the DNA. We can learn much by studying the Ephesian church, which stands before all time with strengths and weaknesses exposed.

Is it possible to move from one model of church to another? If it is possible, how does a church transition? The longer a church has been established, the harder the transition will be. There is a saying church planters often mention when the subject of transitioning established churches comes up: "It is easier to give birth than to raise the dead." Although this is a harsh statement, there is some truth to it; it is far easier to start a new work than to change an old one. I do believe that a church can change, and in the next section I describe some of what that entails.

transitioning models

There are many traditional expressions of church in the United States that are attempting to transition to becoming more organic. Instead of calling them transitional churches, we call them "transfusional churches." The reason for this change is that the idea of transitioning implies simply modifying a model or a system, and we have found that this would be useless without a transfusion of healthy DNA. The problems our churches face in the West are not structural, strategic, or mechanical. A mechanical fix is not a fix at all. The problem is a lack of life in the core, or perhaps a more diplomatic way to describe it is that they are lacking some healthy DNA. So every transition begins not with a structural change but with a transfusion of holistic and healthy disciples infused with the DNA. We want to see them fruitful and multiply enough that there is a growing emergence of health in the church body. Rather than simply use up those disciples in meeting existing ministry needs, we challenge church leadership to release some of them to start groups, perhaps even outside the walls of the congregation itself.

Think about the importance of DNA for a moment. When I speak, I sometimes ask if anyone in the audience would be willing to show us their DNA. Usually people laugh at the thought, and someone eventually stands up with arms extended and says, "Here it is." You see, DNA is in almost every cell of your body.[11] If your DNA were somehow corrupted with a mutation, how would you fix it? You can't conduct surgery on every cell of your body. You can't just take a pill and hope it will fix things.

Changing your church's model or mechanical structure is like trying to take a pill to fix your DNA. It can't be done. But if we could somehow fix someone's DNA, I imagine we would need a more viral approach that brings change one cell at a time. To do this, you would first need to introduce a healthy DNA cell capable of reproducing. The change would be microscopic and slow to begin with, but as each generation of transformed cells reproduces it would build momentum and change would eventually be noticeable.

Once healthy discipleship is under way, leaders can be trained not to get in the way of the growth in disciples, leaders, churches, and movements. This is not as easy as it sounds because most leaders have been trained for decades in a certain way of thinking. At CMA we even talk about going through "detox" at this stage, because we have created such a dependency in our churches that none are self-sufficient or self-replicating. This detox creates a death. We must die to ourselves, to our past, and to our future ambitions in order to be born again to a new way of working. I sometimes even suggest that churches have an official funeral service in which the leaders go first. Everyone then has a sense of anticipation of what God may birth (it is also a good indicator of the willingness of people to change). Lest you think this too harsh, realize that this is the entrance requirement Jesus demands of any who would follow Him.

Phil Helfer, an original co-founder of CMA, is actually the most radical organic thinker on our team. I have learned much from him. Phil leads Los Altos Grace Brethren Church in Long Beach, a church that is more than fifty years old at a facility that has age-graded Sunday school classes and a preschool through sixth grade school on campus. They average between three and four hundred people in attendance weekly. This does not look or feel at all like an organic church, but it is transfusional. Slowly Phil has been training his leaders to think and respond more organically. His leadership team have bought into the organic values and practice them. This church sent us out to start Awakening Chapels. They also launched three other organic church networks and several single-house churches that have yet to become networks. Although a church like Phil's is not likely to start spontaneously reproducing any time soon, she can become a grandparent to movements by releasing the start of networks that look much different from her.

Today there are many churches that are seriously looking at how to become more of an organic church network than a centralized congregation. We are in constant conversation with several megachurches well known for their strong and dynamic leadership that are asking how they can change and multiply.

This subject could easily be an entire book in itself, so I'll not go into more detail. When a church wants to transition from the issue of transfusing healthy DNA into the disciples, there are some structural choices that must be made regarding how the church will function and about its comfort level with decentralization.

In the next chapter I list the advantages and disadvantages of being either very centralized or decentralized. Most churches look to become a hybrid that lands comfortably somewhere in the middle, picking and choosing the pros and cons they can live with. Perhaps it is best in a transfusional church that you begin with an assessment of where you are at currently; I've found the tool developed by Brafman and Beckstrom (*The Starfish and the Spider;* see Figure 6.5 in the next chapter) helpful in that process.

Just as Acts progresses from large attractional and congregational models to organic decentralized and missional networks, I believe God is calling us to a similar shift. The impact is the difference between reaching a single city to transforming nations and ultimately the world. In the next chapter, I develop what it means to become more decentralized.

6

what about church models? part two

from centralized to decentralized

When God said, "Be fruitful and multiply and fill the earth," He did not mean that Eve was to have six billion babies herself. That is not what God meant by multiplying.
—LARRY DEARMEY

CURTIS SERGEANT IS A FRIEND who has personal experience training and coaching national leaders in a rapidly expanding church-planting movement in China. There are not many people in the West who have that sort of experience, so I truly value everything he has to say. He uses an analogy to describe the difference between organic/house churches and cell-based churches that have small groups. Being an avid scuba diver, he likened them to the difference between an octopus and a starfish.[1]

A cell-based church is like an octopus. An octopus is an amazing creature. It is actually delicate and very sensitive to its environment. If the water is polluted or the temperature gets too hot or too cold, it is one of the first creatures to leave or die. It has multiple arms and can reach out in almost every direction. If one of the legs has a part bitten off, it will regenerate and grow back, but if the head is severed the creature will die.

A starfish, by contrast, is not picky about its environment and can survive even in Los Angeles Harbor. It also has multiple arms that can reach out in a variety of directions. If one of the legs is cut off, it will also grow back, but the piece that was cut off will also grow into a new starfish! You cannot cut off the head of a starfish because it doesn't have one. It has a decentralized nervous system that is spread throughout its body.

Some concerned divers in Australia were once frustrated with an explosion of starfish that was starting to kill the Great Barrier Reef. At one point, they decided to get rid of them once and for all and took their knives to cut them into pieces. What they hadn't counted on is the decentralized nature of the starfish's nervous system. They ended up multiplying all their problems manyfold.[2]

The cell-based church, like the octopus, is sensitive to its environment. It thrives only in a culture that is at peace with Christianity. When persecution arises, the cell-based church cannot survive as it is. You will not find them in hostile lands. The organic house churches, however, like starfish actually thrive in hostile environments. In fact, they are the only kind of church that can survive such conditions.

Although the activity in a cell group and an organic church may appear to be the same, there is a difference. When people go to a cell group they are going to a ministry of the church of which they are a part. When people go to an organic church, they are going to the church. Those who are committed to a cell-based church see their small group as just one part of what they do. Those in the organic church do not feel the need for something more. The reproductive rate in a typical cell church is much slower than in an organic house church network, because the small groups are not thought to be mature enough to stand on their own and give birth to the next generation. They still need the central leadership to be a whole church. In a sense, the umbilical cord to the mother church/headquarters is not cut, so they do not have the maturity and fertility to produce the second, third, and fourth generations.

Using examples from the music industry, the Apache Indians, Alcoholics Anonymous, and Websites such as Wikipedia and Craigslist, Ori Brafman and Rod Beckstrom have clearly communicated the unstoppable power of leaderless organizations in their book *The Starfish and the Spider*.[3] Because this book is positioned for the business world, they first present the power of a decentralized organization and eventually yield to the existence of hybrid organizations that retain some of the strength of being decentralized and yet are able to accumulate a profit and hold some command over the organization. For running a business, this makes sense, but for addressing the church I must query, "Why would we sacrifice the unstoppable power of being decentralized for a hybrid?" We have a Head in Jesus who is untouchable and always present for each unit of His kingdom. Therefore we can legitimately be decentralized and not need to build any centralization in our movement. Jesus is our centrality.

Could it be that we want a hybrid for the same reason businesses do: to make money and maintain a level of command? I have found that those who start churches tend to prefer some centrality if for no other reason than they like to have an audience they can preach to, and they want to be paid to do so. I understand this because not only do I like preaching to a large audience, I also like getting paid. It took some strong leading of the Lord to get me to let go of these things so that I could see the bigger picture of what Jesus wanted to truly unleash on the world. In the end, I am communicating to a much larger audience than I ever imagined, and I am well provided for in doing so.

Brafman and Beckstrom present a list of ten questions to help organizations determine just how decentralized they are.[4] These ten characteristics are put together in a simple test that can measure where the organization lands on the spectrum. Organizations can pick and choose which of these ten characteristics are important to them and somehow form a hybrid. The questions are:

1. Is there a person in charge?
2. Are there headquarters?
3. If you thump it on the head, will it die?
4. Is there a clear division of roles?

5. If you take out a unit, is the organization harmed?
6. Are knowledge and power concentrated or distributed?
7. Is the organization flexible or rigid?
8. Can you count the employees or participants?
9. Are working groups funded by the organization, or are they self-funding?
10. Do working groups communicate directly, or through intermediaries?

Perhaps there are other benefits to being a hybrid beyond a paycheck and an audience. In this chapter I examine a variety of organic church models on the spectrum of very decentralized to very centralized, looking at advantages and disadvantages to both. First I describe briefly my own journey into discovering what it means to be missional and decentralized.

awakening chapel's development

As CMA explored a variety of models of church planting over the years, we discovered that all of them fall somewhere on a spectrum from very decentralized to very centralized. The issue is less about the model than it is about the desired outcomes and the disadvantages you are willing to live with on the spectrum. Within Church Multiplication Associates there are churches all along the spectrum. We encourage those who are beginning churches to listen to the Holy Spirit's leading, study the culture, and allow a church that reflects the indigenous culture to emerge naturally.

When I first set out to start Awakening Chapels, I had a completely different idea of what the church would look like than how it turned out. Of course, I have been thoroughly convinced that God's plans are better than mine.

first lesson: missional rather than attractional

The first adjustment we had to make was from an attractional philosophy to a missional one. We had planned to start a coffee house where we could attract young people and relationally reach them in our friendly "spiritual" environment. We rented the space, recruited the team, and were ready to launch a business when the Lord intervened in one of our meetings with a simple but straightforward question that ruined all our strategic plans. He simply asked us, "Why start a coffee house when you can go to the coffee houses that these people you want to reach are already at?" This simple question altered everything for us. In seconds, it deflated all of our planning and turned our entire church model inside out. We became intentionally missional instead of just another attractional church plant that expects the world to come to it. We quickly discovered several ideal café communities where there was little or no influence of Christ's kingdom. You can read more of this story in my book *Organic Church*.

second lesson: decentralized rather than centralized

A second shift in the model of church we were planning was equally profound. Originally, Awakening was to be much more centralized, with disciple-making groups of two or three meeting weekly, a simple church meeting in a home every other week, and a celebration gathering either quarterly or bimonthly. Part of my strategy was in reaction to the busyness I experienced in previous churches, so I thought that meeting every other week would be a relief. I was wrong. When we started reaching people, they were so excited about their new faith that they couldn't wait two weeks to meet with their brothers and sisters. They literally demanded that we meet weekly in homes. Some people would look for more than one group to associate with because they wanted to be together every day if they could. I did not expect this but was very encouraged by it.

Eventually we developed a few organic churches that met either in a home, on campus, or in a business and we decided it was time to launch the larger gathering. I had a worship leader recruit a team of musicians. We rented a space, publicized the opening service, and launched with only one hitch: our people didn't show up. The only people really interested in coming to such a thing were the few Christians we had on the team prior to starting the church. The new followers that we had won to Christ in the city had no inclination whatsoever of coming to the larger gathering. Three times we attempted this gathering, and three times we got the same response. (Sometimes I am like the apostle

Peter in that I need to hear things three times before I get the message.) Eventually I had to listen to the Lord, and to the indigenous church, and let it be the way they wanted it. I want you to hear my story so that you can see that we were thinking just like everyone else when we started. If God had not interrupted our meetings with His better ideas, we would not have learned all that we have about organic church movements.

I didn't know it at the time, but the Lord was leading us to be decentralized rather than centralized. Once we figured out the advantages of being decentralized, we willingly jumped into the Lord's plans with enthusiasm. Since then, I have consistently resisted centralization and pushed the boundaries of being decentralized because most of us are unfamiliar with it. I want to have an example of churches on the far end of the decentralized spectrum and set the tone for others that would follow.

There are organic churches all across the spectrum and all can be healthy and good churches. To us, organic church is not a model; it is a way of understanding the church. Organic church is really a set of kingdom principles that work in any model. Everything that we teach in a Greenhouse can be done in a megachurch or a microchurch. My books are read and used in all models of church. I would like to temper that statement, however, with a little reality that I think you should also know. If you start churches from the harvest using the systems and processes we teach, you will not likely develop a megachurch but rather a network of simple churches. But that network could look very different from another network started in the same town at the same time but by other people.

decentralized versus centralized expressions of organic church

In CMA, we have churches of all varieties. Decision-making power, financial resources, and accountability for correct behavior are channeled either directly through a central office or headquarters in a centralized manner, or they are passed on to the various groupings in a decentralized fashion. Figure 6.1 lists several networks of organic churches and where they fit on the spectrum of centralization when it comes to organization.

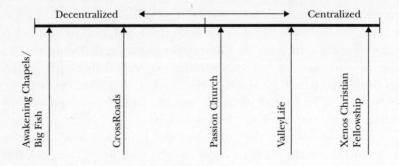

Figure 6.1 The Spectrum of Centralization
Note: The diagram illustrates the scope from very decentralized to very centralized and where various organic church networks fall on the scale.

completely decentralized: awakening and big fish chapels

On the extremely decentralized end of the spectrum, you would find Awakening Chapels (started in Long Beach) or Big Fish Chapels (started in Mesa, Arizona). Dana and I started Awakening with a small team of young leaders in 1999, and Dezi and Susie Baker were the catalysts behind the start of Big Fish. Both of these networks began at about the same time. Because Dezi and I are good friends, we learned much together as we started our churches. These networks of churches are in a chain network, in which each new church is an additional link in a chain of churches. The churches do not meet together or share resources. Each is autonomous. There is no centralized financial accounting or pooling of resources; each organic church can hear from the Lord and decide what it wants to do with the money that is collected. They start other churches by sending out new people, and there is nothing that keeps them together except for the relational tie with the people who went out. There is a sense of identity in these networks that is only truly felt through relationship with the person or people on either side of the links. They use common methodology that is passed down the chain via relational disciple making. With my books and our training events, there is a sense of identity in our churches, but we find that as churches are further removed down the chain these elements might not bind some of them together. Churches start all over the world, in a variety of cultures and languages.

If you ask either Dezi or me how many churches are in our networks or where they all are, we could not answer you. In the early days we could count them because they were still in our own relational grasp, but nearly ten years later we will cock our heads, hold out our hands, and shrug when asked how many. We can identify the beginning and sometimes the first couple of churches down some chains, but that is all. The reason is the open nature of a completely decentralized network, where any-one can start a new church and any new church can just as easily die off.

In *The Starfish and the Spider*, Brafman and Beckstrom say, "Counting the members of starfish organizations is usually an impossible task. It's not only that no one's keeping track, but also that anyone can become a member of an open organization—or likewise withdraw their membership—at any time."[5]

Two years after Awakening began in Long Beach, there were close to fifteen churches. We did a study of the fruit of this one network in the fifth year since the birth of its first church. We found that Awakening had started not only churches but other networks of churches. We were able at this early point in our lifespan to identify five generations numbering close to sev-enty churches started. There were church planters sent to San Francisco, Portland, Salt Lake City, Warsaw (Indiana), and Paris. The church in Indiana was a great-granddaughter of the original church, and it sent people to Seattle, Phoenix, Las Vegas, Chiang Mai, and India. Beyond those churches we do not know where the network went. We found that the people about three or in some cases four generations down the chain knew something about Awakening, but most did not maintain the name of the network. No one was asking for reports or sending resources up or down the chain. Each church was started autonomously and remained so. We found that the mother church would keep track of her church planters' well-being for the most part with email and phone calls but probably never knew the new Christians born in the new churches or the church planters sent out from the daughter or granddaughter churches. There are no full-time or part-time supported leaders in either of these networks. Because pastors are not paid, neither are church planters. Missionaries move and find employment wherever they start churches.

I have personally never received any financial support from these churches. I am not against apostolic leaders being supported. 1 Corinthians 9 seems to indicate it is not just OK but a right of the apostle to receive financial support. Like Paul in that same chapter, I chose not to offer the Gospel at a charge to those I am sharing with. If, after I have moved on to starting other churches in another place, they want to support my ministry, then I will gladly receive it.

mostly decentralized: crossroads

CrossRoads also started in Long Beach and was one of the first born from Awakening Chapels. Brad and Cari Fieldhouse began this work in about 2000. CrossRoads is slightly more centralized but is actually still very decentralized. The churches keep in more communication with each other and occasionally have training events for the church leaders. The churches do collect offerings and can decide what to do with it, but a percentage goes to a centralized account to help support leaders and administration. Although there has been some expansion into other regions of Southern California, CrossRoads is mostly restricted to the Long Beach and Orange County area. CrossRoads has at times supported a leader part-time, and at other times it has not.

equally centralized and decentralized: passion church

A handful of students working with Jaeson Ma and me started a network of organic churches on the UCLA campus. It is more centralized than the previous two examples in that it has a centralized leadership team and is mostly contained by the campus itself. The students meet weekly in their own organic churches. Once a month they conduct an all-network training event. Two to three times a year they have a retreat involving all their churches. They have a single bank account as well, though each church takes its own offering.

Passion Church started more centralized, but the leadership has always valued being decentralized and as the life of this network progresses it is slowly moving in that direction. Students are graduating from UCLA and starting churches off campus, and the result is greater decentralization. Now there are students starting passion churches on other campuses. The future for this network is wide open, and I am excited about its potential, not just for the Los Angeles area but for the whole world as empowered graduates move into positions of influence.

mostly centralized: valleylife

ValleyLife is an organic church network in the Phoenix area started by Ed and Debbie Waken in 1994. Because it began as a cell-celebration church before most of us had discovered organic church as we know it now, it is a transitional hybrid. It is more centralized than either CrossRoads or Passion Church. Churches meet in homes throughout Northern Phoenix, but they are all tied together. None are autonomous but are all a part of the whole network. It is important to note that ValleyLife has always had greater numbers meeting in homes than coming to the weekly service. ValleyLife is a hub network.[6] All the churches gather together for weekly meetings. Although it used to be a more traditional worship service, it now has a variety of agendas for its meeting. They may have a prayer walk one week or meet in a park for a picnic the next week. One week they may all converge on an elderly woman's home and mow the lawn, make repairs, and paint the trim, or on another week they may actually have another worship service. The people of ValleyLife have a sense of shared identity. Communication among the people and with their leaders is much stronger than in the more decentralized networks. ValleyLife supports Ed Waken full-time as an organic missionary to the greater Phoenix area and the world. They also maintain a modest office. ValleyLife has started churches all over Arizona, and most are more decentralized than their parent church. To date, however, there is only one church planter sent out of Arizona (to Colorado), though recently, after about fifteen years of ministry, the church has initiated organic works in India.

completely centralized: xenos christian fellowship

The most centralized organic church I have had the pleasure of knowing is Xenos Christian Fellowship in the Columbus, Ohio, area. I must say this is probably the most unique church I have ever encountered. The moment you think you have it figured out, she will surprise you again. I am a big fan of Xenos.

Three college students at the Ohio State University started Xenos during the heyday of the Jesus movement. The church grew organically among the students, with the three leaders serving the churches. Over time they became a network of house churches. Today Xenos has several acres of property with large state-of-the-art-facilities. They have several thousand members and meet regularly on the weekends. One of the things you will notice, however, is that they do not have any singing of worship or praise songs on weekends. This is not because they don't believe in it; they do. They believe that worship should happen in the house churches, and not at their Sunday meetings. At their Sunday meetings they have a strong teaching time that is equivalent, in their minds, to the teaching of the apostles in the Jerusalem church (Acts 2:42). The church, they will tell you, happens in the homes; what happens on Sunday is not the church. Dennis McCallum and Gary DeLashmet are still leading this church together as co-pastors. Even to this day, in spite of having acres of property and beautiful facilities, I understand that they continue sharing an office.

In many ways, Xenos feels like a megachurch. They have a sophisticated leadership development school, which even grants seminary credit. They have staff with a team of teachers and house church leaders. They obviously have a centralized financial account to support the staff and facilities. But they have managed to maintain through all of this a strong commitment to organic disciple making (Dennis and his daughter, Jessica Lowery, have even written a book by that title[7]) and to seeing church in the homes. They have done some church planting but to date have not been able to replicate this unique church. A few daughter churches of Xenos exist but look different, which is fine. Both Dennis and Gary have encouraged me to use centralized teaching as they do because, they say, I have a teaching gift and people would respond favorably to my teaching. Although I am grateful for their kind words, I want to keep our teaching decentralized, for reasons I discuss below.

There are advantages and disadvantages to being centralized or decentralized, or a hybrid church that picks and chooses among strengths and weaknesses. It is important to remember that CMA has churches of all types along this spectrum; we encourage people to find out which expression best fits their own unique circumstance. As we have watched these churches emerge and develop into networks that vary in decentralization, we are able to witness both the strengths and weaknesses found all along the spectrum.

advantages and disadvantages of being centralized

A centralized organic church network has several advantages. For one thing, they have a greater sense of belonging to one another and to something bigger than an organic church with twelve to fifteen people. They also have a greater sense of identity and visible presence in the community. With this greater presence, they can actually have a more rapid impact regionally. A decentralized network, in contrast, must stay hidden, simmering under the surface for a longer time before they can start to see a difference.

There are a couple advantages that have a two-edged sword to them. The centralized church can pool her resources, but at the same time it demands more money to maintain, so in many ways this advantage can be a wash. The individual churches in a centralized network seem to have greater longevity than in a decentralized network. A decentralized network reproduces much faster. Although individual churches may not last as long, a decentralized network can have a saturating effect that is long-lasting (more on this in Chapter Eight).

Centralized does not necessarily mean attractional, although more often than not this is the end result. A campus becomes a magnet for resources, strategies, and even devotion. It is possible to be centralized and reach out to the community in a missional way, but it is rare. Figure 6.2 lists both the advantages and the disadvantages of being centralized.

advantages and disadvantages of being decentralized

There are some obvious and some less obvious advantages to a decentralized network that merit our attention. The first obvious

The Centralized Church

Advantages	Disadvantages
Better communication	Slower reproduction
Faster regional impact	Higher cost to maintain
Pooled resources	More obvious human ingenuity
More visible in community	More vulnerable to persecution
Greater longevity	More vulnerable to heresy
Feeling a part of something bigger	Slower global impact

Figure 6.2 The Centralized Church

advantage is that the churches multiply much faster in a decentralized network. They can also send churches around the world much more quickly and attain global impact more rapidly. The cost is minimal if anything at all, which adds to the reproductive quality because it allows anyone to do it at almost anytime. Another obvious benefit of being decentralized as a network is its ability to withstand persecution and attack from the enemy. As has been proven time and time again, a decentralized network not only survives persecution but thrives in it. When we were just starting Awakening Chapels and realized the significance of being decentralized, I used to say that I wanted a type of church that, if any persecution ever tried to stomp on it to kill it, would see five more churches spring out from it.

One often overlooked benefit of a decentralized network is that God gets more of the credit for what happens, while in a centralized network human engineering and leadership become far more important, and therefore more noticed. You may not like this last statement, but the New Testament constantly reinforces the idea that weak things allow for God to gain more glory from them, while the stronger things are weaker in God's strength.

Contrary to how we have all been trained to think, a decentralized network is actually more resistant to heresy. I will elaborate on this, but it is always a surprise for people to hear it. One reason we are so surprised by this idea is that we have bought

The Decentralized Church

Advantages	Disadvantages
Rapid reproduction	Weak communication
Less cost of maintenance	Dispersed resources
Global impact much faster	Slower impact on a region
God gets more glory for it	Shorter church life span
Resistant to persecution	Less visible in community
Resistant to heresy	Less connected to a sense of being part of a larger experience

Figure 6.3 The Decentralized Church

into the idea that control is necessary to maintain quality. We have confused order with control. Order is really a DNA issue in the end. Control, no matter how sophisticated the policing, cannot correct the DNA of the disciples, leaders, churches, or movements. Simply killing off unhealthy cells does not release healthy ones in their place. Figure 6.3 summarizes both advantages and disadvantages of being decentralized.

Using Brafman and Beckstrom's ten diagnostic questions to determine an organization's level of decentralization, we can evaluate some of the models presented here (Figure 6.4). In Figure 6.5 I also include a blank that comes from their book, which you can use to measure your own church or network's decentralization.

accountability in decentralized networks

Some resist a decentralized approach to church for fear that a lack of control will mean many more abuses of leadership and teaching as well as breaches in character. They say that there is a need for accountability, and some would even demand a "spiritual covering." These same people would be surprised to see that decentralized networks are more resistant to heresy than their centralized sisters. Why is this? Because in a flat movement

Centralized (C)	Awakening Chapels		Passion Church		Los Altos GBC		Decentralized (D)
	C	D	C	D	C	D	
There's someone in charge		X	X		X		No one's in charge
There are headquarters		X		X	X		There are no headquarters
If you thump it on the head, it dies		X		X	X		If you thump its head, it lives
There's clear division of roles		X	X		X		There's an amorphous division of roles
A unit removed harms the network		X		X	X		The network is unharmed by removal of a unit
Knowledge and power is concentrated		X		X		X	Knowledge and power is distributed
The organization is rigid		X		X	X		The organization is flexible
Units are funded by the organization		X	X		X		Units are self-funded
You can count the participants		X	X		X		You cannot count the participants
Units communicate through intermediaries	X			X		X	Units communicate with one another directly
	1	9	4	6	8	2	

Figure 6.4 Evaluating Decentralization in Three Model Churches

Centralized	Your Church		Decentralized
There's someone in charge			No one's in charge
There are headquarters			There are no headquarters
If you thump it on the head, it dies			If you thump its head, it lives
There's clear division of roles			There's an amorphous division of roles
A unit removed harms the network			The network is unharmed by removal of a unit
Knowledge and power is concentrated			Knowledge and power is distributed
The organization is rigid			The organization is flexible
Units are funded by the organization			Units are self-funded
You can count the participants			You cannot count the participants
Units communicate through intermediaries			Units communicate with one another directly

Figure 6.5 Blank Checklist for Your Church
Source: Adapted from *The Starfish and the Spider,* by Ori Brafman and Rod Beckstrom, New York: Portfolio, 2006.

without any hierarchy, if someone goes off the deep end the person's influence is confined to a few, whereas in a pyramid structure where everyone is accountable to a single leader or team, if the top goes sour the rest tend to follow. For a more in-depth discussion of heresy in organic church movements, I suggest you look at Chapter Eleven.

The term *covering* is not something found in the New Testament. Jesus is our covering and He is sufficient for each of us. Can we trust Him to be the Head without some "subhead" with delegated authority to do His job for him? What is the use of having an ever-present Spirit of Christ if we rely on human leaders to do the job instead? Why would we resort to human-engineered solutions when we can have immediate and imminent access to the Head of the Body? Jesus didn't die and rise again so that He could sit on the bench in heaven and let us do His job for Him.

Accountability is important, but it is far stronger when applied to one another as it should be and is prescribed clearly in the New Testament. A decentralized network will only survive so long as each part is accountable to those around it. If you fear a decentralized movement, you can rest easy knowing that it will all blow up if quality is not enforced at the level of disciples in relation to one another. Of course, there is one other option, and that is for the decentralized network to begin to form a centralized leadership. This is what is allowing much of the heresy people notice in China today. Once some begin to establish themselves as heads of a movement and exert that sort of authority, the movement is then both slowed and vulnerable to heretical teaching.

In *The Starfish and the Spider*, Brafman and Beckstrom use the Apache Indians as an example to show the unstoppable power of a decentralized network. They recount the coming of Cortez and how he killed Montezuma and in a short time destroyed the Aztecs, an extremely advanced civilization that dated back to centuries before the time of Christ. The Incas, another advanced civilization, also could not withstand the onslaught of the Spanish. Once they lost their leaders, these huge civilizations died in just a few years.

The Spanish seemed unstoppable and took over continents in a short period of time—that is, until they hit the much less advanced nation of the Apaches. With no great pyramids, aqueducts, calendars, riches, or complex governments, the Apache people were decentralized and without a single leader. They did have leadership, called a Nant'an, one who had the ears and respect of the people, but no centralized authority. Geronimo was a Nant'an. When a leader was struck down, another took his place. The Apaches not only did not yield to the Spanish but pushed them back from Northern Mexico. This simple, nomadic nation was able to resist the mighty Spanish empire for two centuries.

Eventually the Apaches were overcome, not by the Spanish but by the capitalistic United States. How did they suffer defeat? We gave them the ability to accumulate wealth, and with that they had a need for hierarchy to protect their assets. Once they centralized, even a little, they became vulnerable and were defeated.

Although this description may seem oversimplified, the reality is that the only way to actually defeat a truly decentralized nation is to seduce it into forms of centralization.

The real question is, Which form of accountability is preferable? Is it best to have everyone accountable to a few, or have everyone accountable to everyone else? The New Testament church, though it does have leadership, does not violate the accountability of one to another. I suggest this is a far better approach to accountability. Using open source systems such as Wikipedia as an example, Brafman and Beckstrom say: "On the one hand, there's freedom to do what you want, but on the other hand, you have added responsibility: because there is no police walking around maintaining law and order, everyone becomes a guardian of sorts. You become responsible for your own welfare and that of those around you. In open systems, the concept of 'neighbor' takes on more meaning than just the person next door."[8] Freedom, personal empowerment, and accountability to one another—this sounds right in a biblical way, doesn't it?

I prefer a church where everyone is accountable to one another and to Jesus. With weekly meetings of the Life Transformation Groups, each disciple is accountable to another with a list of questions to talk about each other's past week. We call them Character Conversation Questions.[9] Every week, I am asked;

1. Have you been a testimony this week to the greatness of Jesus Christ with both your words and actions?
2. Have you been exposed to sexually alluring material or allowed your mind to entertain inappropriate sexual thoughts about another this week?
3. Have you lacked any integrity in your financial dealings, or coveted something that does not belong to you?
4. Have you been honoring, understanding, and generous in your important relationships this past week?
5. Have you damaged another person by your words, either behind the person's back or face to face?
6. Have you given in to an addictive behavior this week? Explain.
7. Have you continued to remain angry toward another?
8. Have you secretly wished for another's misfortune?

9. What is your own personal accountability question?
10. Did you finish your Bible reading this week and hear from the Lord? What are you going to do about it?
11. Have you been completely honest with me?[10]

This true and raw accountability is far superior to having a single person or team police everyone. When critics object to what I do because they think it lacks accountability, I have to laugh, knowing that I will face these questions come Monday morning and the people objecting probably never will.

Jesus speaks about addressing a brother in sin, prescribing a detailed approach that any Christian should be able to do:

> If your brother sins, go and show him his fault in private; if he listens to you, you have won your brother. But if he does not listen to you, take one or two more with you, so that "by the mouth of two or three witnesses every fact may be confirmed." If he refuses to listen to them, tell it to the church; and if he refuses to listen even to the church, let him be to you as a Gentile and a tax collector [Matt. 18:15–19].

Nowhere is it said or implied in the passage that it is only those designated as spiritual leaders or elders that are to apply this pattern. In fact, the very pattern itself seems impossible to fulfill unless every Christian is able to put it into practice. Otherwise the confidentiality Jesus seems intent on maintaining is lost when the other church members tattle on the errant brother to the leaders. The context of the passage begins with Jesus instructing against forming rank among those in His kingdom using children to do so. Just think how much purer the church could be if every Christian were empowered to fulfill this teaching of Jesus. Sin would be cut off at the roots, the grass roots. It is quite common for the elders of a church to be removed too much to witness the private sins of parishioners. If all were empowered to enforce this pattern, as it appears Jesus instructed, then there would be a much more immediate and internal battle against sin in the core of all of the church's life— her disciples in relation to other disciples. The immune system of the body of Christ would be healthy and active. We would rarely hear of problems because people closest to one another would immediately address them. The body would be purer, healthier, and more resistant to infection.

When we consider the nature of God's church and of her relationship to Christ, we find that a decentralized organizational structure has more potential than any other sort of movement. Consider this:

1. Christ is the Head of the church. There is no greater authority in heaven, on earth, or under the earth.
2. Christ as Head is fully capable in communication, power, and quality of work.
3. Christ is fully present in each follower and in every church.
4. A church is merely the gathering of His followers into a missional family, not an organization or program, and Christ is in their midst.
5. He loves us, cares about our needs, and is powerful enough to do whatever is necessary for the success of his church.
6. If every Christian is connected to the Head, and Christians are connected together to form a church, then in fact every church is also connected to Him directly.
7. He can communicate, authenticate, and empower each of us for the work He asks of us. He can do so far better than any of His pastors or leaders are capable of doing.
8. We actually have all we need to be a radically decentralized, expanding network of spontaneously multiplying churches. If so, none can stop us from bringing the powerful good news of His kingdom to the entire world. Each new Christian and consequential church is equally empowered and able to do the same.

Why then would we want to stop all of that to form large centralized organizations where everyone has to listen to leadership in a human headquarters and run every decision past said leadership? Granted, it is all that the world has presented to us as an organizational model, and we have bought into it for centuries (wherever there is not persecution). Now we are informed and know better.

If I can be vulnerable for a moment, I want to share with you my greatest phobia. Until now, this was a secret known only to my wife and three kids, but it is time for full disclosure. I am not afraid of large dogs, strange people, or standing in high places. I have no problem in the dark or an enclosed place. I have a phobia about bugs. There, I said it. An individual bug doesn't really bother me. I am glad to remove a spider that one of my daughters finds in the bathroom, without hesitation. It is when bugs swarm that I am creeped out. This has always been my greatest nightmare. Even as I write this and imagine it in my mind, I feel shivers on the back of my neck. The feeling of ants all over my legs is the worst! I hate it.

The truth is we should all be a little freaked by swarms of insects; they are so overwhelming that there is almost no defense. You can have a double barrel shotgun and an automatic machine gun at the same time and you are absolutely defenseless against a swarm of killer bees. You can shoot at the swarm, and you may even hit a couple of the bees, but the swarm doesn't even need to duck when you shoot. It will come without any slowing or adjustment after you have fired all rounds. This is also why a decentralized movement can be literally unstoppable.

Most ask me if we ever have larger meetings than our organic churches, which is a question I address more fully in the next chapter. Some of our networks do, and others do not. Instead of trying to figure out how to centralize organic movements, maybe we should all start thinking about how to decentralize our current organizations, for therein lies a power that could fill the earth with the glory of Christ's presence and be virtually unstoppable.

7

what about larger gatherings?

from one-size-fits-all to tailored groups for effective function

Never doubt that a small group of thoughtful,
committed citizens can change the world; indeed,
it's the only thing that ever has.
—MARGARET MEAD

I am often asked whether organic churches have regular gatherings of the small groups to form one large congregation. I suspect this question is more a reflection of past church experience that is weighted toward centralized worship gatherings than a concern about strategy. We are so accustomed to having a larger gathering for worship and teaching that it is hard for us to imagine church without it.

From the beginning of my writing, I have never been opposed to larger gatherings of Christians, for worship or anything else. I have, however, felt that we need to determine the right size grouping for the right need, and not confuse them. I believe we have put too much of our investment in a less-than-effective way of making disciples and transforming the world: the Sunday service and sermon. In this chapter, we will look at groupings that are geared to the variety of functions found in a movement. Jesus understood the natural laws of size of group and function, and we must too. But first, it is important to understand that there is a natural order to the development of these groupings.

the natural order of social groupings

People are social beings and cannot survive alone. We are drawn to one another by God's design. We are also drawn together in groups of a variety of sizes to accomplish what is necessary for us, as individuals and as an entire group.

In our experience, we have found six natural sizes for social groupings that should be multiplied and networked together into today's organic church movements, if we are to accomplish all that is necessary in His kingdom. Each grouping has its own natural function that is necessary for the body of Christ. People participate differently according to the size of the group. I like the phrase coined by the publisher and unique conference organizer Tim O'Reilly, who began the TED (Technology Entertainment Design, known for its invitation-only conference) conference, when he refers to developing "an architecture of participation."[1]

Correctly applying the activity and behaviors of discipleship in the grouping can have a significant impact on the overall life of the church as well as her impact on society as a whole. The absence of key groupings robs the church of a needed interaction and participation in significant spiritual behaviors, and it results in a lack of fruitful influence on people's lives.

Clay Shirky, author of the book *Here Comes Everybody*, comments, "The centrality of group effort to human life means that anything that changes the way groups function will have profound ramifications for everything from commerce and government to media and religion."[2] I assert in this chapter that if we match the Christian life function and interaction with the best-sized groupings, we can relieve other-sized groupings from false expectations and release healthier growth for the whole of the church.

The best-sized groups for various functions are mentioned in the New Testament specifically tied to Jesus' minstry, but that information alone is not enough to develop an entire theology of group-size dynamics. Tied to those same groupings is a context that helps us see why these numbers are important. A survey of literature today in this field reveals it is more than coincidence that these sized groups are mentioned in the Bible. With this in mind, I want to emphasize with great concern that I am not prescribing a model of church, but instead offering some guidelines to consider when we ask this central question: How can we see the best development of people for the specific challenges associated with the church's entire mission?

the base unit of life: two or three people

Two become three. This is how every family begins. In fact, all of creation begins with a twosome, male and female, life on life. Life, however, begins even before that.

God exists in a community of three: Father, Son, and Holy Spirit. God was, is, and always will be the Trinity. The Lord God said, "It is not good for the man to be alone. I will make a companion" (Gen. 2:18). Prior to this passage, God had called everything He made good: the sun, the moon, the plants, the animals, everything! Then He saw a person all alone and said, "This is not good." People are made for partners.

"Let us make man in our image, in our likeness . . . He created them" (Gen. 1:26a, 27c). The beginning of the human race was a party of two (Adam and Eve) created by a party of three (Father, Son, and Spirit). The group of two or three seems to be the spring of life in every way imaginable.

Both the Old and New Testaments use the phrase "two or three." It is interesting that at least ten times "two or three" is suggested as an ideal size at which to conduct ministry. The Bible does not say "two or more" or "three or less," but regularly "two or three." In the wisdom literature, Solomon shares, "Two are better than one, because they have a good return for their work. . . . Though one may be overpowered, two can defend themselves. A cord of three strands is not quickly broken" (Eccl. 4:9–12). It seems that for effective ministry God wants to give us choices, but not too many options—two, or three.

The New Testament Scriptures contain several more reasons for two or three being the ideal size for effective fellowship and ministry.

Accountability and confidentiality are stronger with two or three. Whether concerning an accusation against a brother or sister in the church (Matt. 18:15–17) or an elder (1 Tim. 5:19), instruction around handling these issues requires two or three.

Two or three enjoy simpler and more balanced communication. Two or three is the perfect group size for clear communication and for everyone to participate. With the several perspectives that all the persons bring, the group can have a more balanced conversation and find it easier to reach conclusions. Paul wrote this regarding gatherings of the church:

> When you come together, everyone has a hymn, or a word of instruction, a revelation, a tongue or an interpretation. All of these must be done for the strengthening of the church . . . two—or at the most three—should speak, one at a time. . . . Two or three prophets should speak, and the others should weigh carefully what is said. . . . For God is not a God of disorder but of peace [1 Cor. 14:26–33].

A group of two or three also has flexibility and can schedule time together easily. In addition, Jesus says, "For where two or three come together in my name, there am I with them" (Matt. 18:20). Jesus promises to join the meeting when two or three come together, no matter where or when it might be.

A group of two or three is also important for mission in the New Testament. There are several examples of this. "[Jesus] sent them two by two ahead of him to every town and place where he was about to go" (Luke 10:1b). Jesus didn't send a large group or an individual; He sent a team of two. This greatly simplifies the creation of a spring of life; we only need to discover *one* other harvest-minded person in the place we have adopted. The results of these ministry teams were extraordinary. Luke notes that the spiritual accomplishments were so great that Jesus was "full of joy" upon their return (Luke 10:21). People often wonder, "How much can just two people accomplish?" It's clear when the teams of two are directed by Jesus they can accomplish much—to the point of filling Him with joy.

In Acts, we see how church leaders were directed in the composition of the first missionary team: "The Holy Spirit said, 'Set apart for me Barnabas and Saul for the work to which I have called them.' So after they had fasted and prayed, they placed their hands on them and sent them off" (Acts 13:2b–3). The Holy Spirit instructed a group of *five* to send a team of *two*. Paul and Barnabas operated as traveling evangelists covering fifteen hundred miles (Acts 13:4–14:28), and their efforts bore much fruit. Later, Paul and Silas formed a missionary team, as did Barnabas and Mark.

We see in these examples that as God seeks to expand His work in the world, He calls and sends workers two by two. Jesus described the kingdom of God with the parable of the mustard seed, which starts small and then eventually grows very large (Mark 4:30–32).

Much as many small springs may be the source of a powerful river, so the kingdom of God starts with the smallest of groupings: two or three. Jesus reinforced the principle that the kingdom must start small and grow via multiplication to have great and expansive influence. Not surprisingly, this is consistent with who He is and with His wisdom as articulated throughout the Scriptures.

Why not take a moment, flip to the back page of this book and write down the name of another disciple who could partner with you to launch a spring of life in your chosen missional place?

In addition to its biblical basis, there is the practical matter of communication. The difficulty of managing communication is roughly proportional to the number of possible social interactions found in a group.[3] Each additional person increases the number of possible interactions. With two people, there is nothing to manage because there is only one possible social channel. With three, the number of social interactive channels jumps up to four (three possible two-person interactions and one three-way connection). When you add another person, you suddenly have eleven possible connections, so it takes far more energy to maintain the depth of relationships. It is easy for a person to drift into the background with four or more, but more difficult with three. It is also possible that groups start to isolate into pairs with four, but this is not so likely with three.

In *Here Comes Everybody*, Shirky uses a simple trip out to the movies with friends to illustrate for us this dynamic. With just two people, it is far easier to pick a time and movie because you only have two opinions. When you add a third and fourth person, the complexities of a simple decision become far more fragile. He writes, "Two of you love action films, two hate them; one wants the early show, three the late one, and so on. With two people, you have only one agreement to make. With four you need six such agreements. Other things considered, coordinating anything with a group of four is six times as hard as with two people, and the effect gets considerably worse as the group grows even moderately large. By the time you want to go to a movie in a group of ten, waiting for forty-five separate agreements is pretty much a lost cause."[4]

It is Satan's maniacal strategy and our own foolishness that kept the church bogged down for centuries, making the work of God depend on committee decisions. If God had to wait for a committee to lead us, we'd all still be out in the wilderness of the Sinai walking in circles. My friend Tony Dale quips, "Jesus didn't say, 'I came that you may have more meetings and have them more abundantly.'"

A group of two or three is ideal for the most intimate and accountable relationships. Communication is more easily managed. The merit of unimportant ideas is debated less. Distractions are reduced. Preferences are less likely to bog down the group. If the most important behavioral practices of the Christian faith, such as accountability and disciple making, can be accomplished in a group with the least amount of possible breakdowns, we have a powerful grouping for the good of the whole. This is all part of God's design and why the numbers two and three are so frequently mentioned in the Bible when it comes to accomplishing the important spiritual disciplines that the faith is built on.

Here is a summary of many of the reasons the Scriptures identify this group as the ideal size for effective fellowship and ministry that will penetrate the rest of the church and ultimately the kingdom of God:

- Community is stronger with two or three (Eccl. 4:9–12).
- Accountability is stronger with two or three (1 Tim. 5:19).
- Confidentiality is stronger with two or three (Matt. 18:15–17).
- Flexibility is stronger with two or three (Matt. 18:20).
- Communication is stronger with two or three (1 Cor. 14:26–33).
- Direction is stronger with two or three (2 Cor. 13:1).
- Leadership is stronger with two or three (1 Cor. 14:29).

God has designed all of creation to reproduce at the level of two. It is also true that if you cannot reproduce disciples at this level you are not likely to reproduce them at all. This grouping is the beginning of all life. A church that ignores this fact is a church that bypasses the springs of life necessary for health, growth, and reproduction.

the leadership team: four to seven people

Groups of four to seven tend to function in more of an auxilary dynamic, where they feed and fuel the other groups, but the organic development of groups does not need to pass through this particular stage. Research indicates that a group of five is the best size for consensual decision making.[5]

When it comes to a small group with decision-making responsibility, the math seems to indicate that the ideal size for this team is five.[6] A group of five has enough diversity to represent a variety of personalities and yet is small enough to reach a consensus in making a decision.[7] Once the group goes beyond five, there are just too many possible social interactions that require maintenance. Some people will be stifled for the betterment of the group and its decision-making process.

Business consultant and blogger Christopher Allen says: "Groups below this size can function effectively, but risk not having enough manpower to deliver a result that everyone is happy with, or having insufficient viewpoints to avoid group thinking. . . . It is typically at this size that the first signs of leadership in a group informally emerge, but the leadership usually isn't overbearing at this level, nor does there tend to be any rebellion against it—perhaps because the group may be too small to elicit multiple leaders."[8]

For a representative leadership team in which all participants are equal in status, this is the best group size. Once decision making is done in larger groups, a type of hierarchy must be developed that excludes some input for the sake of the group process.

The folks at Intuitor.com[9] like to take on mathematical challenges and debunk commonly held beliefs that are actually mythical. They applied mathematical analysis to determine the best group size for making decisions. They say:

Large groups require skillful leaders and formal structure in order to function effectively. Formal structures, such as parliamentary procedure, work by deliberately stifling many of the possible social interactions. Unfortunately, this can also stifle creativity and insures that decisions will be dominated by the most politically skilled individuals even when they don't have the best ideas.[10]

Does the five member group have any biblical precedence? Peter, James, and John represented an inner circle, but on occasion a fourth disciple was added to the group: Andrew (Mark 13:2–4). Two sets of brothers and one mentor formed a group of five. The four plus Jesus represent another sort of group, a team that has enough diversity of personalities, gifts, and voices that it can serve much larger groups of people with solid representation and yet remain small enough that consensus is not impossible.

A quick scan of the Gospels shows that Jesus did treat this special team differently. They were included in all interactions with the twelve, but there were special times when this important group gained unique access. Jesus revealed his inner self to them in much more vulnerable ways (Matt. 17:1–2; Mark 14:33), and they were allowed to witness things that the others were not (Mark 5:37, 9:2; Luke 8:51). Jesus rarely if ever asked anything from others. One of the rare exceptions is when he requested that this team pray with him in his intense emotional need the night before His arrest, trial, and execution (Mark 14:32–42). Unlike any others, these men were called out to help Jesus in a time of crisis, in a sense more as peers.

There is another five-member team in the New Testament. In Ephesians 4:11, five roles are laid out as the equippers necessary for the body of Christ to form, mature, and adequately represent Christ to the world. There is not one that is higher in authority than the others; they serve as equals each representing the gifts necessary to equip the whole body to reflect Christ to the world more accurately. They are apostles, prophets, evangelists, shepherds, and teachers, commonly called the APEST or fivefold team.

To provide leadership for the Hellenistic members of the Jerusalem church a team of seven was appointed (Acts 6:1–6). The leadership team of the breakthrough church in Antioch was a team of five (Acts 13:1) as opposed to the twelve who led the Jerusalem church. These five were able to find quicker consensus and immediate obedience for the mission God had for them, unlike the larger committee of twelve stuck in Jerusalem that took way too long to get mobilized.

A nuclear family in the West is often this size, but prior to the rise of the industrial age, given the higher mortality rate, the need for more hands in an agricultural environment, and the lack of any birth control, four to seven would seem very small for a family. I believe that for a strong sense of family when grouping people to function as Christ's body the next category is far better. We do often see spiritual families healthy at this smaller group size, but those that are healthy usually grow to twelve to fifteen persons.

the family unit: twelve to fifteen people

Even though it is not the best-sized group to make leadership decisions, twelve to fifteen is a much better size for caring for one another's needs. When one wants to maintain a level of intimacy and yet have enough diversity to be able to work effectively as a group, this is the best size. It is also often the size of an extended family, small enough that all parts can intimately know one another, yet large enough to have significant diversity and group dynamics. Across the world, house churches everywhere have twelve to fifteen members. It is a natural size to operate as a spiritual family on mission together, whether you are Baptists, Calvinists, or terrorists. The weaker ones are cared for by the stronger in a setting that ensures all will get the care they need. You have enough diversity of strengths to make the whole better, without too many people decreasing the effectiveness of the intimate family dynamic.

This, however, is not the best team size for leadership and decision making, as we've already discussed. Following Christ's pattern, some have taken to forming leadership bands of twelve people with one mentor. Called G-12, this strategy is admirable in following Christ's pattern but breaks down in assuming that twelve was the best context for leadership decisions. Christ never really used the twelve to make decisions or to function as a leadership community. That would more accurately resemble the four-to-seven group size, which would include Peter, James, John, sometimes Andrew, and Jesus Himself.

Christopher Allen says that in a group size of twelve

no one ever feels like they get a fair share of the time. Studies show
that at this size participants underestimate the amount of time they
contributed to the conversation, and thus will come out feeling like
they were unfairly ignored despite having a fair share of the conversation. Groups of this size risk people being lumped into categories
and ceasing to be trusted as individuals. In addition, problems start
with the development of "too many chiefs," yet there is not enough
variety of non-chiefs for them to direct. Furthermore, many leaders
may struggle for hierarchical status, increasing the conflict in an
already troublesome group.[11]

A group of twelve has a greater tendency toward dysfunction.
Allen points out that a possible solution is to allow more time
to be casual and socialize in order to shake off the tensions of
this size group and improve the dynamics.[12] Of course, this puts
the correct emphasis on the funtion best suited for a group this
size: to relate together casually and less formally, much like an
extended family.

In the church, we often run into problems because we
expect too much from this grouping. The Western church is littered with dysfuntional and disgruntled groups of this size, perhaps because we expect so much to be accomplished by a group
that is not best suited to do that. When it comes to life-changing
accountability, this size cannot hope to compete with the grouping of two or three. When it comes to leadership, this size group
cannot compete with a grouping of four to seven. But this size
has an advantage over all others: it contains enough diversity to
meet a number of needs and yet is small enough to maintain a
high level of intimacy. It is easy for all of its members to keep
track of everyone's health. It can accommodate breaking off into
smaller groupings and yet remain intact. If a tighter, task-oriented
agenda and a higher expectation of production is placed on a
group of this size, it will likely break down. Viewing a group of
twelve to fifteen as the only one necessary and capable of doing
all that God desires of a church is like trying to be able to have
the performance of a sports car yet carry the passenger load of
a minivan combined with the toughness and luggage capacity of
an SUV. You really cannot find such a car, or group of twelve. If

we have strong life growth and accountability in the group of two or three, with leadership and equipping forming a specialized team of four to seven, then a group of twelve to fifteen can relax and be the family it is meant to be. But if the only group we have for everything is twelve, we are expecting way too much. In most church contexts this is considered the small group of the church. As I have already demonstrated, there are actually two smaller-sized groupings that are necessary prior to this one. It is unfortunate when we place too much expectation on this size of group for all that a church should experience.

the training group: twenty-five to seventy-five people

When it comes to training and mobilizing leaders according to giftedness, where all feel part of the same team even though they may not work side by side, a group of twenty-five to seventy-five represents the most efficient size to get across pertinent information, skills, and relationship, while still maintaining quality. When it comes to training leaders in a region through, say, monthly leadership meetings, this is the size that works best. The median attendance of churches in America is seventy-five, which puts it at the maximum of this size grouping and just below the network size.[13] The huge megachurch phenomenon is what drives the numbers higher than they used to be.

Again, Christopher Allen has some insight on this group size. He says it is quite clear that this grouping is mostly nonexclusive, which means it is likely not to be a permanent group or the only group that its members are part of. This can change if the group is mobilized in a stressful environment that glues the people together, as on the field of battle. He writes that with this number "more energy is required to keep a tightly knit community together; either the community agrees to a higher level of commitment and grows to the next level, or the community splits apart."[14] This size and all that follow also require more concerted and directive leadership to function.

In ancient Rome, the military was organized around the idea of one hundred men led by a "centurion." As the years went by, however, centuries tended to reduce in number to include seventy or eighty soldiers.[15] Because there needed to be some relational crossover where it was necessary for the people within a group of one hundred to know well the members of another group of one hundred, the size had to be scaled down to close to seventy. After many years of experience in military action, the Romans learned that if the men have too many relational connections within their assigned company then the connectedness of the groups themselves is weakened because humans can synthesize relationships with only a limited number of people.

Allen hypothesizes that the optimal size for an active group where the members are creative and specialized in their task is between twenty-five and eighty. "Anything more than this," he writes, "and the group has to spend too much time 'grooming' [social care and interaction] to keep group cohesion, rather than focusing on why the people want to spend effort on that group in the first place . . . anything less than this and you risk losing critical mass because you don't have requisite variety."

This size is ideal for short-term assignments involving specialized training and mobilization. It was a group this size that Jesus trained and then deployed by twos to saturate a region with the kingdom of God (Luke 10:1–20).

the relational network: 100 to 150 people

There is an abundance of evidence throughout history that 150 people is a very serious boundary when it comes to group dynamics. Perhaps the most seminal work was done by the noted British scholar Robin Dunbar. He is so well cited now for his research that the number 150 has even been labeled "Dunbar's Number."

His assumption is that the human brain has the capacity to handle only so many relational connections at one time. Using historical evidence combined with psychology, neurological study, and the study of primates, he says: "The figure of 150 seems to represent the maximum number of individuals with whom we can have a genuinely social relationship, the kind of relationship that goes with knowing who they are and how they relate to us."[16] He likens this kind of relationship to how you feel welcomed to invite yourself to sit with a person in a public place if you happen to bump into them. This is the level of relationship we can have within the context of a group of 150. In a group larger than that, we lose this sort of relational connection with people.

Malcolm Gladwell, in *The Tipping Point,* writes almost spiritually about the significance of the number 150 in the development of movements throughout history; he calls it "the magic number 150."[17] It is also mentioned in Mark Buchanan's *Nexus: Small Worlds and the Groundbreaking Science of Networks,*[18] as well as Duncan J. Watts's *Six Degrees: The Science of a Connected Age,*[19] as well as his *Small Worlds: The Dynamics of Networks Between Order and Randomness.*[20]

There is also anecdotal evidence from organized crime to demonstrate the consistency of the number 150. The Genoveses number 152, the Gambinos retain 130 members, and the Lucheses have a total of 113 gangsters, according to FBI reports.[21] It is also not a coincidence that the average church size in America is close to this number. Today it is driven higher—183— than it has been for decades thanks to the recent rise of the megachurch phenomenon, which has altered the statistics.[22]

One example of the universal significance of the number 150 given by Dunbar is the Hutterites, a conservative Christian denomination who live in farming communities of South Dakota and Manitoba. They regard 150 individuals as the limiting size for their communities. When a community reaches this size, they look to start a second daughter community. Part of the reason for this practice is that a group growing beyond this threshold can no longer maintain a level of internal accountability. Beyond this number, the community needs a police force to maintain as high a level of quality as can be kept internally with a group of 150 or less.[23]

Most organized armies have a basic unit of about 150 men. The smallest independent unit in modern armies (the company) invariably contains one hundred to two hundred men. Dunbar writes: "This I suspect, is not simply a matter of how the generals in the rear exercise control and coordination, because companies have remained obdurately stuck at this size despite all the advances in communications technology since the first world war. Rather, it is as though the planners have discovered, by trial and error over the centuries, that it is hard to get more than this number of men sufficiently familiar with each other so that they can work together as a functional unit." Of course, armies can and do have a greater number of troops than this, but to get them to work together stronger hierarchical structures are necessary, with rules and police. According to Dunbar, "At this size, orders can be implemented and unruly behavior controlled on the basis of personal loyalties and direct man-to-man contacts. With larger groups, this is impossible."[24]

We too have found by experience that a network will very rarely grow beyond fifteen house churches (or 150 people). This boundary is natural, God-designed. The kingdom does not stop at this boundary. What is necessary beyond this threshold is to reproduce more networks, rather than try to add more house churches to an existing network.

As I mentioned in a previous chapter, on the basis of the number of greetings Paul presents, it appears that the network of organic churches in Rome might have numbered about fifteen (Rom. 16:1–16). The key to multiplying networks is to raise up leaders from within who can start and lead new emerging churches in an entirely new network.

The number 150 is really a maximum that is hard to maintain. In Dunbar's research, he mentions that this size requires an extensive amount of "grooming." It is actually at this size that a shepherd, for example, is maxed out in the role of caregiver. Beyond 150 relational connections becomes overtaxing. It is indeed a rare shepherd who can even accommodate this many people. Jesus Himself left behind a flock of 120 disciples when He ascended to heaven (Acts 1:15).

the occasional public gathering: 200–500 people

The next largest gathering would be in the hundreds, though probably not more than five hundred. Two or three networks of 150 would form this grouping. At this level and all levels above, stricter hierarchical leadership is necessary to keep the groups together and behaving properly, unless of course all such leadership is done in smaller groups. As groups grow beyond 150, the associations become quite shallow without the smaller-scale groupings at work underneath. Because of the large size and the lack of relational connectivity, a few are activated to address the entire group which becomes passive and immobile. One can speak to them, but keeping them together for more than an occasional pep talk is nearly impossible, and getting them to accomplish something together at this size is futile.

It is a design of our enemy, not God, that so many churches strive to be in this size without the foundation of having smaller groups in place. One can gather a crowd but not form disciples in groupings of this size or larger. Because we are seemingly compelled to make disciples this way, we have wandered from the relational context that is clearly prescribed in the New Testament and resorted to the belief that if we simply pass on information and run programs people will become godly disciples on mission together. This is fallacy and foolishness . . . and it is killing us. We have sacrificed the role of a shepherd for that of a rancher that corrals and herds the masses rather than leading them out in front from among them.

A group beyond 150 requires much to maintain. It is also nearly impossible to mobilize any sort of practical function for any length of time with a group this large. Drawing out creativity, mobilizing talent, or coordinating productive activity with a group this size costs much in resources and can be sustained for only a short time. Allen says, "It is possible for a large company to force groups up to this size by expending lots of energy (which is to say money) to keep it healthy. Apple did this during the invention of the Macintosh, the first OS X operating system, and the iPhone, but the intensity required of such large teams is not sustainable for long periods of time."[25] Any regular gathering of this size will automatically devolve into a passive audience without the undergirding of relational development among the previous smaller groupings. Even with reinforcement of the small-scale groups, it is nearly impossible to do more than just speak to a group of five hundred and perform for it.

Shirky points out that

> as organizations grow into the hundreds or thousands, you also have to manage the managers, and eventually manage the manager's managers. Simply to exist at that size, an organization has to take on the costs of all that management. Organizations have

many ways to offset those costs—Microsoft uses revenues, the army uses taxes, the church uses donations—but they cannot avoid them. In a way, every institution lives in a kind of contradiction: it exists to take advantage of group effort, but some of its resources are drained away by directing that effort. Call this the institutional dilemma—because an institution expends resources to manage resources, there is a gap between what those institutions are capable of in theory and in practice, and the larger the institution, the greater those costs.[26]

There is a time and a place for huge groups. In a mostly volunteer organization, when we attempt to influence a group this size we can usually cast a vision, raise awareness, and collect resources. The group itself remains passive at this size; members are receptors of information but have little or no way to participate except by casting a vote at a business meeting, donating money, or receiving the activity of the leaders. Only by breaking the large group down into smaller groups can we even start to call for volunteers to donate time and energy and manage those investements.

The only mention of a group this size in the New Testament is when Jesus came and appeared to a group of five hundred followers after His resurrection (1 Cor. 15:6). In a very powerful manner, He cast "a vision" that would carry through the millennia. There is no evidence that Jesus had other meetings with a group this size. The one meeting He did have with them, however, was memorable to say the least. It is assumed that during this encounter the group had little or no expectation other than to receive the revelation. Jesus was the one who bore the responsibility of presenting the revelation.

When people do come together in this size grouping, there are some other advantages. They feel a sense of being part of something that is big. They can have a sense of belonging, much as Lakers fans feel a sense of camaraderie when they see others who have the same T-shirt and team loyalty. But they do not know each other personally and may not share much else in common. Just because someone at a restaurant wears a T-shirt with your favorite team emblem on it doesn't mean you will join the person at the table. It may merit a smile and a gesture of camaraderie, but that would be about the limit.

As I said before, I have never been against larger gatherings of this size or bigger. I would warn that we not start with them, or think of them as the main event. I strongly recommend that gatherings of this size or larger be considered secondary to the smaller groupings already mentioned. If we start at this size, we skip all the sound relational transformation and development of community and mission necessary on the smaller scale. A church that starts this way is built on a lack of participation and contribution from the majority of its people; therefore it is not built on the life change that results from a high-bar expectation of participation. An occasional gathering of this size is very exciting and helpful, but it has never been the impetus of changing a society. True cultural transformation occurs with people devoted to one another in much smaller groups.

unlimited multitudes

Beyond five hundred, a group is a mass. It is a gathering together of the other smaller groups for the purposes of annual conferences, occasional worship, and teaching celebrations, saturation of cities with the Gospel, broader impact on a culture, and so on.

Ross Mayfield, an emerging expert on social software, networking, and business, has a blog where he addresses the "ecosystem of networks." He lists three categories of networks and relates them to contacts in the sphere of blogging: political, social, and creative. The political network is a scale-free network, meaning it is not restricted in size at all and can be numbered in the thousands. This would be seen in using blogs as mass media to support a candidate. A social network, by contrast, stays around 150, which would represent what he calls classic blogging. Rarely can we actually carry on a typical blog interacting with known contacts beyond this number. The third category, the creative network, which he refers to as the "dinner conversation" blog, remains around twelve.[27] Even in the world of electronic socializing, the scales for involvement and participation remain about the same. When it comes to servicing thousands at one time, we are frankly limited in what we can do. We communicate to them in mass media such as radio, TV, or Internet traffic, but relationships are lost at this level.

Jesus healed the multitudes (Matt. 15:30; 19:2). He taught them (Matt. 7:28; 13:1–3). He even fed them a couple of times, which was quite a faith-stretching venture (Matt. 14:13–21, 15:32–39). But this was the limit to his public service to them (beyond his redemptive sacrifice). It was not lack of love on His part that kept Him from staying with the crowds, as His redemptive work demonstrates (John 3:16). It was not strategic for Him to invest at the level of large, faceless, and unconnected crowds.

Not that Jesus didn't attract large masses. It seems that whenever a large crowd gathered to Him he would find a way to retreat from them or send them away (Matt. 14:23; 15:39). This is the very opposite of how most Christian leaders respond to the multitudes today. We seem to think that the larger the masses we speak to, the greater the influence we are having. But Jesus understood that this was a shallow effect and that He could not change the world with such a crowd. He would speak honestly to them about their consumeristic values (John 6:26–27). He would hide spiritual truth from these crowds (Matt. 13:10–17). He would even say things to intentionally offend them and reduce the followers to just a few (John 6:59–66). Jesus walked as one who was contrary to our current church growth mentality. He invested in the few rather than the many, not because He didn't love them but because He *did*. He knew that the best thing He could do for the world was to ignite a movement of transformed disciples in relation to one another. Large gatherings are not the place to begin a movement, as Malcom Gladwell says; it starts with the "law of the few."[28]

Figure 7.1 illustrates that these universal groupings can be found in society, and in the New Testament. There is an interesting phenomenon that is noticeable when one looks at all of these groupings together, developing from the micro to the macro. The main quality of these groupings alternate from being more relationally oriented (2–3, 12–15, 100–150) to more task-oriented (4–7, 25–75, 200–500). There is a natural and constant ebb and flow from relationship focus to mission focus throughout the emergence of God's people.

When we look at the formation of organic movements from the grass roots to a global network, it is imperative that we understand the importance of each size of group and plan accordingly. If

	Social Relations	Military Command	Christ's example
2–3	Companion	Buddies	Sent out in pairs
5–7	Band	Special team	Jesus' inner circle
12–15	Family	Squad	The 12
25–75	Clan	Platoon	The 70
120–150	Tribe	Company	The 120
500–2,500	Society	Battalion	The 500
Multitudes	Nation	Regiment/brigade/division/corps/army	The multitudes

Figure 7.1 Grouping Comparisons in Society

reproduction at every level is desired, it is best that the impetus for giving birth to another group of the same size come from growth within, by reproduction of even smaller units, rather than enforced from outside by some programatic mechanism. This internal imperative is the difference between organic reproduction after its own kind and cloning or franchising from an external source. Each group must be self-organizing and self-propagating.

For instance, for a time in small-group training it was taught that every group starts with a leader and an apprentice. As the group grows and reaches fifteen people, the apprentice is to take half the group and leave to begin a new group. This has been taught as multiplying, but in fact it is division. It is virtually impossible to find succesful reproduction to multiple generations using this externally enforced dynamic. People will probably only let you do this one time. After that they will resist, because from a group's perspective it feels more like a divorce than reproduction. A far better way to reproduce a group of twelve to fifteen is when the disciples within the group are infused with a whole DNA—including apsotolic mission—such that they are unable to keep from reaching out to others in need. When this natural, Spirit-led impulse meets an opportunity to reach a new pocket of people, the group can send a much smaller team to fulfill its internal desires and birth a new group. This is much more natural, motivated from within, and feels like something worth celebrating. Rather than feeling weakened as a spiritual family by starting a new group, people feel stronger, much as a family feels even better when it has grandchildren in the mix. Therefore, having internally motivated ways to reproduce groups beginning at a smaller size is essential.

Writing about the rise in social network communication tools, Shirky comments, "By making it easier for groups to self-assemble and for individuals to contribute to group effort without requiring formal management (and its attendant overhead), these tools have radically altered the old limits on the size, sophistication, and scope of unsupervised effort (the limits that created the institutional dilemma in the first place)."[29]

Therefore, in designing systems that can catalyze healthy reproduction, it is best to allow the effectiveness of each group size to be the core reason for of the group's existence, so that if the group outgrows its effectiveness people will feel the void in their experience and naturally want to get back to a right-sized group. If the accountability, character formation, and spiritual disciplines necessary for the Christian life are instilled at much smaller sizes that can self-manage and self-replicate, they will not need external professional management to enforce Christian life and behavior. We could unburden the larger group contexts of much of the expense (and need) that we currently place on them. Cost would drop immensely and spiritual life expectations placed on individual disciples would grow proportionately. At the same time, even the larger group meetings could concentrate on the very things that make them so special rather than expecting unrealistic results from them. We simply must become smaller to influence the bigger, and create groups that accomplish the life-changing dynamics in a self-managed way (Figure 7.2).

For instance, a Life Transformation Group that has mutual accountability to confess sins to one another naturally remains small. Two or three is best; as it gets larger, the intimacy of the group is lost and members long to return to the natural size. An inherent invisible sense of glue for each group is needed, so that we do not feel forced to police group size from the outside. A spiritual family will lose the intimacy and sense of group involvement necessary to be a family if the group grows to twenty or beyond.

The key is for group members to have a natural, internal, and inherent motivation to maintain the size that is proper and have

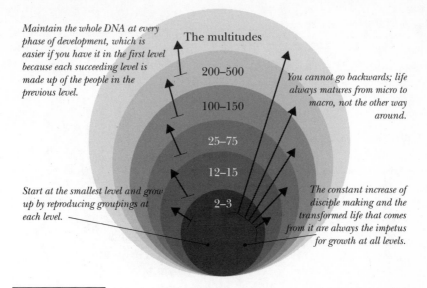

Maintain the whole DNA at every phase of development, which is easier if you have it in the first level because each succeeding level is made up of the people in the previous level.

The multitudes

200–500

You cannot go backwards; life always matures from micro to macro, not the other way around.

100–150

25–75

12–15

Start at the smallest level and grow up by reproducing groupings at each level.

2–3

The constant increase of disciple making and the transformed life that comes from it are always the impetus for growth at all levels.

Figure 7.2 Strategic Size Groupings for Providing Care at All Levels

within all members a DNA that includes growth via reproduction of disciples. Without this DNA, all hope of reproducing groups at any size is hopeless and self-organization is lost.

One size does not fit all. What we need is to find the right size group for the God-given needs of the people so that they naturally want to remain in such a group. Expecting one size to meet all needs is not only unrealistic but disappointing to all involved.

CMA has developed and deployed catalytic systems at all levels of these groupings (Figure 7.3). We build everything on the foundation of making fully devoted followers who can reproduce using Life Transformation Groups. On this foundation, we form organic churches that are spiritual families. We also have the Greenhouse, which is a training and mobilizing system that not only spreads the seed of organic church but develops trainers of trainers. We have found from our experience that a network of churches started from scratch will grow to a maximum of fifteen churches, or 120–150 people. To grow beyond that, the network must birth new networks. We have an annual conference with upward of five hundred people who come to catch the vision,

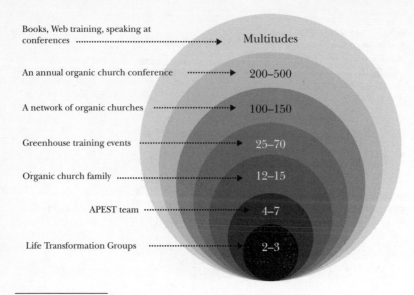

Books, Web training, speaking at
conferences ....→ Multitudes

An annual organic church conference ················▶ 200–500

A network of organic churches ········ ··········· → 100–150

Greenhouse training events ·········· ·········· → 25–70

Organic church family ················· ········ → 12–15

APEST team ·············· ········· ▶ 4–7

Life Transformation Groups ··········· ········ 2–3

Figure 7.3 CMA's Strategy for Providing Care at All Levels

share ideas, and best practices. Beyond this, we use publications, Websites, and conferences as means to address the multitudes.

following christ's pattern

Jesus sent the disciples out in teams of two (Matt. 10:1–2; Luke 10:1). He invested most in an inner circle made up of Peter, James, John, sometimes Andrew, and Himself, which makes a team of five. He lived every day with a spiritual family of the twelve disciples. He personally trained and deployed the seventy. When he ascended into heaven, he left behind 120 disciples. He appeared in person at one time to more than five hundred followers after his resurrection. Although these groupings were the main focus of his life and ministry in order of priority, he also healed, taught, and fed the multitudes in numbers ranging from three thousand to more than twenty thousand at a time (Figure 7.4).

Leaders and leaders of leaders can and should follow Christ's example. Too often we focus on the larger groups, which gives us

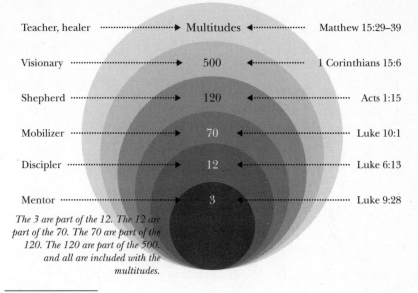

Teacher, healer	Multitudes	Matthew 15:29–39
Visionary	500	1 Corinthians 15:6
Shepherd	120	Acts 1:15
Mobilizer	70	Luke 10:1
Discipler	12	Luke 6:13
Mentor	3	Luke 9:28

The 3 are part of the 12. The 12 are part of the 70. The 70 are part of the 120. The 120 are part of the 500. and all are included with the multitudes.

Figure 7.4 A Leader's Ability to Influence at Each Numerical Level, with Jesus' Example

the most accolades and pressure to perform but also produces the least results. Figure 7.5, which is adapted from *Organic Leadership* as well, demonstrates the variety of leadership roles one can have in the church and ties them to the number of people one can influence in those roles. It is most important, as you can see, to invest the best and most of your time in the center of the target.

We need to see church as connections of people for a variety of purposes and in groups whose size varies with the purpose. For far too long we have seen church as only one thing, and the goal was to grow that one thing every year. There is much more to the church than that (Figure 7.6).

the perils of violating these natural patterns

Trying to go backwards results in hollow programmatic development rather than natural life and transformation. When churches begin with large groupings and then try to estabish smaller groups after the start, the small groups are not a source

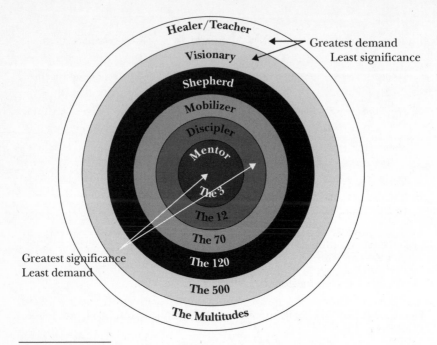

Figure 7.5 Leadership Roles and Number of People Influenced

Reproduction should occur naturally at every succeeding level of complexity, beginning at the smallest and simplest level. It should never stop at any level but continue to fuel the whole through reproduction of units at each stage.

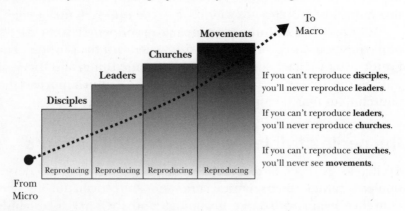

Figure 7.6 Natural Phases of Organic Church Development

of life, growth, and reproduction and therefore are merely a means of programming spiritual life rather than releasing it.

Trying to accomplish comparable results with the wrong-sized grouping wastes energy and resources and leaves nothing to show for it. For instance, when churches try to make disciples using groups of twenty-five to seventy-five and skip the size of two or three, then much of the true power of relational accountability and obedience is traded for a sort of group exercise that may train people in skills but not in holistic discipleship.

Morphing from one size to the next without maintaining the smaller sizes sacrifices the future. The needs of the smaller groupings never go away. When we have people graduate from a small group to a larger one and no longer maintain the original size, then the power and dynamic that caused growth in the first place is forfeited. I have talked with literally dozens of church planters over the years who have regretted the fact that they lost something when they grew to a larger church gathering, and no longer had the intimacy and spiritual vitality they had when they started in a home. The solution is not necessarily not to grow but to maintain the right size groups for the most effectiveness.

Bypassing the micro units cuts out the transformation that makes all other levels more meaningful and also derails all true growth via reproduction. The kingdom of God expands on the shoulders of a changed life. Deeper life change can occur only in the lowest levels of church organizational life. If we target only the larger groups, we trade transformational growth for informational growth, which doesn't really change a life or a society.

The important thing to do is make sure there is health at every level and progress from an earlier level (smaller size) to the next level with the growth and reproduction of the previous one. In other words, you form a small group of twelve to fifteen by first multiplying groups of two or three. This growth from one level to the next need not be sequential; it can start with the smaller groupings first. Going from the largest to the smallest is not only backward but causes a number of problems. It places too high a priority on the larger gathering at the expense of relationships, and it derails reproduction.

Of course, we are all leading busy lives; to mandate weekly meetings for all sized groups would be crazy and cruel. The intentions of some groups do not demand weekly or even monthly meetings. The level at twenty-five to seventy-five people is best serving an occasional need. As you prioritize the groups, keep in mind that the smaller-scale groups of two or three and twelve to fifteen are indeed more conducive to transforming lives than are larger groups in the hundreds and thousands. I recommend that you place a higher priority there than in the larger groups, which can perhaps meet all needs less often than with weekly meetings.

Forming expanding networks of disciples, leaders, churches, and movements can occur only if we pay close attention to how God created people to interact. For far too long, the Western Church has ignored these important concepts and in the process forfeited a real opportunity to change lives, and consequently transform neighborhoods and nations.

part three

pragmatic concerns

8

what about evangelism?

from drawing converts to catalyzing movements

It is the duty of every Christian to be Christ to his neighbor.
—MARTIN LUTHER

IN THE BEGINNING of his seminal work *The Forgotten Ways,* Alan Hirsch asks a profound question: "How many Christians were on the planet in 100 A.D.?" He then asks, "How many were on the planet just before the reign of Constantine in 310 A.D.?" The answers are a lesson for us all:

- In 100 A.D. there were as low as twenty-five thousand Christians.
- In 310 A.D. there were as many as twenty million followers of Christ.[1]

The Gospel of Jesus Christ went from 0 to 10 percent of the world's population in just over 250 years. Then he asks the question that the rest of the book addresses: "How did they do that?"

A movement such as this is not about making converts; it is about transforming people into active followers of Christ and messengers of the Gospel. For too long we have had a different view of how to expand Christianity. Whether we take people to church services or to crusades in a stadium, we have been trying to convert people from unbelief to belief. In the past, we have been more concerned with getting people *saved,* but I am not content with that mission. I also want to have people *sent.* I believe that simply getting people to convert is a short-sighted goal unworthy of the Gospel. We simply must put more stock in the Gospel and understand that it carries enough power within to change someone from the inside out, forever. That change in itself is potent. Instead of trying to get people out of the world and into the church, we need to get people out of the church and into the world. So long as they are Jesus people, they will be fine in the world. Not even Jesus tried to take people out of the world (John 17:15), and Paul saw such an endeavor as foolish (1 Cor. 5:9–11). Evangelism is not enough; we need to release movements. The word *evangelism* derives from two words: good news and messenger. It is not just about converts; it is about igniting new messengers of the good news.

apostolic genius

Hirsch coins a new expression for the missional church: *apostolic genius.* It is defined as "the built-in life force and guiding mechanism of God's people."[2] He calls it "that unique energy and force that imbues phenomenal Jesus movements in history."[3] Alan's work is masterful at laying out the environments and priorities that must be in place to witness such a movement, so I'll not even attempt to duplicate his own genius.

In essence, apostolic genius is found within each Christ follower and carries the potential of igniting a movement. Apostolic genius is not just an apostle with a high IQ; the genius behind apostolic genius is the presence of Christ's Spirit within us. If this is true, then why are we not seeing an unleashing of movements? Environmental factors must be in place to release the apostolic genius in us all. We need catalysts to grease the channels that apostolic genius travels on.

In his follow-up book, *The Forgotten Ways Handbook* (with Darryn Altclass), he elaborates much further on what he means by apostolic genius.[4] If you passed up the second book because you thought that a handbook would simply be worksheets based on the content of the first book, you are missing out on a great read. More than a publisher's chance to make additional money on an already successful book, it gives Hirsch the opportunity to develop all his important ideas in a deeper manner. He lists five "apostolic habits," each with a subset of practices that further inculcate what he calls "apostolic envioronment."[5] Although I concur with all he says, I also believe there are ingredients to the catalytic nature of the apostolic gift that are foundational to movements and that need to be unpacked further.

Taking his cue from Brafman and Beckstrom's *The Starfish and the Spider*,[6] Hirsch describes the apostle as the catalyst of apostolic movements. Even though this is right, it is actually not the apostle's personal presence that is the catalyst within an apostolic movement. A catalyst maintains its own integrity as it interacts with other elements to increase their effectiveness while not losing its own potency. The influence of the gifted apostle can start a catalytic reaction, but the apostle himself or herself does not spread with the movement. For example, as Paul matured in his apostolic gift he traveled less, not more, staying in a place for an extended time. By doing this, he let others carry the work in all directions farther than he could ever go—and his influence spread exponentially, much further than his earlier missionary trips.[7]

It is the extended influence of the apostle, not his or her actual physical presence that sparks the movement and gives it the wings needed to fly throughout a region or people group. Paul even wrote a letter to a church that started under his influence (as its apostle) even though most of the people had never met him (Col. 2:1). Paul's foundation was laid without his physical presence being necessary. Hirsch understands this in describing the apostle as one who initiates vision and ideas *and then steps back*.[8]

More than any other gift, the apostle delights most when disciples carry the work on to others, and everything he or she does is designed with this in mind. The New Testament describes the apostle as a foundation layer (Eph. 2:20; 1 Cor. 3:9–13; Rom. 15:20), which means he or she lays the principles down that will allow the missional DNA to carry throughout the development of the church. It is especially important to understand this quality at this time, when so many people claim apostolic authority, but in fact they expect everyone to be drawn to and directed by him or her. A foundation does not cast a shadow. It is not the most noticed part of a building; it is usually ignored and walked all over. This is often the response to a true apostle (1 Cor. 4:9–13). Not looking to be the center of attention, the true apostle wants others to be the messenger of the movement. For this reason, I believe that part of the apostolic genius is not so much the apostle's own hands-on ministry as it is his or her ability to get others to spread the message. It is not the apostle as a person but the influence that is the true catalyst of a movement. Granted, it is nearly impossible to separate the two. In this chapter I focus on the part of apostolic genius not yet elaborated by Hirsch.[9]

I want to describe some of the elements of apostolic genius that form the foundation of movements. I offer some of the sociological principles that reinforce the ideas I have come to believe are necessary to catalyze movements. After that, I use our own movement (CMA) to illustrate these ideas and flesh them out. By presenting CMA in this manner I am not presenting *the* model of apostolic genius. I do not share these examples in any sort of prescriptive manner; I am merely describing what we have done with the principles discussed in this chapter. Simply copying us will not be sufficient. As we did, you must first grapple with the principles, listen to the Lord's voice, and figure out what will work in your own context with your gifts and callings. That is the most prescriptive statement I will make in this chapter!

Please keep in mind that I'm not presenting these ideas in this chapter like some slick Madison Avenue attempt to create buzz. If indeed these ideas are sound, then we should see how Jesus displayed the apostolic genius that would spread so rapidly. In the next chapter I turn the light on some of the ways in which Jesus Himself showed His apostolic genius by answering common questions about what we do with baptism and communion in organic church movements, because these practices and ideas (as well as some others) are the mark of true apostolic genius.

the catalyst of movements

When I was a teenager, we used to reshape and repair our own surfboards. We would apply the resin to the fiberglass and add a catalyst, which caused the resin to harden in a few minutes. You had to be careful that you were ready to add this ingredient because once you did, it would be too late to correct anything; it worked too fast. The truth is, the resin was going to harden anyway, but the catalyst accelerated the process. A catalyst maintains its own potency while interacting with other properties in increasing their rate of effectiveness. In other words, a catalyst accelerates a natural occurrence, without being consumed by the process. Designing catalytic ideas and methods is basically my role in our movement. I am an architect of ideas, with catalytic elements to fuel the acceleration of Jesus movements everywhere.

I have found through years of trial and error that there are six characteristics of a catalyst that spark movements. By catalyst, I mean an idea, a product, or a practice that catches on and spreads virally so that it suddenly blossoms into a movement, which is when that something spreads from one person to another. This spontaneity is why the apostle himself or herself cannot be the actual catalyst so much as the engineer of it. Internet marketing expert Seth Godin remarks, "There's a difference between telling people what to do and inciting a movement. The movement happens when people talk to one another, when ideas spread within the community, and most of all, when peer support leads people to do what they always knew was the right thing." He goes on to say: "Great leaders create movements by empowering the tribe to communicate. They establish the foundation for people to make connections, as opposed to commanding people to follow them."[10] The tools, methods, or strategies that enable people to connect together and pass on memorable ideas are the catalysts I am talking about.[11]

With Church 2.0, we evaluated a church's success by how many people attended and how much money they left there. Because Church 3.0 is a movement, success is not measured by how many people come, but instead by how many go! We want to measure the church's sending capacity more than its seating capacity. We ask: "Are the message, the method, and the mission spreading from one person to the next and then on to the one after that?" For such a release to happen, apostolic genius must be released, engineering good catalysts that can ignite a movement.

The reason I call these ideas and tools catalysts is that the method may not actually be the cause of the spread, only the thing that accelerates it. I firmly believe it is only the Spirit and Word of God (which are core to apostolic genius) that carry any true spiritual movement. Because we all have these potent missional properties, the potential of a movement is within each of us (see Chapter Four). Jesus understood this concept and even spoke of it when he used the analogy of leaven. Leaven is a catalyst when added to dough, causing it to rise (Luke 13:20–21). Only a small amount of the catalyst is needed because it maintains its own property and multiplies its influence. This chapter (and the next) focus on the catalytic elements that enable the people to pass apostolic genius on to others. Importantly, apostolic genius is the potent force of real movements. The catalysts are tracks that allow the power to spread. Both are necessary. Apostolic genius would incite a movement alone, but the catalyst accelerates the process.

six qualities of a good catalyst to ignite and accelerate movements

Through trial and error over the past twenty years, I have found six ingredients of a good catalyst.

a good catalyst is simple

Simple things reproduce. You cannot pass on something complicated from one person to another and then another and so on. The more complex an idea, the more people will think they are incapable of mastering it. As a result, they will not be empowered to tell others for fear of getting it wrong.

In the book *Made to Stick: Why Some Ideas Survive and Others Die,* Chip and Dan Heath also start with this fundamental characteristic. Simplicity is not just about being able to pass something on. There is more to it. There is something powerful about the editing process that creates a simple and yet potent thing. It is not just about what is excluded but about what you deem so significant that it is included, that makes an idea potently simple. The Heath brothers say: "To strip an idea down to its core, we must be masters of exclusion. We must relentlessly prioritize. Saying something short is not the mission—sound bites are not the ideal. Proverbs are the ideal. We must create ideas that are both simple and profound."[12] This process of relentlessly prioritizing solidifies into something so important that it cannot be ignored. Seth Godin also articulates this when he says, "The art of leadership is understanding what you can't compromise on."[13] Antoine de Saint-Exupéry, best known as the author of *The Little Prince,* once said, "Perfection is achieved, not when there is nothing more to add, but when there is nothing left to take away."

Sanity is knowing what to fight for. Insanity is fighting for anything. Cowardice is not fighting for anything. Some things are worth fighting for. Some things are even worth losing a fight over. A few things are worth dying for. I'm convinced that you are ready to lead when you are able to know the things that are worth dying for, and the things not worth fighting over. You will find that after you have lived enough to know these things more people will receive your message. Your authority increases as you realize this is what you know to be true, and all else is secondary.

I recently had breakfast with a leader in our movement who was frustrated because others were not so capable of casting the vision for the city-reaching ministry he started. He did not have a problem in recruiting people to the vision; he could do that too well (in my opinion). Others could not internalize the vision and pass it on to their friends as if it were their own. To help him simplify his vision I asked him, "What are you willing to risk offense for? What are you willing to be hated over? What prevents you from associating with a given church or ministry?" When we ask these questions we are chipping off excess marble to reveal the masterpiece that lies within the hard rock. When we get down to the rock bottom of ourselves, then we are able to state things with bold clarity. Others will not only understand our message but also relate to and in turn verbalize it themselves.

Coming up with a vision is easy. Releasing a movement is more of a challenge. A vision does not sell itself and become a movement unless it is something people can buy into and then sell as well. If you cast your vision, you may get followers and draw a crowd to your work. A movement is much more. In a movement it is not *your* vision; it is a vision all want to spread, because they have come to own it themselves. It is as much theirs as it is yours.

To get there, you can't just add more attractive things to the vision. Quite the opposite: you have to cut out attractive things. If you can cut everything out but the most important core, you have something simple and profound at the same time. Package this idea in something so simple anyone can do it memorably, and you have a catalyst of a movement. It's that easy—and that hard. It's easy to describe this but hard to pull it off. Most of us need to learn the difficult lessons of valuing the editing process more than we value our own ideas. We have a vested interest in the components that are less valuable. We tend to want to slide some of our own cherished things into the mix, and then the whole idea becomes more complex and less powerful, and it does not spread. So the scrutinizing process also involves objectivity that is often at your own expense. This is what makes it hard.

You and I are not the initiators of our movements. Jesus is the King, and He is the one who has given us the message of our movement. It is remarkably simple, so simple a toddler can understand it and buy in. The Gospel is profound enough that theologians spend their lives trying to work it all out. Nevertheless, it is simple.

a good catalyst starts small

I am a big thinker. Some people assume that because I do church in a small way I am opposed to big things, and this is vastly untrue. I will not be satisfied until the whole world is changed, and you can't do that in a single church; but you can with many small ones. The way to effect global change is to start with the microscopic.

Seth Godin boldly declares, "Small is the new big."[14] Contrary to the way we usually think, the way to big is really to go small. Of course this is counterintuitive. So we generally try to make something grow bigger and end up doing less than we could. Jesus used the parable of leaven to show the effect of a small thing on a massive scale. He also often referred to the smallest known seed as having huge potential for earth-shaking results (Matt. 17:20).

In his hugely successful book *The Tipping Point: How Little Things Can Make a Big Difference,* Malcolm Gladwell identifies three characteristics necessary for an epidemic-type spread of a trend, an idea, or even a virus itself: "one, contagiousness; two, the fact that little causes can have big effects; and three, that change happens not gradually but at one dramatic moment" (he calls this moment the "tipping point").[15] He devotes an entire section of his book to "the law of the few," in which he cites example after example of how huge epidemic-type movements began with very few people. In fact, it is the only way they begin.

Not every small thing is powerful. It matters what is within the small package. A grain of sand and a grain of wheat are both small. One has the God-given potential to eventually feed the hungry world; the other can be the catalyst to create a blister or a pearl—but only once. The catalytic package of being small is not enough if the apostolic genius is not carried within each person.

Before we can change the world, we must be able to change a single life. We must change a life in such a way that the same life is able to do it all over again with someone else. This is best done in small ways that eventually affect the world. If you are looking to spread an idea virus by coordinating larger groups to do so, the whole process breaks down. If it is as simple and small as one life to another, the virus can spread easily, with every person carrying the contagion.

AIDS, a tiny microscopic virus, is bringing an entire continent made up of dozens of nations to its knees in Africa. Passed on from person to person in an entirely predictable manner, this virus spreads almost unhindered because those infected continue doing what spreads the virus. In combating AIDS, we are not just trying to figure out a way to stop the virus itself; we want to stop the behaviors that spread it—and that is the hardest part, because it is against the natural drive in people.

Why is small so big? Small does not cost a lot. Small is easy to reproduce. Small is more easily changed and exchanged. Small is mobile. Small is harder to stop. Small is intimate. Small is simple. Small infiltrates easier. Small is something people think they can do. Big does not do any of these things. We can change the world more quickly by becoming much smaller in our strategy.

Seth Godin even warns of moving from small to big too fast.[16] If you outgrow the viral nature of your idea too quickly, you may corrupt the very things that make it contagious in the first place. You can shift from a viral approach to a more conventional means before the infamous "tipping point" occurs, and you will lose everything in the process. Do not despise the day of small beginnings (Zech. 4:10), and do not be in too big a hurry to get past them.

a good catalyst is surprising

There is a problem with the status quo. Even when you read the words you feel some disdain, don't you? Status quo doesn't stimulate any excitement or creativity. It is the curse word of the new millennium.

The Gospel is all about transformation—*change*. The Christian life and the status quo are opposites. If I read my Bible correctly, any life that stays the same is not Christian. Nevertheless, much of the religious world values not rocking the boat and maintaining the status quo. We, of all people, should be the ones who not only embrace change but bring it with us wherever we go. Our reputation, however, is the opposite. "Religion" says Godin, "at its worst reinforces the status quo, often at the expense of our faith."[17]

To incite movements, we must acknowledge the spot we're in and then set off on an alternative course. At the risk of the obvious: to stay put is to not move. We cannot be a movement and remain in the status quo.

We must present an alternative that is surprising enough to capture the curiosity of others. In *Made to Stick,* the Heath brothers say: "We need to violate people's expectations. We need to be counterintuitive . . . we must generate interest and curiosity . . . by systematically 'opening gaps' in their knowledge—and then filling those gaps."[18] Christianity is an invitation to launch a mysterious journey from which we will never return. Our message should be memorable because it is not what was expected. When someone finds an unusual solution to a dreaded problem, it is hard to forget. In fact, it becomes hard to keep it to yourself.

The Gospel is a solution to death—not just eternal death, but a life slowly dying day after day because of inescapable sin. Freedom from the captivity of sin is Good News worth telling. It is a surprising proposition that we are set free from death because a perfect Proxy, sent from a loving God, died in our place and then rose from the dead! How could we not want to tell people this powerful and surprising idea?

It is a sin to present the Gospel in a boring way. Everything about the Good News is surprising, and transforming, and should incite movement. The Gospel is not an invitation to walk down an aisle or a sawdust trail; it is an invitation to the adventure of a lifetime! The Gospel introduces a journey that will end with great significance and a life lived well. It is an invitation to an intimate relationship with an eternal God who adopts you as his beloved Son or Daughter. The Gospel presents the opportunity to have Christ's intimate presence at all times and in all circumstances. The greatest surprise in all of life is called a mystery by the apostle Paul: it is Christ in you, the hope of glory. Who can resist that?

a good catalyst is significant

It is not enough to have a simple process packaged in a surprising and small way, if indeed you are passing on something of little or no value. After fiercely scrutinizing your ideas to the core, you will find that if the core is potent then you have a significant principle.

From my point of view, what we are spreading must be important, although importance is given less value in the burgeoning literature on viral marketing. Some write about the spread in popularity of Hush Puppy shoes,[19] or an innovative vegetable peeler,[20] but those are fads, not a movement. A movement does more than change your footwear; it moves you to do something or be something. It asks more of you than to just buy a product; it wants you to buy into an idea. It lasts longer than a fad and leaves a lasting mark on society. This can be a good mark or a bad one. The Nazi youth movement in Germany was not a good thing, but it left a mark on history.

The difference between a fad and a movement is in how it changes people and leaves a mark on the world. A fad, like the Hula Hoop, simply comes and then goes away. Today it is seen in nostalgic footage meant to reminisce about the good old days. Yes, you can still find a Hula Hoop in some places, but you are not likely to see a commercial for it today because so few are interested in buying one; the fad is over. "Been there, done that, bought the T-shirt."

If you drop a stone the size of your palm into a small, calm pond, you will see the water ripple outward until the energy is expended at the shore. Within a few minutes all the energy is absorbed, the reaction is gone, and the pond is left unchanged. The same is true of a fad. If you drop in a tablet of chlorine the same size and weight of the stone, you will see the same ripples come and go, but there will also be a chemical chain reaction that will cleanse the water over the course of hours. This is what a movement is like; it creates a chain reaction that changes things.

Many ask me if the organic church movement is just a fad. I believe that if we see lives transformed then it will not be a fad. If we just see Christians meeting in homes and doing the same thing they previously did in church buildings—or more significantly, still not doing the things they didn't do before—then we will be a short-lived fad. The key is, do we change lives? Are people so moved and changed that they cannot go back to the old way? Ultimately, it is not the missiologists, the theologians, or even the statisticians that determine whether or not you are a movement; it is the future historians. Simply doing church in a home rather than a cathedral is not enough of a significant principle to incite a movement, only a fad. Let us hope we are passing on transformative ideas and methods that will birth a movement and not just a fad.

Although there are plenty of good ideas in the kingdom of God, I have personally found the most transformative idea is always the Scripture itself. How could we miss that? When we devise a simple process involving a small group that allows the Word of God to speak for itself, then it is something that not only can spread but is worthy of spreading. Working on these things for two decades now, I discovered that this is not hard to do at all. The Scriptures are given to spread throughout the world. We simply need to place our faith in them rather than in our own ideas. Later in this chapter, I present examples of how the Scriptures can be the significant principle that speaks for itself as a catalyst.

The truth is that if we have the truth then we have the most significant principle of all. As I pointed out in my earlier work, *Organic Church*, Sir Walter Moberly, a non-Christian educator, once said to us as Christians: "If one tenth of what you believe is true, you ought to be ten times more excited than you are."[21] We should ask why we are not seeing more movements. I suppose the answer is that we are not letting out the most significant part of our faith: God's revealed word.

a good catalyst has "sticky" potential

In the breakthrough book *The Tipping Point,* Gladwell introduced an idea that was so descriptive and helpful that it "stuck" with us. He called it the "stickiness factor." His terminology became sticky itself. There are more and more books using the language. Larry Osbourne has a book called *Sticky Church,* and I have referenced the Heath brothers' book *Made to Stick;* each is influenced by Gladwell's sticky terminology.

The stickiness factor has to do with the memorable quality of the idea, product, or method that is spread in a movement. When the idea is so intriguing that it sticks with people—they can't forget about it—a movement can happen. This is (pardon the pun) the glue that makes a movement come together. If the idea itself is not such that people want to tell others about it, then you cannot start a movement. You can sell products, ideas, and even ministries with advertising and mass media promotion, but that is not a movement. To ignite a true movement, the idea itself must spread from one person to another—only sticky ideas can do that.

Chip and Dan Heath's book on this very subject pays homage to Gladwell for applying the word *sticky* in this way. They go on to examine all the traits necessary to make an idea stick; some of them (simplicity, surprise, importance) are already included in my own six characteristics of apostolic genius, but they also add three others that I think are worth mentioning.

1. Concreteness: an idea can be solid to people when we make it clear, using concrete images that relate to life experience, so that it is understood and believed in instantly.
2. Emotions: people must feel something for the idea or it will not land very deeply in their memories.
3. Stories: people remember stories, not facts.

The reality is you do not need an assessment tool to discover whether something is sticky or not. All you have to do is examine how you feel about it. If it doesn't stick to you, it probably won't stick to someone else. That said, there are some things that are sticky only to certain tribes of people. If you're the one motivated enough to create something in a specific field and it doesn't stick with you, it's time to go back to the drawing board. Of course, the ultimate test of an idea's stickiness is its spread or lack thereof. It really is easy to find out if it is sticky or not; just hand it off and see what happens.

Within CMA's history, we have invented many viral methods and ideas. We found that the ones that were truly sticky we did not need to publish or produce in any formal manner. They were passed along verbally (usually diagrammed on a napkin). In fact, we will not even publish an idea until we have seen it already going viral first. Once we do see something truly sticky that is spreading on its own, then we begin to think of ways to publish it and accelerate the process.

The movie *Pay It Forward* is a good story of a sticky idea that spawns a movement. It is the story of a middle school boy who is challenged by his sociology teacher to come up with an idea that can change the world. He does. His idea is called paying it forward. It works using all the basic movement principles listed here. One person helps someone else, but it has to be something important. Then the one helped, instead of paying it back, pays it forward by doing something really big for three other people. Those three in turn pay it forward to three others as well, and a movement is catalyzed by a simple, memorable idea that is significant, spread in small packages using natural pathways. The important thing making the idea viral is that you have to do something really big for the other people, something they couldn't do for themselves. This is what makes the idea sticky. If it were just a little thing, like helping a lady across the street or holding the door open for someone else, it would be acknowledged and then quickly forgotten; it wouldn't be sticky.

Having a sticky church is not enough to ignite a movement. Even if the church is healthy and enjoyable enough that people want to tell their friends about it, all they can do is bring their friends to the church. Stickiness alone is not enough; the church must also have the other attributes mentioned in this chapter if you want to release a movement. That said, it is a good thing if your church is so good people can't help but tell their friends.

a good catalyst follows strategic relational pathways

In *Organic Church* I spelled out the idea that each of us is connected to people who are connected to others.[22] In fact, as you have probably heard before, we are all only six degrees separated from any person on the planet. In other words, between you and any other person on the planet—a gondolier in Venice, a pygmy in the Congo, or the prime minister of England—are five or fewer intermediaries. This concept can open your mind to the powerful idea that we are connected to everybody and capable of reaching thousands or even millions by reaching just one.

This powerful truth is amazing, but what makes it all work is not "everybody" but instead what Gladwell calls "the law of the few." He breaks these few into three types: the connectors, the mavens, and the sales people. The real reason for such a phenomenon is that some people are so extraordinarily connected they make up for the rest of us.

I have a friend whom I mention often in my books because she is a mentor and powerful woman in God's kingdom. Her name is Carol Davis. You probably either know her, or someone you highly respect does. I am only partly exaggerating. Carol has never written a book, though I always encourage her to get her ideas down. She does not have a doctoral degree or a position in some large organization. She is not wealthy or politically powerful. Carol has a keen understanding of people and God's kingdom. Many people value her wisdom. You won't find her name on the cover of any books, but you will often read it in the acknowledgments of books by dozens of well-known authors. Carol's most incredible gift is that she knows people, naturally assesses their unique qualities, and likes to connect them—and she knows *a lot* of people.

We often joke that every person on the planet is separated by six degrees unless you know Carol; then it's only two. God has created and placed these key people in the world for a purpose higher than selling products. Carol is what Godin would call a "powerful sneezer."[23] He teaches that viruses spread because people sneeze, and he likens the key people in an idea virus movement to sneezers. There are two he describes: "the promiscuous sneezer," who likes to sell anything and everything; and someone like Carol, "the powerful sneezer," who really propels a true movement.

Powerful sneezers will not sell just anything. They have particular tastes based on deep and highly respected knowledge. They are careful with their recommendations because they know they have a reputation. They highly value all their friends and would never want to recommend something that is not helpful. When they do find something that they value and they start telling others about it, their range of important friends will buy it because it comes from them. When you get the promiscuous sneezers also spreading the same idea, then you have a movement. This is the pathway of a movement. If a few of these types start sneezing your idea, a rapid movement will be released.

I always give Carol free copies of my books. I do so because she is my friend (and she is probably mentioned somewhere in the book), but also because she is a powerful sneezer. In the case of a couple of my books, she has done more to generate interest than the entire marketing department of the publishers.[24] As for other books of mine, she was grateful for the gift. Even friendship doesn't guarantee influence, and this is why I will buy any book she tells me to get. I trust her recommendations implicitly, and so does her vast array of friends around the world.

the six catalytic qualities in cma

From our early days, CMA has been searching for and designing catalytic methods and ideas. It is what we do best. Not that every idea works; we have more that do not succeed than that do. We use these six catalytic characteristics to scrutinize everything. Here I list some of our successes, but you must know that for every success there are ten failures collecting dust on the Shelf of Shame in our offices.

a simple process: seven signs of john

The Gospel of Jesus is the flame that burns at the grass roots of the apostolic movement. Having a means of igniting that flame in such a way that those who catch it can spread it on the same day is an extremely valuable catalyst. We felt we needed a means of unveiling the true Christ to a person open to it, one that was simple enough that everyone could do it in any culture, language, or generation. That is a tall order to fill. We found our answer in the Bible, specifically the Gospel of John.

The seven signs of John are based on the words that the apostle writes near the end of his Gospel. He said, "Therefore many other signs Jesus also performed in the presence of the disciples, which are not written in this book; but these have been written so that you may believe that Jesus is the Christ, the Son of God; and that believing you may have life in His name" (John 20:30–31).

Apparently, although John was with Jesus from the start and saw all the miracles performed, he selected these particular miracles and included them in this specific order[25] for a purpose: to open the eyes of the unbeliever to have faith in the real Christ and gain eternal life. This is not my opinion; this is what the Scriptures themselves say. Consider it this way: the Holy Spirit is telling you that the miracle stories in the Gospel of John are the stories that are best adapted to present the true Christ to an unbelieving heart. It is quite common for American Christian leaders to exaggerate the effectiveness of a method, but in this case it is the Holy Spirit making the claim, not me.

The signs are:

1. The turning of water into wine (John 2:1–12)
2. The healing of the royal official's son (John 4:46–54)
3. The healing of the paralytic at the pool of Bethesda (John 5:1–17)
4. The feeding of the five thousand (John 6:1–14)
5. Jesus walking on water (John 6:15–25)
6. The healing of the man born blind (John 9:1–41)
7. The raising of Lazarus (John 11:1–46)

How this method works is that the person or persons you are sharing with are encouraged to read one story a day for a week. In the first week, they read, say, the story of Jesus turning water into wine. At the end of the week, when you meet and read the passage again together, you ask four simple questions and discuss the passage. The questions:

1. What does this story say to you about *people?*
2. What does this story say to you about *Jesus?*
3. What does this story have to say about *you?*
4. Who needs to hear this story?

This can be done easily by meeting once a week over a cup of coffee with anyone who is a spiritual seeker. Every organic church I have ever started began going weekly through these stories and simply asking the questions. I have yet to do so and not see someone commit to following Christ. I am not guaranteeing you the same results, but we can take the Holy Spirit's word for it that these stories will help people believe in Jesus.

This profound ministry tool crosses all cultural barriers because it is simply the Bible speaking for itself (a significant principle!). It reproduces because anyone can ask a few easily remembered questions. This is not a model of church or a human curriculum. It is merely unleashing the power of God's word to do what it does in a life. The only way you could say that this doesn't work cross-culturally is to say that the Bible doesn't work cross-culturally. Even in an oral culture that is not literate, this tool will still work because it is basic storytelling.

start small: life transformation groups

The mission of the church is not to convert the lost but to make disciples of them. A small reproducible pattern that allows every disciple to make other disciples almost immediately and that connects each disciple to the Master Himself is a potent catalyst for apostolic movements. A Life Transformation Group (LTG) is that. Ultimately every church is only as good as her disciples. We need a simple disciple-making tool that has a small enough pattern to easily reproduce disciples: life on life.

An LTG is made up of two or three people, all of the same gender, who meet weekly for personal accountability in the areas of their spiritual growth and development. A group should not grow beyond three but multiply into two groups of two rather than a single group of four. If a fourth person is added to the group, it is recommended that the group consider itself pregnant and ready to give birth to a second group. Once the fourth person has demonstrated sufficient faithfulness (two to three weeks), the group should multiply into two groups of two.

There is no curriculum or training needed for the LTG. The Bible and a simple bookmark that stays in the participant's Bible are all that are needed.

The LTG consists of three essential disciplines for personal spiritual growth: confession of sin, a steady diet of repetitive reading of the Scripture, and prayer for others who need Christ.

The pattern is simple and small. Two or three meet. They have a card with character conversation questions on it and anyone can read the questions. All answer. They also choose a book of the Bible they will read on their own the following week. They try to read twenty to thirty chapters in the week. If one person doesn't finish reading all the chapters, then everyone will read the same book again for the next week. They continue this process until all three complete the reading in the same week. Then they move to another book. Some people think this is a lot of reading, but the idea is *not* to finish each week. The amount of chapters read is supposed to be a stretch, so that it takes a few weeks to finish. Each person identifies three people she or he wants to see come to Christ and writes those names on all three people's LTG card. Every day they each take one of the names and pray for the person.

a surprising proposition: our sayings

One thing I commonly mention when I am talking to an audience is, "We have a saying in our movement." I will then go on to state one. This is actually by design. I could just say the words without singling them out as a "saying in our movement," but I want to clearly identify that these sayings are meant to be passed along. In a sense, I am more interested in people stating it themselves as if it were their own than repeating it as a quote from Neil Cole.

We have developed these sayings over the years. Each one is meant to plant a memorable seed thought that carries an important idea. They are proverbs of the organic church movement designed to shock your senses and present an alternative way of seeing things. Here are a few:

- "We want to lower the bar of how we do church so everyone *can* do it, and raise the bar of what it means to be a disciple so that everyone *will* do it."
- "If you want to win this world to Christ, you're going to have to sit in the smoking section."
- "Bad people make good soil for the Gospel; there's a lot of fertilizer in their lives."

These sayings have legs. It is common to find them repeated in other books, blogs, and training events. For instance, you can find more of our sayings listed in David Garrison's book *Church Planting Movements*.[26] Feel free to say them as if you thought them up. That's the idea.

a significant principle: god's word

We truly believe that God's Word is as powerful as it says it is. We learned long ago that the Word of God is the seed of eternal life and needs to be planted in fertile soil. All that is necessary for life, health, growth, and bearing fruit is found within the seed that is God's Word. Many plant a seed substitute—a message about the Word, but not the Word itself. It is as if God needs our help interpreting His word because He can't seem to get His thoughts across without our help. This is lazy thinking and misplaced faith, putting more confidence in your own teaching than in the Word you teach from.

It is for this reason that we design things such as the seven signs of John and LTGs, to simply plant the Scripture in people's hearts without any intermediary to interpret it. We let God's Word speak for itself, and it does just fine without us. I remember when Myles Hamby, a student at UCLA doing some of our training, read Hebrews 4:12:

> The word of God is living and active and sharper than any two-edged sword, and piercing as far as the division of soul and spirit, of both joints and marrow, and able to judge the thoughts and intentions of the heart.

After reading those words, he paused, looked up at the audience of mostly underclassmen, and asked, "Can *you* do that?" Everybody laughed at the odd thought that any of us could have such power; yet we operate in the church as though our curriculum, sermons, and methods have such an effect. Why else would we so regularly give that stuff to people rather than the actual Word itself?

a sticky potential: the tlas

Over the years CMA has developed powerful training materials. Instead of holding on to them and protecting them, we give everything away—regularly. We have only one caveat before giving it away: the person must first start five organic churches. We want to multiply significant powerful sneezers, but we do not want to empower professional consultants who have never done the work themselves. A powerful sneezer must have credibility.

When we give our material away to others, we also grant permission to change and adapt it. We even allow them to change the name of the material (we do ask that somewhere they identify that it is adapted from our material). In our value system, if there are more people spreading the organic church virus then this is a good thing. We value our mission more than we value credit for our mission. We have only one strong recommendation to the people we give the material to: you can delete anything or add anything, but think very hard before you change the TLAs! Usually I get a bewildered look, so I explain what a TLA is: a *three-letter acronym*.

Our most significant ideas are TLAs: DNA, CMM, LTG, POP, 411, 10–2b, and 7SJ. I've already explained DNA, CMM, and LTG. 7SJ, as you may have figured out, is seven signs of John.

To give you an idea of our significant principles, I will explain briefly the POPs and the 10–2b because these two TLAs are not just great examples but also are all about spreading epidemic-like movements, and they are most often taught together.

The POPs are based on Christ's teaching in Luke 10 and Matthew 10. In both sermons, Jesus explained missional principles for extending His kingdom in dark places to catalyze a movement. You can read much more detail about these principles in *Organic Church*, so I will not go into great depth on any of them.[27] We have isolated six principles from the texts, each of three words whose initial letters spell out POP:

1. *Pockets of People:* identifying the social groupings that people are naturally inclined to form and go to them with the Gospel of the kingdom rather than extracting people from them to form our churches.
2. *Practice of Prayer:* Luke 10:2 says, "The harvest is plentiful, but the laborers are few; therefore beseech the Lord of the harvest to send out laborers into His harvest." When we teach this we spread the 10–2b virus. This is an idea based on the latter part (b) of this verse. When teaching on this, I first sneeze really

loud and exaggeratedly. Then I announce that I have a very contagious virus that I can't get rid of; it's called the 10–2b virus. I then give them the virus. The idea is that we all set our mobile phone alarms to go off at 10:02 AM every day. I tell them that when the alarm goes off, whatever I am doing I stop for a minute, turn my thoughts to heaven, and beg my father for Him to call out and cast out new workers for His harvest fields. I also explain to whomever I am with why I am doing this, and I have them program their phone alarm too. At that point, I tell my whole audience to take their phones out and give them the time to set their alarm. If I am with people who are not yet followers of Jesus, instead of having them pray I ask if there is anything they would like me to pray for on their behalf—and then I pray for them. This is a great example of a viral catalyst. It is simple, small, surprising, significant, sticky, and spreading. As I travel around the world I spread this virus so that every time zone is infected. Every hour of every day, Heaven is being bombarded by the prayers of God's people, begging for workers.

3. *Problems of Planning:* Jesus specifically sends the disciples in twos without any resources except one another and the presence of the kingdom. They are not to bring money, plans, or ministry tools. He tells them specifically to simply announce, "the kingdom of God has come." The idea is that they were to either demonstrate God's power or leave looking like fools, but certainly not to demonstrate any power of their own. We usually make the mistake of doing the opposite. We come to people with plans, brands, resources, and expensive strategies. When we do this, those we reach are instinctively taught to believe from the start that expensive resources of this sort are what are needed to reach people, so the movement stops before it starts. We must learn to let Christ's power shine rather than our own, and to do this we must learn to come in weakness and faith.

4. *Power of Presence:* Jesus told his disciples to go to a town and proclaim that the kingdom of God has come. Can you imagine the audacity of such a thing? Talk about a surprising proposition that would capture everyone's attention! The idea is that wherever you go the kingdom of God (the reign of our King) goes with you. There is power in just showing up. Light always

overcomes the darkness, and you are a light to the world. Your greatest significance is found in dark places.

5. *Person of Peace:* Jesus taught, "Whatever house you enter, first say, 'Peace be to this house.' If a man of peace is there, your peace will rest on him; but if not, it will return to you. Stay in that house, eating and drinking what they give you; for the laborer is worthy of his wages. Do not keep moving from house to house." The person of peace is the influential sneezer of a kingdom movement. The instructions are clear. We are not to go from house to house; the Gospel is, but we are not. The person of peace is the key to that. We call the person of peace the first domino in a chain reaction to the Gospel of the kingdom. We strategically teach people how to discover a person of peace.

6. *People of Purpose:* the result of this kingdom strategy of Jesus is a new church born in the context in which the people are found and in such a way that it can spread from there to other such pockets of people. Jesus understood the catalytic principles of an apostolic movement.

I have heard others teaching our TLAs in a variety of contexts. A fine example of rejoicing when others spread the catalysts in their own way is Jaeson Ma's great little book, *The Blueprint,* for student-led campus churches. DNA, POP, LTG, 10–2b, and 411 are all found in the content of Jaeson's book, which is in many ways a contextualization of our Greenhouse training.[28] You can find our DNA and LTG mentioned in Tony and Felicity Dale's excellent book *The Rabbit and the Elephant.* LTGs are mentioned in numerous books, including recently *Exiles* (Mike Frost), *The Forgotten Ways* (Alan Hirsch), *Movements That Change the World* (Steve Addison), *How to Multiply Your Church* (Ralph Moore), and *Missional Renaissance* (Reggie McNeal). I am only mentioning this to demonstrate that the TLAs are sticky, and some powerful sneezers are spreading their message.

a spreading pathway: greenhouse training events

The Greenhouse is our method of training in organic church practices. At the time of this writing, we have conducted 209 weekend events and trained more than twenty-one thousand people in the catalytic ideas found in this chapter, in just eight years. From the outside, it appears that the Greenhouse is our front door to the world and our means of spreading the seed of our movement, and indeed it is. In my opinion, it is the behind-the-scenes portion of Greenhouse that is the best part. You see, once we do the teaching we watch to find out who takes the ideas and runs with them. Those who are faithful in implementing the principles and starting a network of churches (three or more) we invite into our training to become a Greenhouse trainer.

We usually have at least two presenters for each training. It helps to hear from people with contrasting styles and experiences. But the more important reason we have two presenters is that we are constantly training new trainers. We believe that you learn more by teaching than by being taught, so we enlist people to be involved in spreading the catalysts. At first they just supply "color commentary," which means they help answer questions and tell a story or two, all the while listening to the same material again for at least the second time. The next time, they teach two or three parts they are most comfortable with, all under the watchful eye of an experienced lead trainer. The following time, they go over the material at least for the fourth time and are asked to teach parts they have not taught before. Finally, they become lead trainers themselves and begin to teach not only other audiences but new trainees.

The best part of this is that it is infecting these influential people with the catalysts at a deeper level. They then become the organic church movement evangelists. We give them permission to teach this stuff all the time. I do not want to take anything away from these strong leaders; they do not just teach our stuff. They are given permission to change the way it looks, add their own stuff, and give it another title. All over the country (and now the world) are training events by another name that are presenting much of what is in the Greenhouse: Catalyst Training, Blueprint Training, Student CPx, as well as many others. All of these trainers come to a deeper level of ownership with the material because of the freedom we give them to adapt it. Some of our best trainers are so good that they headline events, while I am just the warm-up speaker. At the time of this writing, we have almost sixty of these powerful sneezers spreading the message of organic church movements.

9

what about baptism and communion?

from sacerdotal rituals to apostolic genius

> *The church exists for nothing else but to draw men into Christ, to make them little Christs. If they are not doing that, all the cathedrals, clergy, missions, sermons, even the Bible itself, are simply a waste of time. God became a Man for no other purpose.*
> —C. S. LEWIS

I HAVE STARTED MANY CHURCHES in the past ten years. It seems that a church doesn't really feel like a church until we baptize our first new disciples. We have had several baptism parties in this decade, and I know that nothing makes the church family more joyful.

One night, a young lady named Alice, struggling with her sexual identity, decided to follow Jesus while at a coffee house in Long Beach. We felt that the best thing to do was baptize her, so we let all her friends who were there know that we were heading to the beach to baptize Alice. This was a curiosity to a lot of the regulars, so several cars drove the mile down to the beach to witness what was happening.

About fifteen or twenty of us gathered on the shore in a circle. Alice was asked why she wanted to be baptized. She told us that she had chosen to follow Christ and wanted to tell the world. We prayed, and she followed her disciple maker into the ocean. It was a magical night. Bioluminescent plankton in the water gave off a fluorescent glow as the two waded in. She was baptized to hoots and cheers from the people on the beach.

They came back out of the water and we gathered again in a circle, joined hands, and prayed. The message of Christ's atoning death and resurrection was presented once again, followed by a challenge to follow him. Two more people who had come decided to follow Jesus. They waded out with Alice and another in their street clothes and were also baptized.

This is not a rare occasion for us; it is actually more common to have people accept Christ and get baptized in their street clothes than not. If more of us presented the opportunity, we would all get to have the same kind of party and experience this same joy. In this chapter I will demonstrate that Jesus gave us certain practices for the express purpose of presenting the truths of the Gospel in memorable and challenging ways. If we use these methods as they were prescribed by Jesus, it may be more common to see the kind of results that the practices were originally intended to incite.

Perhaps the most dangerous ground a church revolutionary can tread on concerns the "sacraments" or "ordinances" of the Christian faith: baptism and communion. Hundreds if not thousands have literally lost their lives over the centuries because of these practices commanded by our Savior. At the risk of offending many, I would like to take a look at Jesus' instructions from a slightly different perspective and see if there is more to them than our religious leaders have shown us.

In the previous chapter, I laid out some catalytic principles that can ignite and accelerate the spread of epidemic movements. I also shared one of our tools called POP, which presents six missional principles from Jesus' teachings that actually exemplify all of the catalytic characteristics. I have already shown you how Jesus understood and used these principles, but I believe we have more to learn from the genius behind apostolic genius. What we are about to unfold in this chapter is a fresh and alternative way to view some very old religious practices. You may or may not agree with me, but at the least you can learn a new perspective of our Lord's genius.

the genius apostle behind apostolic genius

We all know that Jesus was a genius and an apostle. He is also the one who instills in each of us the powerful apostolic genius that carries the movement of His church. He succeeded in starting a movement, as we have already pointed out, but did He employ the six catalysts we've just discussed that accelerate the transfer of apostolic genius from one person to another? The answer is that He did, in many powerful ways, but unfortunately these catalytic ideas and practices have been buried in church dogma and hidden behind stained-glass windows.

I believe that Jesus established a few things that are simple and reproducible and able to carry a message that expands His kingdom and changes lives. These practices are transferable; anyone can do them, and they are meant to be set loose.

Unfortunately, Satan has done everything he can to keep them from accomplishing what Jesus intended. We have hidden our Christian practices, which in the New Testament were carried out in the marketplace for all to see. We have "sanctified" them—our preaching, our baptism, our communion meal—and moved them behind stained-glass windows. We've even developed doctrines to keep them reserved for the saints and dispensed by special holy men with collars and robes.

Our true Enemy has been hard at work trying to pull the teeth out of the potent practices that Jesus established. The Enemy's scheme is to remove them from the context where they are indeed dangerous to his cause. Baptism was meant to be public. Communion was meant to be a shared everyday meal, which can "proclaim the Lord's death until He comes" (1 Cor. 11:26). In the New Testament, preaching is always for the purpose of presenting the Gospel of God's kingdom to those who are trapped in the darkness. It was not done from behind a pulpit to an audience of Christians to help inspire them in their own personal sanctification.

on baptism

As I said, I believe more people have lost their lives over the issue of baptism than any other spiritual practice. In many parts of the world where being a Christian is illegal, it is not uncommon for someone to accept Jesus with few repercussions, but if the person chooses to be baptized he or she reaps all manner of persecution. Throughout history some of the great heroes of our faith (Luther, Calvin, Zwingli, and others) would have people drowned or executed in some other way because they wanted to be baptized as adults. My own denomination has had several splits over the issue of how baptism is to be done properly and to whom it is acceptable.

Even today in Los Angeles there is heat involved with being baptized. I have had Muslim converts get excited about following Jesus and obey everything but baptism, because they fear being completely ostracized from their family. I have seen fear in the eyes of people who surrendered to Christ from a Roman Catholic background when it is suggested that they be baptized as adults in obedience to their new faith; they fear their parents will disown them. Recently, I even had a young man in my church receive strong abuse from his parents, who are part of an independent Christian church, because he wanted to be baptized. His parents' pastor stepped into the mix and said that our organic church people are "novices" and "heretical" and that the young man should be baptized only by those who have the "spiritual covering" of their church. What does that even mean? Where is it in the Bible?

Baptism is so important to some people that they have adopted the term to identify themselves and thus separate themselves by it; they are *Baptists*. Of course, now we have so many varieties of Baptists that we need other words to clarify which brand we mean.

Why would such a simple act be so volatile? Why are secular and religious people, denominations, institutions, pastors, and historical figures so threatened by an action that is over in a matter of seconds?

Even as I write this, you (like many others) may be tempted to say, "Forget about it. This is just a symbolic act that is done one time; it isn't worth all this hatred, division, and spilled blood." That sounds calm and rational, but it may very well be exactly what Satan wants. You see, I think there is a reason the true enemy, the Devil, has done so much to keep baptism from being what Jesus always intended.

As I explore the significance of baptism in this chapter, I expect it to raise some heat in my own life because baptism is at the heart of each disciple loving Jesus—following Him in obedience, and telling others about Him and thus making more disciples. If Satan can disrupt all that from the very start, he will disrupt a great deal more. This is why the idea of baptism is the target of so much hostility from the Enemy and why dismissing it as unworthy of the struggles it generates is a mistake.

last words of our savior

The Great Commission is important. It is the last word of Jesus to His disciples before He left them on earth to carry on His work. I recently had the people in my church read the words of Matthew 28:19–20 out loud. Afterward I told them that all the Greek words in the passage were translated into English, except one: *baptizo*. The Greek word means "to immerse" and was used in ancient times to describe a sinking ship or a garment that is being dyed. It is more than pouring or sprinkling; it means being completely submerged. We are not talking about tie-dyed clothing in the first century.

When the Bible was first being translated into English, the translators couldn't just translate the word because they were no longer immersing people. They were sprinkling infants at the time, so they simply transliterated the word—making an English word out of the Greek one. That is where we get the word *baptize* from.

It did not really take the Enemy long to attack the simple practice of baptism and knock Jesus' direction for it off course. Before the close of the first century, the church had already parted ways from the New Testament pattern and not only delayed baptism but reserved it for people who really proved themselves to be Christians. It became something akin to the Old Testament practice of circumcision, and done to infants shortly after birth. Because a newborn baby cannot be immersed, they began sprinkling the baby with water. Soon only the ordained holy men with special robes and ceremony could do it. By the time the New Testament was to be translated into common English, baptism no longer meant immersion. So they coined a new word for it.

Baptism is not just a church ceremony; it is a key element of disciple making. It is at the core of the Great Commission. If you take it out of the hands of the ordinary Christian and reserve it for only the clergy, you take disciple making out of the hands of the ordinary Christian. I am amazed at all the pastors who want their people to fulfill the Great Commission but then do not allow them to do so because they will not permit them to baptize.

I have found that if you give people permission to fulfill all of Jesus' commands, they will rise to the occasion. We will never fulfill the Great Commission and live up to the last words of our Savior until we put the work into the hands of everyday Christians.

weirdness in the church

The practice of baptism is not something Christ gave to the "clergy," church organization, or institutions, but to all disciples. One of the sayings in our own church-planting movement is, "The Bible doesn't command us to be baptized but to be baptizers" (see Matt. 28:19–20).

There is absolutely no biblical support for the idea that only the clergy in the local church can baptize. Though our traditions and experience may reinforce such standards, the Bible does not. In fact, it is my opinion that the Bible is slanted in the other direction. Those who are seen to be the leaders in the New Testament are often not the ones who are doing the baptizing; instead their disciples are. Jesus didn't baptize; his disciples did (John 4:1–2). Paul states that he is glad he only baptized a few in Corinth (1 Cor. 1:13–15).

It is amazing how much damage the simple idea of baptizing another has caused through church history. People have been killed, cults have been initiated, denominations started and split, heretics burned at the stake, and parachurch organizations have been formed—all because we view baptism in a strange, unbiblical fashion. If we would only read the Bible and take it for what it says literally, rather than defend our "sacred" traditions, the church would be healthier.

We have created spiritual boundaries to manage spiritual practices, but these boundaries are not in the Bible. As false boundaries begin to take on a biblical sense of authority, they grow quite insidious. We accept them as truth and even rise to defend them, as though they come from the Bible when they do not. Unfortunately, we are often willing to submit to these false divisions more than to Scripture itself. This is how the subversive strategy of the Enemy causes so much damage. Because we have allowed artificial boundaries to separate Christian groups on the basis of illegitimate organizational differences, weird things happen.

For instance, one motto for a parachurch ministry was "to fulfill the Great Commission in this generation." This seems honorable, except that they have rules in place that prevent them from ever fulfilling the Great Commission in any place. Right in the middle of the Great Commission is the command to baptize disciples, which they strictly forbid in order to maintain their "parachurch" status because (in their view) only churches can baptize.

quick baptism

I think we are guilty of protecting new believers from depending on God. If we were to follow Christ's example and deploy new believers immediately in ministry, we would see how quickly they are forced to pray, trust in God, listen to the Holy Spirit, and find answers. This would solidify their commitment on a much deeper level from the very start. They will have an unbreakable bond to the Head of the body, Jesus Christ. They will also learn to suffer for Christ's sake, which is part of the important pattern that Jesus and Paul set for us (Phil. 1:27–29).

Perhaps this is why baptism was done so quickly in the New Testament. It was a chance for a brand-new believer to make a stand publicly for the new Lord, driving a figurative stake in the ground to declare allegiance to the Triune God in front of peers, family members, and coworkers. I fear, once again, we have wandered too far from the plain truth of the Scripture, with dire results. Simple observance of the plain pattern of the New Testament would serve us well in all areas of church practice. In our movement, we baptize as quickly as we can and as publicly as we can. It is not uncommon to have people accept Jesus right there at someone else's baptism and be baptized themselves while still in their street clothes.

baptism *with* salvation, not *for* it

One of the questions that have plagued the church through time is whether baptism is essential for salvation. Part of the problem is that the institutional church, from at least the days of Constantine, used baptism as a sacrament that empowered the church and its leadership over the people. This has caused confusion for almost all of our history.

But this is not the whole explanation. One reason the institutionalized church has been able to get away with this is because the New Testament itself connects baptism and salvation so closely together (Acts 2:38; Rom. 6:24; 1 Pet. 3:21). We cannot escape the fact that baptism and salvation are connected; the question is, *how?*

I do not think that the water is magical. I do not think that baptism conveys any special grace beyond the grace that one reaps from following Christ in obedience. Nor do I believe that any work we do, even baptism, merits salvation.

Being baptized is not the way to be saved, but it is an outward action to make the decision more than just a thought—and salvation is indeed more than just a thought. Salvation involves the whole person: thoughts, emotions, and will. It should be considered the first step of a new life, a life of obedience. Baptism and public confession are the willful expression of an inward faith, a public declaration of the decision. It is a step that announces a life of allegiance to the King.

Paul tells us it is not important just to believe with our hearts; there should be an act of the will, which actually cements the faith with a dose of reality. I think this is something of what Paul meant in Romans 10 when he said:

> If you confess with your mouth Jesus as Lord, and believe in your heart that God raised Him from the dead, you will be saved; for with the heart a person believes, resulting in righteousness, and with the mouth he confesses, resulting in salvation [Rom. 10:9–10].

Baptism is a clear way for the new believer to confess publicly that she or he has an internal belief in salvation. In the New Testament the disciples who made a decision to follow Christ took their first step into the water. Baptism is, in a sense, much the same way walking an aisle for an altar call was a few years back. Once again, we have an example of our substituting a nonbiblical practice for the one first established by Jesus. The "sinner's prayer" is another example of this. Neither the altar call nor the prayer is an adequate substitute.

Baptism symbolizes so much: a cleansing, but also a tomb (death and resurrection), and a womb (being born again). It is being completely immersed in the name of the Triune Godhead with nothing held back. It is the end of an old life and the birth of a new one.

Baptism reflects Christ's apostolic Genius. It is:

- *A simple process.* Baptism is really the most natural of processes. It is as common as bathing. It would have been a common practice of the day and something everyone would know how to do. It is as simple as down and up.
- *A small pattern.* Baptism, as a core part of disciple making, is no more complicated than one to one. It is the smallest pattern possible in community and is the beginning of the most basic unit of life in the church: one disciple in relation to another.
- *A surprising proposition.* Jesus took a common practice and thrust into the midst of it some things that change everything. First, He has us do it in the name (singular) of the Father, and the Son, and the Holy Spirit. God is one and is three persons at the same time. That's a surprise. Yet it shouldn't be. Why? Because God is love, and God is eternal. For Him to be both love and eternal, He would have to be able to love someone before time began. You cannot really love void of relationships. So when God made us in His image, He made us relational. This is why He said it isn't good for us to be alone. It wouldn't be good for God to be alone either. He is relational and He made us relational in His image. A Triune God is the only way for us to have a relational God that is only one God. We are to be relationally one with the other as the Godhead is (John. 17:20–26). A second surprising principle is that we are to die to find life, which I would say is a surprise; baptism represents the death to our old life, buried with Him and then risen again to new life.

- *A significant principle.* Baptism is a picture of a truth that is foundational for all others: that we have chosen to follow the Triune God at the expense of all else.
- *A sticky potential.* Baptism is a scary thing for a new follower to do. It is meant to be in a public place, before all your peers and family members. The fear is supposed to be part of it. Starting off your new life with an act of faith, at great risk and personal expense, sticks with you. It is an emotional story lived out for all to see. You don't forget it, and neither do those who witness it.
- *A spreading pathway.* The whole idea behind baptism is that a disciple baptizes the next one, who is then commanded to obey the commands of Jesus, which includes making another disciple who is also to be baptized. In other words, you cannot obey the command without reproducing disciples via baptism.

communion

Near the end of Jesus' public ministry, He took a turn in a radical direction and it so offended the majority of people that most turned away from Him. The great teacher, miracle worker, and healer suddenly sounded more like a vampire than a messiah.

He talked of eating His flesh and drinking His blood. The truth behind the words was to be shown to the disciples in a short time, at a dinner where He would break from the normal Passover pattern and initiate a new pattern. He took the bread, broke it, and said that it represented His body, which was to be broken for us. Then He took the cup of wine, and as He passed it along the table He instructed that it represented His blood, shed for us. He told us that as often as we do the same thing, we are to remember Him. Jesus instituted a new practice for His disciples. It was symbolic of the very heart of the Gospel, and it was to be repeated. We have repeated it, at least in some form, all these years. But in most cases, we are far removed from the context in which it was originally intended.

from the table

We call it the Lord's Supper, because it is based on the dinner experience where Jesus first instituted it. But it is also called a supper because it was always meant to be part of a supper. The early church called it the *agape,* or love feast. Today we have so reduced the manner of this practice that it is now just a thin wafer of Styrofoam-like "bread" and a thimble of grape juice passed down the aisle of a church building. Yet we still have the nerve to call it a supper. Somehow I expect more and better food from Jesus at His dinner parties.

The Lord's Supper was originally part of a common feast for the church family to enjoy together, remembering what Jesus did for them and the great supper we will all share when He returns. There is no doubt that Jesus intended for us to eat together, because this is what families do. So much can happen at a dinner table that cannot happen sitting in rows and seeing the back of the head of the person in front of you. When communion is taken out of the context of a family seated in a circle around a table and put into an auditorium with rows of pews, it loses much. We have replaced a common table with a sacred altar, but that is not the context in which Jesus broke bread and passed the cup. When church is removed from everyday life in a home, it becomes convoluted and mutated.

When Jesus began this practice He took elements common at every meal and made them spiritually significant. The staple diet of the first-century person would include bread and wine. Jesus used the most common elements of the most common practice of life, and He gave them powerful symbolic meaning. Why? He says, to remember Him.

We have taken His intended practice and made it anything but common. Usually only the priest or pastor will be able to bless the elements. We have removed them from a table in a home and placed them on an altar in a cathedral or "sanctuary." The Lord's Supper was meant for all to partake of, but now we actually threaten to punish people if they are not among the special group that we are part of. In many cases, we have toned down the ingredients so that it is no longer a meal but a barely edible cracker and a sip of unfermented grape juice—more in common with a very bad kindergarten snack than a loving feast. Instead of a couple times a day, it is now a special service done once a week at the most, and in many cases it is performed only quarterly. Communion has all the trappings of a religious ritual and none of the everyday life appeal that it was meant to have.

all to partake

A misused passage from 1 Corinthians has caused us to reserve this sacred rite just for the brethren, and the good ones at that. In Corinth, some wealthy church members who had no regard for the poorer brethren, most of whom were slaves, had a monopoly of the meal. They would leave nothing for the others who worked all day serving the rich and could not join the meal until much later, after the food was gone. What was meant to be an inclusive meal that unifies all of God's people in love had become exclusive and selfish. For this reason, some were sick and even dying because of sin.

The passage reads:

> Whoever eats the bread or drinks the cup of the Lord in an unworthy manner, shall be guilty of the body and the blood of the Lord. But a man must examine himself, and in so doing he is to eat of the bread and drink of the cup. For he who eats and drinks, eats and drinks judgment to himself if he does not judge the body rightly. For this reason many among you are weak and sick, and a number sleep. But if we judged ourselves rightly, we would not be judged. But when we are judged, we are disciplined by the Lord so that we will not be condemned along with the world. So then, my brethren, when you come together to eat, wait for one another. If anyone is hungry, let him eat at home, so that you will not come together for judgment. The remaining matters I will arrange when I come [1 Cor. 11:27–34].

For a long time, we have applied this passage to mean that the communion is only for insiders who have a clear conscience. We often warn any unbeliever in our midst not to partake for fear of great punishment. But the reality in Paul's letter is that the ones who were being judged are clearly Christians who were being divisive in their selfishness and not sharing the meal with others. Is that not an irony? We use the verses that are teaching us it is dangerous to not share the meal, and use it as an instruction to intentionally not share the meal. Not that very many people are hungry for a paper-thin cracker and a single sip of grape juice anyway.

It is almost universally taught that unbelievers are not to take the bread and the cup, but the Bible never says this. Its only warning is for the abusive Christians who were not sharing with others. In fact, it says, "For as often as you eat this bread and drink the cup, you proclaim the Lord's death until He comes" (1 Cor. 11:26). Doesn't that sound like a great message for someone who is not yet a follower of Christ? It is remarkable when you think of it, but at the core of the Gospel message is that we share a meal with others. In a hungry world, Christianity is supposed to be generous, which symbolizes the love and sacrifice of Jesus for us all. This is why when some Christians were selfish and hording they became sick and even died under the discipline of the Lord. This is very serious to our Lord, who paid a great price to give this all away.

It is especially noteworthy that when Jesus first instigated the practice, He himself handed the bread to Judas Iscariot (John 13:18, 26), who clearly was not a Christian (John 13:11). If indeed Jesus set the pattern that we are to follow, then excluding unbelievers is not the right thing to do. We should be more careful about excluding people than including people, because the warning passage is directed against those who kept some from eating the feast.

digesting the gospel

There is no indication anywhere in the Bible that specially anointed Christian leaders are to be the ones who administer the Lord's Supper. I believe that this practice was meant to be so common that anyone can do it, and in fact does do it more than once in a day. It was a transferable method for sharing the good news at an informal table with any guests who were welcomed.

Think of how easy it would be to invite a friend who doesn't know Jesus to eat with your family. In that very beautiful and generous setting, as the bread is broken and passed, you remind the table of its important meaning. Then, as the cup is prayed over and passed, you also remind all at the table of its significance. In this way, anyone can share the Gospel in an informal and highly relational manner. It is simple, powerful, and easy to spread to the next table.

The guests not only hear the Gospel in a safe and loving context but get to taste it as well. The message has greater influence because it is carried on multiple sensory channels into the heart and mind as well as the stomach of the invited guest. They digest the Good News in more ways than one. The welcome smell of bread and wine will trigger an important memory in us all. Every time they eat and drink afterward they will again be reminded of the Good News.

stoking the flames of love in god's family

Jesus did not say, "By this will all men know that you are My disciples: by your great knowledge, bumper stickers, T-shirts, or WWJD bracelets." It is by our love for one another that we show our devotion to Jesus (John 13:35), not our doctrine or denominational label. Communion is meant to be the wind that stokes the flames of love in our souls.

One reason they called the Lord's Supper the love feast is because the bread and cup of communion are intended to remind us of Jesus' love and sacrifice for our sins. There is nothing that can turn your eyes off yourself and on to Jesus like the Gospel. John says, "We love because He first loved us" (1 John 4:19). The Lord's Supper reminds us every day of the forgiveness of our sins. Jesus tells us that whoever is forgiven much, loves much (Luke 7:46–48). These meals were to be so full of love that any who would come could not help but fall in love with the people and Jesus. How we do communion today has the exact opposite effect. It has become an individualistic act, consumed in silence and solitude and done for God, instead of a community expression of gratefulness for how much Jesus has done for us. How do we raise the elevation of the love quotient in our church? Discovering the great qualities of the people there is not the answer. Concentrating on being positive toward others will not get you there. Reading books about love and increasing your understanding of it will not increase the actual love in your life. Feeling guilty or ashamed about your lack of love will never stoke the flames of love in your life. We must remember Jesus and His sacrifice for our sin to find the love for others that is so needed. The Gospel is the source of love, and love is the fulfillment of the entirety of the Christian life. As Paul declares, "For I have determined to know nothing among you except Jesus Christ, and Him crucified" (1 Cor. 2:2).

as often as you take of it

There is one other thing I need to expose about this practice. One reason the Lord chose to use the mundane act of eating and drinking the food and drink that was most common to their diet is because we need the reminding of His sacrifice often—as often as we eat and drink. This special act of breaking bread and passing the cup was to be a daily part of life, not a once-a-month or quarterly practice.

Here is what Paul said of it, quoting Jesus:

> "This cup is the new covenant in My blood; do this, as often as you drink it, in remembrance of Me." For as often as you eat this bread and drink the cup, you proclaim the Lord's death until He comes [1 Cor. 11:24–25].

The more we saturate our souls with the Gospel, the more we will love others. This is why Jesus tied the remembrance of His sacrifice to an act that everyone would do more than once a day. Could it be that every time we eat bread and every time we drink a beverage we are to take a moment and remember the love of Jesus demonstrated in His sacrifice for us? Wow, what a thought! How that would change us if we were to actually reflect on the Gospel every time we eat and drink. Imagine the opportunities you would have to mention the Good News of Jesus' death and resurrection, whether you are at a family dinner, or going to a friend's home for dinner, or even at a lunch meeting.

The Gospel is not just for evangelism. Paul calls it the power of God for salvation, to everyone who believes (Rom. 1:16). It is power for us believers, and frankly I say we need power in our lives. Perhaps if we gave thanks to Him for His sacrifice every time we eat or drink, we would be a different kind of person.

Let's run the idea of communion as we have just looked at it through the criteria of apostolic genius:

- *A simple process.* You cannot get more basic than a meal together.
- *A small pattern.* This is meant to be a real meal where people can share together in fellowship and love. A family is the ideal environment.

- *A surprising proposition.* "Eat my flesh and drink my blood" is about as surprising as you can get. It is provocative, and certainly memorable.
- *A significant principle.* Jesus' substitutionary atonement is about as significant a message as there is. Taking in the life of Jesus in exchange for His death is significant. His body broken for us so that we can become His healthy body is amazing. Communion is the very picture of the new covenant (1 Cor. 11:25), where God dwells with us and partakes of life among us, and puts His life and word in our hearts. It is His sure promise that we are His and He is ours.
- *A sticky potential.* You cannot find a more compelling and emotional story than the substitutionary atonement of God's only begotten Son. It is a story of redemption, with good overcoming evil in the end against all odds and after a harsh struggle. This is a story that all of history has been shaped by.
- *A spreading pathway.* All pathways on the planet pass through the dinner table. After someone has heard and tasted the Gospel at a Christian's dinner table, she will be reminded of the powerful message every time she partakes of a meal after that. Even to this day, I cannot help but think of Jesus when I slice a piece of bread at a table.

the lord's prayer

Another transferable practice is the Lord's Prayer. At least in this case, the institutional-minded church hasn't taken the practice out of the hands of the ordinary Christian, but it has taken much of the power out of the practice by making it a superstitious form of penitence.

The disciples saw the special intimacy of Jesus with His Father, every single day. It was such a beautiful thing that they had to ask Him how it worked. They asked Him how to pray. In response, Jesus gave them this example:

Pray, then, in this way:
"Our Father who is in heaven, hallowed be Your name.
Your kingdom come, your will be done, on earth as it is in heaven.

Give us this day our daily bread.
And forgive us our debts, as we also have forgiven our debtors.
And do not lead us into temptation, but deliver us from evil.
For Yours is the kingdom and the power and the glory forever.
Amen" [Matt. 6:9–13].

Is this just a prayer to be said from rote memory? Or is it more? I believe it is more, a beautiful example of Jesus' apostolic genius giving the disciples a pattern to follow that is reproducible and powerful in its outcome. In reality, I believe the Lord meant for it to be a pattern for His people to commune together with God. It makes for a great pattern of an organic church meeting. They asked Jesus to show them (plural) how to pray, and He did just that. We are so individualistic in the West that all we can see is personal and individual application. But that would not be a correct application of what Christ is giving to us in this passage.

Here is the breakdown of the simple pattern Jesus gave us:

- *Exaltation of God in worship of who He is:* "Our Father who art in heaven, hallowed be Thy name."
- *A joint missional accountability and surrender to His reign in life:* "Thy kingdom come, Thy will be done, on earth as it is in heaven."
- *Prayer together for daily needs:* "Give us this day our daily bread."
- *A radical relational inventory and accountability to reconciliation among each other:* "forgive us our debts, as we also have forgiven our debtors."
- *Prayer for guidance and protection in the ongoing spiritual battle:* "lead us not into temptation, but deliver us from evil."
- *Acknowledgment of the Lord as our king and our lives as belonging to Him:* "For Thine is the kingdom, and the power, and the glory forever. Amen."

Notice that the prayer is completely in the plural voice ("our" and "us"), it is not meant to be something done individually but as a family—all under the headship of the Father. Jesus is not just showing us what to say when we pray; he is giving us a pattern for how to exercise our spiritual life as a family with *our* Father.

I think this is really quite similar to the way my friend Andrew Jones describes living a missional life that ends in starting churches: make friends, throw parties, tell stories, and give gifts. In his own apostolic genius, Andrew has simplified what it means to do church planting in a simple, repeatable, yet profound manner. It is a pattern that almost anyone can follow because it encompasses patterns already present in our lives. It is concrete and familiar.

A description of making friends, throwing parties, telling stories, and giving gifts makes the work seem entirely possible for regular folk—even fun. Telling people to start churches (with all that this implies in our current world's experience) sounds awful to most people. Instead, make it simple and concrete and powerful. Connect God's infinite complexity and power to simple and ordinary people who are capable of doing something easy and normal. Let God be the complex part that gets all the glory, and let us be the simple part that doesn't deserve any credit because we're doing nothing beyond the norm. We are the clay pots that carry the glory of divine truth in us. The more complex and important we make our actions and our ceremonies, the less glory God gets because the methods take center stage.

The Lord's Prayer is something almost half the world can recite, and yet it remains powerless in some regards because it is not followed as Jesus intended. I do not think this is a tragedy but an incredible opportunity. If this is indeed meant to be a pattern for how to connect together as a spiritual family with the Father, and half the world already knows it, just think how easy it will be to start new churches once the light turns on! In a sense, God has already laid the foundation of a rapid global church multiplication movement; all we need to do is get people to see what it is they already know how to do.

Here's how the Lord's Prayer looks as a catalyst:

- *A simple process.* Six simple sentences, that's all it is. It is so simple that it is already being said all over the world, countless times today.
- *A small pattern.* It sets in place a pattern for the grouping of a spiritual family (twelve to fifteen). It must be applied in a context of community and involves accountability to one

another. In spite of what occurs the world over, the prayer is impossible for one person alone to use without changing the pronouns. There are some fairly strict limits on the size of a group that can adequately apply the pattern.

- A *surprising proposition.* God, the infinite all-powerful and all-knowing Creator, will meet with us in intimate relationship, care for our needs, restore us to fellowship, protect us from the evil enemy, and take us out on mission together in His power and for His glory. He wants to be our Father, an incredibly exciting and surprising proposition.
- A *significant principle.* Connecting together with God in intimate relationship. You can't get more significant than that.
- A *sticky potential.* It is simple, memorable, and concrete; it connects us all with an emotional story that is no more complicated than a Father's love for His children. In spite of the prayer not being used in its intended manner, it has maintained its sticky nature, as evidenced by the billions who can recite it at any moment.
- A *spreading pathway.* The family is the basic building block of all societies. It is universal and desirable to all cultures. Wherever there are families, there is a chance for this pattern to be put in place.

It is my hope that as I walk through these simple processes Jesus initiated, explaining their natural context and intent, you can see just how much the Enemy has stolen from us. What a travesty that we have taken such powerful ideas and removed them so completely from the very people they were intended to influence. What a loss that we have cheapened them so much and distorted them to such an extent they are not even recognizable when seen through the experience of Jesus.

Perhaps the greatest shock of all is that some reading this will think it is I who have trampled on the sacred and polluted the holy. I hope not, but I suspect that it may turn out that way for some.

What would happen if every true follower of Christ began to make disciples and baptize them in front of family members and friends? What if some of them also became followers and were baptized? What if they then gathered fellow disciples in the home for a meal in which they pronounced Jesus' sacrifice for them all as the basis for their love for one another? What if they followed the pattern of worship and prayer together regularly as a spiritual family? What if it were that simple and everyone could do it without needing permission granted from some human hierarchy? Is there enough of the Good News born in these practices that if given over to the common Christian they could release a potent movement of reproduction that goes way beyond the shadow of an institutional church? I believe so. Why else would Satan work so hard to keep them away from people? The meaning behind these demonstrations of apostolic genius may actually be something worth dying for.

We need to take back the apostolic genius of Jesus and let it loose again. Our spiritual leaders have to step out of the way, hand back to God's people these powerful catalysts, and let them ignite and accelerate the movement that Jesus began two thousand years ago.

10

what about kids?

from a scholastic model to a spiritual family

New Testament believers viewed the church as neither an edifice nor an organization.
—STANLEY GRENZ

As THE TUTTLE FAMILY DROVE through downtown Los Angeles at night, the sight of Skid Row captured their attention, especially for eight-year-old Andrew. He was alarmed seeing many homeless people sleeping on the sidewalk, some in cardboard boxes, some without shoes. He fired questions at his mother and father. "Why are they on the street? Why don't they have homes? Where are their families?" Then he asked a question that changed the Tuttle's life: "What can we do for them?"

Tim was at first tempted to say to his son, "The problem is bigger than us, and we can't do anything. There's nothing you can do for them, Son. Just pray." Rehearsing the response in his head, he realized how it would affect Andrew's future views on life. The consequences were too grave to follow through. Instead, they all prayed that God would show them what to do. Andrew's concern ignited a spark in Stacy, his mom, whose thoughts turned to mobilizing resources to make a difference.

Andrew's questions and his parents' response led to the start of a ministry called Campaign for Care,[1] which creates and distributes blankets and foam mattresses for the homeless. It wasn't the grown-ups who ignited this ministry, but an eight-year-old boy looking at the world with the faith and imagination of a child. His wise parents were willing to listen to their son and encourage him to follow the Lord.

One of the sayings we often repeat in our movement is, "When a child receives the Lord, the child doesn't receive a junior-sized Holy Spirit and a Jesus action figure." The child receives the full power of the Spirit of God and is no less spiritual than any adult. Marrying this Divine empowerment with childlike faith is a world-changing mixture, to say the least. Children are our future, but they are also potent agents of God's kingdom in the present.

One of the most frequently asked questions we receive about organic churches is, "What do you do with children?" I imagine people ask that because they know we don't do Sunday school or the usual age-segregated teaching systems that are common in most churches. The question also seems to imply that because we are not using those pedagogical methods we must be depriving our children in some way; I would argue that the opposite is true.

Most churches (and other institutions) in the West seem to assume that adults and children must be segregated when it comes to teaching and learning. Apparently, grown-ups can't learn anything if their kids are present, and vice versa. All of us have been educated to group children by age and tailor the content and its delivery accordingly. We don't deviate from the curriculum, and as kids we don't mix with children older or younger than ourselves. We don't typically question these assumptions, but I would argue that this is a very small-minded approach, one that is blind to other ways, perhaps even better means of education.

We all can see easily from a cursory reading of the Bible that children are especially important to God. So when He chose to place their nurture and development into the care of an institution, He did not choose a school, but a family. From the beginning, it is clear that the best environment for the growth and development of children is a family setting. This is problematic in a world where the family as an institution is rapidly decaying. Schools have become more responsible for being the place where children grow and develop. According to Hillary Clinton, it no longer takes a family to raise a child but an entire village, and by a village she means public community services (especially schools).

Dana, my wife, is a teacher on the frontlines of education serving the Los Angeles Unified School District and working in South Central L.A. She can attest that children from broken families have a much more challenging road ahead of them in education than those who have a whole and healthy family. Our society tends to put the responsibility for the health of our children on the shoulders of our educators, but God does not. He chooses the family. Instead of following that choice, the church has followed society's lead in giving the spiritual development of our children over to the Sunday school teacher, to an event that occurs once a week. Unlike the church in the New Testament, which uses the idea of family as the essence of what it was to be and do, church has become a religious event that takes place once a week, rather than a spiritual family on a mission together. The entire experience of church—for adults and children— culminates with a teaching lesson. We even use school language ("Sunday school" and "Christian education") to describe what takes place.

This model of church is understandable since those starting and leading churches are trained in academic institutions (schools). Church leaders wanting to know how to lead a church attend seminary and learn in a school context how church should function. We produce what has been modeled for us, and we end up with a teaching institution instead of a spiritual family. The goal of an educational institution is to teach; this also appears to be the primary goal of most churches. We have so invested in this idea that we often equate knowledge with maturity.

We must shift back to a New Testament understanding of church, for the sake of our children and their parents.

integration is better than segregation for children

I have three kids, and they are growing up fast. They have always been a part of church, in a large megachurch, a small traditional church, and a simple organic church. They can tell you the best part of each experience and the worst as well.

In the traditional Sunday school approach, they learned many things for which I am grateful. It was often cognitive learning rather than experiential. They knew facts about Jesus, David the giant slayer, and the lions in Daniel's den, but they did not learn how to love their sister or how to share the Good News with a friend at school. They may have learned about love, but real love is not something you just learn about; you have to learn how to do it, in real life experience. They learned about character qualities but never actually had the opportunity to experience them and see them lived out in others; that is, until they went home.

A few years ago, my family received a call to a new kind of ministry. At the time, we lived in a suburb determined by the FBI to be one of the fifteen safest cities over a hundred thousand in population in the United States. We had our own house, with a nice yard on a quiet street.

Our new call was to urban Long Beach, a place where gangs not only got started but also franchised around the country. We moved into a rented back house with an alley instead of a yard. Instead of crickets chirping we had helicopters flying overhead with spotlights beamed on our block most nights. Many would think this was not the best move for our children. I have to admit, there were a few moments where I myself wondered. But deep inside I knew it was the right decision. We were following the Lord of the harvest, and He loves my kids even more than we do.

Looking back, I wouldn't have traded the experience we had in that back house for any other. The lessons learned on the streets of Long Beach have left a lasting mark on each of my kids. They did not learn to avoid the world and huddle in the Christian ghetto. They have had a different sort of Christianity modeled for them, a missional version that is willing to take risks and incarnate the truth in difficult circumstances. They not only believe in the Gospel with their minds but also literally believe in its power to change lives because they have seen so many lives changed. They are also more sober about the reality of sin, from seeing so many fall away. This is an education you cannot buy with tuition. It is learned in a deeper place than most Bible studies and Sunday school lessons can reach, because the people in these lessons have names, faces, and stories that are real and that my kids have seen lived out in front of them.

When we moved to the city and started organic churches, our kids began to learn in a more experiential fashion. They saw lives transformed. They listened to people share their horrid stories of abusive lifestyles and then watched them live for Jesus. My son has even had a few temporary roommates along the way who needed some stable and loving home life for support. He has learned something about love, kindness, and hospitality that he never could learn with a flannel graph story of a Good Samaritan.

In organic church, we expect great things from our children and we are usually not disappointed. It is common for the kids in our church to have the best questions and share the most profound thoughts. One time, when we were on a tangent about the rapture thanks to the Left Behind series of novels, my middle child, Erin (who was twelve at the time), had a puzzled look on her face. She asked, "If the rapture comes, do people all go up?" I said, "That's what is usually taught." You could see the wheels turning in her head behind the puzzled look in her green eyes. Then she asked, "Well, if the earth is round and we all go up, doesn't that mean that we're all going to different places?" I've never been asked that question before. It took the beautiful mind of a child to think it up. I assured her that if the rapture does come we will go to the same place and she won't be left behind without us.

When we have toddlers in our church, rather than send them to another room with a baby-sitter or a Veggie Tales DVD, we let them be a part of the church. They worship with us, pray with us, and usually waddle from one lap to another. To be honest, I can't remember a single disruptive moment. Because the kids are trained with this sort of church, they just know how to be a part of it. I will never forget the time a small boy had surgery to correct his lazy eye. He came to church and couldn't wait to say something during the praise and prayer request time. He sat on the edge of his seat, his feet barely touching the floor. Opening his eyes wide, he said with great wonder, "Jesus fixed my eyes," as he slowly turned his head around the room to show everyone. We all thought, Wow, what awesome worship! Jesus must love this.

Why on earth would we want to send that person away to watch the latest Veggie Tales video in the bedroom?

Early in the beginning of our movement, my associate Paul Kaak was concerned with how organic church would work out for his young children, Elijah and Jeremiah. Their family went on vacation for a couple months in a rural part of California and decided to start a church during the vacation. At one gathering, they were all praying intently when he noticed how quiet it was. With small children, quietness, though often desired, is not always a good sign. Paul opened his eyes to see if Elijah was getting into some trouble. To his amazement, he saw the boy sitting right in front of him, fascinated as he watched his mom and dad praying for others. So many kids in America see their parents pray only at the dinner table, if at all. Paul was convinced right then and there that integrating kids into church was powerful.

We have forgotten that much of the Christian life is "caught by example" rather than taught by fill-in-the-blank, pop-up, coloring books. It is a real blessing for kids to see their parents worshipping God, and I am always moved to great joy and tears when I listen to my own children as they sing praise to their Savior and pray for other people. I could never go back to the days when we sent them away to another room to be entertained while we took God seriously without them.

There was a moment in the Bible when Jesus' disciples wanted to keep children away from Him so that He could attend to more important things. He rebuked them (and us) by telling them not to take the children away, for all of us need to learn from their kind of faith (Matt. 19:13–15). He is telling us that we need the kids and can learn from them, not the other way around! All my children will tell you that they love being a part of this kind of church.

A few years ago, while I was doing ministry in Japan, I had a dream that my older daughter, Heather (who was almost fifteen years old), started a church with her friends in Huntington Beach, California, where she went to school. After I returned, I told her about the dream as I was saying goodnight to let her know I was thinking about her while traveling.

The next day after school she came home and said to me, "Dad, my friends want to do it." I asked, "Do what?" She replied,

"Start a church." She told me that they were tired of the old boring type of church (her words, not mine) and wanted to be a part of starting a new church. Because she had seen organic churches start a few times, I told her, "Well, you know what to do; go do it, and I will be available to help if you need it." The next day, she came home from school and said they planned church to start the following Thursday in Huntington Beach in her friend's living room. They invited many others from their high school and arranged for a friend who was a musician to lead worship. On that Thursday, their new church was born.

My children have learned things by being a vital part of the beginning of new churches that they could never learn in a traditional Sunday school. They have watched people come off the streets addicted to speed and then turn and follow Christ. They have seen people transformed into powerful agents of the kingdom of God. They fully believe that God is powerful and able to change lives, not just from the stories in the book of Acts but also from the stories of people's lives they have seen. They now have a very real faith and compassion for lost people. I know many churched kids who are actually afraid of lost sinners, but my kids have learned to love them and have a sincere desire to connect with them.

One evening, Dana and I went out on a date and left the kids at home. After dinner, we called them to make sure Zachary, our youngest, was getting ready for bed since it was already getting dark. Heather answered the phone and said that Erin and Zachary were still out back in the alley. I told her to get the kids and bring them in immediately. A dark alley in urban Long Beach at night is not a safe place for a young child.

When Zach got on the phone, he told me excitedly, "Dad, when the mean old lady across the alley backed out of her garage, she said mean things to me and Erin." Instead of asking him what he was doing in the alley at all, I just asked, "Why are you in the alley so late?"

Zach said, "I was waiting for her to return because we had made things for her." Zach said he had made her a picture to try to help her to become a little happier, and Erin had written a message to tell her about Jesus.

When I told Zach that he needed to come in and get ready for bed, he burst into tears and said, "But, Dad, she is old and doesn't believe in Jesus. She probably doesn't have long to live, and I want to tell her about Jesus. We've been praying for her and want to give her these things." He was sobbing for the soul of a person who had treated him like dirt. I know few adults who have wept for the souls of lost people, let alone those who have treated them unkindly.

These kids obviously were filled with the Spirit because they had deep compassion for someone who had consistently been cruel to them. I was tearing up as I talked to my son (and I am tearing up again as I write this). I let him take the picture to her the next day. It didn't change her demeanor at all in the moment, but over the course of a few years she seemed to lighten up a bit.

This sort of compassion is not learned by completing a fill-in-the-blank photocopied sheet of Bible curriculum. It must be modeled and experienced in real life. You must choose to live on the alley if you want to learn the lessons that only an alley can teach you.

A few years later my son was listening to a P.O.D CD and heard the song "Youth of the Nation," about the sad end of many young people who live without Christ and die without hope. He was so moved by the song that he came into our bedroom late because he couldn't sleep. He shook me awake. I asked him what was wrong, and he said he'd decided that he wanted to go back to public school so he could help young people like those in the song.

Out of respect to the Lord's leading in this fifth-grader's life, we took him out of his Christian school and enrolled him in a public middle school the following fall. He has done well there, in spite of transferring in from a small Christian school. Today he is a senior in a large high school. He has played in three sports and is well respected by his teachers and peers because of his godly example; some of his friends have come to Christ, and together they are starting their own organic church.

These attitudes are embedded in my children because they made sacrifices to bring the Gospel to lost people, and they have seen lives change so dramatically. They know the power of the Gospel, and they believe in it. The lessons they have learned through experience will stick with them for the rest of their lives.

Instead of just hearing the stories of other people's faith thousands of years ago, they are walking stories of faith lived out today. Even the lessons they learned from the failures they witness in the crucible of real life are valuable lessons.

It is my hope that these children will grow up and see church differently than previous generations did. Instead of viewing church as a spiritual entertainment center, to be evaluated by how well it suits their own individual needs, they will see church as a missional community to which they bring something special. They will not evaluate church as consumers looking for a good product, but as a family that is on an important adventure together, each with special abilities needed for the success of our common mission. I have learned that if you treat children as if they are weak and helpless and need a baby sitter, they will act that way. If you treat them with respect because the living God dwells in them, and if you wish them to be examples of faith to us all, they will rise to that expectation.

integration is better than segregation for adults

Integrating children into every aspect of a church community is not just good for the kids; it's also beneficial to adults in ways you may never have thought. We live in a time when families are falling apart and parenthood is a lost art. It seems that with each succeeding generation things get worse, at an exponential rate. Dysfunctional parents pass on their flaws to the next generation, only to be added to before they are passed along to the grandkids. This rolling snowball of dysfunction is gaining speed as it races downhill and is destroying many lives and our society as a whole.

Part of the reason for this dire state of affairs is that it is more challenging than ever to find a good model of parenting. The church is not helping with the situation. We may have programs, seminars, and books to help teach about parenting, but we are not getting good examples in church. How could we when we send the kids off to classes with other kids their age, while parents go to another class? We aren't in situations where a new parent can actually watch a seasoned vet respond to her or his children and teach by example.

If we are honest with ourselves, we can see that the reason many of us resist having small children in our church meetings is that the experience could be disruptive. We've been trained to think that what goes on during a worship service is sacred and holy and not to be upset by loud children. This is not true just in sacred halls with tall ceilings and stained-glass windows. Paul Kaak remembers visiting a church in India that met in the open. They rolled out a rug and gathered on the rug to worship. Afterward, the kids were running around as kids will do, and one happened to run across the rug. A church elder grabbed the child by the arm and scolded him for running in church! We do allow the sacredness of religiosity to invade our minds in some rather peculiar ways. If for no other reason, simply being reminded that church is to be a family rather than a religious ceremony is a positive reason to include children in the life and experience of church gatherings.

It is especially challenging to include children, however, when you have some young children with parents who are less than responsible themselves and do not know how to train their children. My own church is full of people who came to Christ from marginal backgrounds of drug addiction, suicide attempts, gang violence, and various sexual addictions, so I do know what it is like to have immature (and themselves poorly parented) people with small children. Nevertheless, I cannot remember a time when the children were an interruption in nine years at this church—which began in the home of a drug dealer.

The reason that kids are not an interruption for us is simple: there is nothing to interrupt! Oh, don't get me wrong; we do have a learning time discussing God's Word, but it is not a monologue by a gifted teacher that demands silence and respect. Instead, it is a community learning time that involves the entire family, including the children, so there is no such thing as interrupting it.

If you think of church as a family rather than a weekly religious event, you begin to see differently the whole idea of what it should be. Children do not interrupt family because children *are* family. Family learns from one another, and that includes other parents. In an organic church, young parents who were raised with poor role models can learn how to parent children well, but not if we separate the family according to age-appropriate educational groupings. It takes a lot for a young couple to admit they do not know how to raise their children in a healthy manner, so they will likely not ask for help unless they have actually seen parents who appear to know what they are doing. The earlier in their children's lives they encounter such role models, the better.

There are moments (although not too many) in our church context where a mom or dad will pick up a small child and go outside for a couple of minutes. Occasionally, I may even take someone else's child out to read a storybook while mom and dad stay and participate in the group learning. We allow kids to go out back and shoot baskets if they want to. Often children draw pictures while we discuss the Scriptures. They are kids and they act like kids; we would expect nothing else.

For us to view church as a spiritual family, we must include children in the mix and allow them to be kids. I personally believe that the familial interactions in church are a more potent way to change lives than listening to a sermon once a week. I know this may cut against the grain, especially for the pastors who spend so much time and energy developing important sermons. But consider this: if you were to list all the passages that refer to teaching the Word to Christians and compare them to the passages that admonish us to love and serve one another, you would find the latter far outweighing the former. Of course, we need to teach one another, but the best form of learning involves putting the lesson into practice, and an organic church context is far better suited to this type of learning.

It's also true that the children often teach the adults. In fact, as many will tell you, there were numerous times when my own small kids were the mature ones in the room. That is really more a reflection on the hurting people we were reaching than on our parenting skills. If we allow our children to carry some of the responsibility of church life, then they will learn and share in the church experience. Our churches will be better, both now and in the future as these children grow up and take on leadership as adults.

practical ideas

Practical ways to include children in the life of a gathered church merit an entire book in itself. Here are a few suggestions to help get started:

First, realize that the kids are there and as much a part of the church as the adults. Keep them in mind as you share your time together. Make a point to ask questions that the children can engage with, not just the adults. Make plans ahead of time for how the kids can be involved in the experience together. Solicit important prayers from them so that they realize how powerful their prayers can be. Let them share their own prayer requests and praises, and take them seriously when they do. While children are as much endowed with the Spirit of God, nevertheless their cognitive development is not as complete. Take that into consideration without treating them as inferior. You can give younger kids a task to do during the time together; for example, drawing a picture of something they think is important for the church to understand. Then give them a moment to share their picture and why they think it is important.

Second, if you listen to the songs your church sings regularly while driving with the kids, they will become more familiar with them and will enjoy participating during the times you praise God together. We sometimes hand out a variety of percussion instruments and let the kids have a chance to "make a joyful noise" for a song or two. We also let them select the songs they enjoy singing.

Third, there are times when it is appropriate for the kids to let the adults have time without them. If you plan on discussing something that is not appropriate for young children to hear, excuse them and provide something for them to enjoy doing. You may have adults take turns investing in the children during these times, but do make sure that these adults are not only responsible but a wise choice. You may set up a place where the kids can find something fun to do each week when a church gathering goes longer. This may be close enough for them to listen while they play. If that is the case, you may need to instruct them how to play quietly. If that is not practical, then perhaps someplace more removed will be necessary. I highly recommend that others in the church take responsibility for sitting with the kids and give mom and dad a break every now and then. We are a family.

Finally, it is important to know that there is not one right way to do this. Be flexible and learn as you go. Listen to the Lord's leading, and vary things to keep them interesting. Every child is different, and so you will need to address each child's development with constant prayer and listening to the Lord as a whole spiritual family. This is not just the work of the mom and dad but of the entire church. In fact, we should take time as a church to pray for each child and listen to our Lord for each one. If you do hear a word "from the Lord," measure each given word with wisdom, Scripture, and maturity. Often, what may appear to be an interruption may indeed be a teachable moment from the Lord. Be flexible and allow for spontaneity and the Lord's leading in the life of your organic church. You cannot expect spontaneous growth if every moment is scripted.

Erin wrote this poem when she was only thirteen to express her own feelings about our church, which is called Awakening. As you can see, she felt strongly that this was *her* church.

MY AWAKENING

Every Friday night about six-thirty or seven,
I meet and have church with believers of heaven.
We worship and gather together and share,
Of all sorts of things that just need some prayer.
There could be a few of us, maybe five or ten,
Or maybe, on occasion we'll be thirty again.
All of the people used to be lost,
But now they love God at any cost.
Before we begin we sing praises to God,
I play the drums and everyone's in awe,
At what Jesus did for us on the cross.
To not accept that would be a great loss.
This changed my view of what church should be,
I learned that God loves everyone, not just me.
Church doesn't have to be repetitive or traditional,
But sharing God's love, that is unconditional.

11

what about heresy?

from better-trained pastors to better-trained people

All great discoveries start as heresies.
—GEORGE BERNARD SHAW

FOR REASONS NOT ENTIRELY CLEAR (and I'd rather not speculate), a few years ago a segment of a U.S. denomination decided to go looking for heresy in our organic church movement. No one ever called me (or anyone else) to ask what we teach. Instead, they just publicly posted a letter online denouncing us as "a fast growing and biblically errant movement that is appealing to young people." In other words, we were labeled heretical.[1]

After searching a multitude of Websites and reading from a plethora of articles written by dozens of church leaders, these investigators found two things that were enough to label false doctrines. First, someone taught that church is a family; therefore a family must be the beginning of a church. Second, they found out that one person who was teaching about Christ at a breakfast used the elements of the table for communion, namely, pancakes and syrup.[2]

There followed some upheaval in the offices of the denomination's church planting arm. A McCarthy-style investigation uncovered sympathizers and organic practitioners. Some were forced into early retirement. Others resigned. Church planters were not allowed to use the words "organic" or "simple" to describe church (but "pancake" was OK if you were referring to the "bad guys"). When a large denomination starts outlawing words, you know they have already lost the war.

I for one do not see that either of these two practices is heretical. Actually, a pancake is a flat bread and probably is close to what Jesus would have used. Granted, syrup is not a product of grape vines but maple trees instead. The irony, however, is that if a pastor or missionary actually used the cup that Jesus used in communion in this particular denomination he could lose his job for drinking alcohol. This is a case of being damned if you do and damned if you don't. I guess grape juice, not syrup, is the officially sanctioned replacement for wine.

Heresy is put forward today as the cancer of Christ's body, for many the most feared outcome of church. Entire ministries are established for the sole purpose of rooting out the heresies for the rest of us. It is an important concern and one that Jesus and the apostle Paul addressed.

I get asked about heresy more than almost anything else when I am teaching about organic church. The common understanding is something like this: if we rely on uneducated leaders and teachers, won't we allow heresy to run rampant in our churches? Of course this is a risk, but I believe there are simple ways to lower the risk of such an infection. A healthy body with a strong immune system fights off infection better than a sick one. It is a natural function of the body, inherent in its very makeup. There is a better immune system for the body of Christ than what we have been comfortable with for so long. That is not to say that we can ignore concerns about heresy; I want to address it in an intelligent and articulate manner because it is so important. The organic church movement is not going to last if we simply ignore the challenges it faces. If the organic church movement does not move forward toward better health and wholeness, then it is not worth pursuing at all. I firmly believe that we can upgrade our church health in this new movement, including our theological integrity.

what is the true threat?

In reality, there is no way to eliminate heresy 100 percent from the church. Jesus told us there would always be false teachers (Matt. 24:4–5, 11). The enemy is a liar (John 8:44) and he works in clandestine ways to infiltrate our ranks (Jude 4, 10–13). If the liar can put something other than truth into our minds, then he can keep us from being all that the resurrected Christ intended for us. Unfortunately, I fear he has succeeded in doing just that— ironically under the banner of avoiding false doctrine.

The best solution to heresy in the church is not to have better-trained leaders in the pulpits but better-trained people in the pews. Although many say that the key to better-trained people is having leaders who equip them, this unfortunately is most often not the whole reality. We do need better leaders who empower and equip common Christians to know the truth, spread the Word, and prepare others for the work of ministry (Eph. 4:11ff.), but that is different from the sort of leaders who screen all beliefs and are the gatekeepers of God's Word. When a few are held responsible to determine what is right and wrong with everyone else, then we create an environment more, not less, conducive to heresy. So long as our leaders are considered the gatekeepers of truth, we leave the majority of God's people in the dark and susceptible to leaders who do the thinking for them—because that is what people have been trained to do. It is ironic that the very thing we think will prevent heresy actually feeds the problem.

There is no gatekeeper for God's Word. When the apostle Paul was behind bars, held in place by a keeper of the gate, he said "the Word of God is not imprisoned" (2 Tim. 2:9). The truth is, I do not need to protect God's Word; it protects me! (Eph. 6:10–18). People have been attacking God's Word in every generation. Entire empires have launched full-scale war against God's Word and fallen, yet the truth of God's Word stands. The thought that God's Word needs my individual, personal help is truly foolish. People have not kept God's Word pure; it is God's Word that has kept people pure (Ps. 119:9–11; John 17:17). We are sadly lost if we ever lose sight of this fact. We need God's Word more than it needs us. In fact, if God's Word is so weak as to need my stewardship to survive, then it is not something worthy of my faith or yours.

The Word of God in the hands of His people is *not* a dangerous thing! To me such an idea reeks of Satan. Keeping the Word
out of their hands is a dangerous practice, which is something we
immediately need to repent of. Good men and women throughout history have lost their lives for the right of others to have
God's Word freely. Let us not cheapen their sacrifice by refusing
to entrust God's word to ordinary people.

Of course it's true that God's Word can be twisted to suit
human purposes. Satan has done that from the very beginning
(Gen. 3:3), and he will not stop until he is doing laps in the lake
of fire. What should we do about that? It is clear that the letters of
the New Testament take false teachings head on. So should we.
The question isn't whether we should do something about false
doctrine, but *what* it is we do. Our knee-jerk reaction for a couple
thousand years has been to tighten up the reasoning of our few
scholars and let them do battle for the rest of us.

Just yesterday, I was warned of two particular heresies that
threaten the organic church movement. The funny thing is
that they have been widespread among conventional churches
for a long time. I was asked what I would do about it. I will probably do nothing at this time. Why? Because I believe in the freedom to believe in what you choose. I would rather have free
people who are wrong than people in bondage who are right. Of
course, I would prefer even more to have free people who know
the truth. I think that if options (good and bad) are not presented
before us we will not be challenged to think well. Lazy minds are
not good minds. The startling truth is that heresies have always
been good for us. False doctrines have been good for true doctrine. As strange as this sounds, it has historically been true. Like
an inoculation that injects a small amount of the bad stuff to
strengthen the good stuff in our bodies, false teachings actually
crystallize and sharpen our thinking and cause us to articulate
truth more clearly. If it were not for the heresies of Arius and
Montanus, we would probably not have the Nicene Creed.

Of course, a weak immune system may not be able to handle the inoculation. You have to be healthy enough to withstand
the inoculation. I believe we have not been healthy enough to
withstand germs in general, so we have taken to living in a bubble protected from outside influences. Church 3.0 is a shift to a

healthy immune system so that we can withstand the false doctrines that come our way. The secret to a strong immune system
is to have people strong in the truth, not just the experts. I am
not willing to trust a few people to care for such an important
issue. In a sense, we must trust God, His Word, and His people.

Perhaps we need a healthy and strong enough environment
to debate the doctrines without fear of being brutalized and
ostracized. I know that this type of open culture is lacking in my
own denomination, where some attack others without recom-
pense and everyone else is afraid to say much about it. We cannot
have open communication and learn from one another when we
are so afraid of losing our dogma.

I do not put my trust in a few people for a strong body of
Christ. Do we actually think that the way to protect the church
from human frailties is to make sure that people rely on others
(with their own frailties) to think for them? This is like trying to
solve a problem with more of a problem; it is like trying to put
out a fire with a bucket of kerosene.

Maybe the church of the West has sacrificed the power
we need because we have not trusted in the power and the purity
of God's written revelation. Instead, we have placed our trust
in the ability of certain people to interpret, teach, and system-
atize the Bible. There is no power inherent in these people or
in their systems. God's Word stands alone, and we must learn
again to trust in it. We have sacrificed the power of God's Word
for mere human teaching about God's Word and wondered
why the people of God are ineffective in influencing society. The
sad irony is that all this is done out of a misplaced respect for
God's Word.

The concern I have heard about organic churches is that if
we have leaders who are not seminary trained we are open to
all sorts of bad teaching. The reality is that many heresies were
born in seminary. Some would argue that the whole fundamen-
talist movement was born out of a reaction to the liberal and
heretical teachings coming out of many of the seminaries, particularly in Germany during the early twentieth century. We have
been trained by our seminaries to think that we are incapable of
holding off heresy without their help. Seminary as an institute
for higher learning, however, is a relatively new phenomenon

in church history, and I would venture to guess that we have not had less heresy since its invention. Although I do not believe that seminary is a bad thing (furthering one's education is always helpful), I also do not believe seminary is a cure for heresy. To put so much pressure on this institution is not fair to seminary or to the church. I wonder what would happen if the amount of effort and resources poured into training a select few leaders over the past hundred years were invested instead in training all Christians; what would our churches look like today?

One can argue that legalism is the heresy fought against with the greatest fervor in the New Testament. Legalism, the Galatian heresy, is a view that our spirituality is built by our own efforts, that we can accomplish our spirituality by ourselves with concerted effort. It says that salvation is by Jesus, but spiritual growth is by keeping the Ten Commandments and being a good person. This is a lie.

Legalism is a false doctrine that is countered harshly by both Jesus and Paul more than once. Nevertheless, it is quite common today to find churches and entire denominations that have reduced the Christian life to simply managing sin and keeping things in order, which is actually a clear expression of human-made spirituality. Much of what is done on Sunday mornings in the name of God would go on next week with or without the Holy Spirit. Ask yourself: Can we do what we call church by ourselves without a special empowering of God? When others come into our midst, are they struck with the miraculous nature of our spiritual community, or do they see people doing what people can do? Do not be deceived; this kind of spirituality is as much legalism as telling people that they cannot get to heaven without doing good works to earn their way—even with an orthodox statement of faith for your doctrine.

We could have misread what the real threat is of false doctrine that infiltrates the church in the West. Sometimes we can espouse the right words and live by the wrong ideas. Having correct statements of faith in your creed is not all there is to being orthodox.

In Titus 2 the apostle Paul exhorts us to communicate sound doctrine, which he goes on to elaborate for us. I include the complete chapter below because it is not that lengthy and is revealing. Take a minute and read what Paul considers "sound doctrine":

> But as for you, speak the things which are fitting for sound doctrine. Older men are to be temperate, dignified, sensible, sound in faith, in love, in perseverance. Older women likewise are to be reverent in their behavior, not malicious gossips nor enslaved to much wine, teaching what is good, so that they may encourage the young women to love their husbands, to love their children, to be sensible, pure, workers at home, kind, being subject to their own husbands, so that the word of God will not be dishonored. Likewise urge the young men to be sensible; in all things show yourself to be an example of good deeds, with purity in doctrine, dignified, sound in speech which is beyond reproach, so that the opponent will be put to shame, having nothing bad to say about us. Urge bondslaves to be subject to their own masters in everything, to be well-pleasing, not argumentative, not pilfering, but showing all good faith so that they will adorn the doctrine of God our Savior in every respect. For the grace of God has appeared, bringing salvation to all men, instructing us to deny ungodliness and worldly desires and to live sensibly, righteously and godly in the present age, looking for the blessed hope and the appearing of the glory of our great God and Savior, Christ Jesus, who gave Himself for us to redeem us from every lawless deed, and to purify for Himself a people for His own possession, zealous for good deeds. These things speak and exhort and reprove with all authority. Let no one disregard you [Titus 2:1–15].

Sound doctrine is truth lived out in our character to the betterment of others. I would love to be a part of that church, wouldn't you? Many have said over the centuries that all we need for better churches is better doctrine. I must conclude that if we all have the type of sound doctrine Paul describes in this passage, we really would have better churches. This unique passage devoted to explaining sound doctrine is as notorious for what it does not include as for what it does. Notice that there is no mention in the paragraph about the order of end times events or of the triune nature of the godhead. There is not a single petal of the Calvinist "tulip" mentioned. Not that these things are unimportant, but true and sound doctrine is "adorned" in our character and lived before others, not simply written out and cognitively agreed on.

when is it best to teach biblical interpretation skills?

Just because I am a big proponent of having ordinary people encounter Scripture directly doesn't mean that I don't teach interpretive skills. But it is not the first thing I do. First I set disciples to reading the Scripture without any middleman. Once the sheep hear the Good Shepherd's voice, they will follow Him for life. There is a significant imprinting that needs to take place from the very beginning of a new life. In the natural world, a bonding occurs with a newborn to its mother. All of the memory of the creature is forever shaped and influenced by the connection to the first creature seen. This is sometimes called imprinting. Like the baby ducks that will follow their mother, new disciples must connect with God's voice early in their new life—not the booming voice of their pastor preaching *about* God's Word. In most churches, people are told to read the Bible but rarely develop an appetite for it. I hear the common mantra of "I try to read my Bible, but I never understand it. It makes so much more sense when I hear my pastor explain it." These are sheep who know their pastor's voice, but it is *not* Jesus' voice.

We do not worry overmuch about whether disciples misunderstand Scripture; of course they will. I did too when I was a young disciple. Maybe we need to realize that we will spend the rest of our lives trying to understand an infinite book that has no end to its depth. Perhaps we should allow people the freedom to make a few mistakes, leave with a few questions, and learn as they grow. I remember my first Bible study that I ever taught. It was bad, to say the least, perhaps even heresy! I even managed to utter a four-letter word in it. I am glad someone gave me a chance to do better the next time. I am still embarrassed by my first sermon. If you held me to everything I believed in my first pastorate, I would be a stagnant and stunted disciple who is not learning. I now understand things better than I did at first, and I am hopeful that in ten years I will see even more clearly. It is actually when we are unwilling to allow mistakes that we stop learning and become stagnant in our biblical understanding. Any theologian who believes we have already cemented all our understanding of Scriptures and found every doctrinal answer should retire early. Why not? He or she has nothing more to learn. I believe that a church that is stagnant in its theological learning is worse than an errant but learning one.

When I teach about organic church, I often ask members of the audience to raise their hand if they have ever misinterpreted Scripture. Most times all of them do so. Rather than burn them at the stake, I usually just ask them to give others the same courtesy of learning by making mistakes.

I think that, ironically, we will have healthier doctrinal practice in the body of Christ by allowing people to make mistakes in interpreting the Scripture than by trying to eliminate all mistakes. When we impose a high standard requiring absolute correctness without room for any mistakes, we scare people into not reading the Bible. It is safer for them to simply listen to the experts who are entrusted with true interpretation. This, in turn, allows a few to be responsible for the many and virtually eliminates healthy internalization of God's word by God's people.

If 100 percent accuracy is held forth as our standard, we are all disqualified. No one is learning and no one is thinking. If you were a careful student of church history you would be surprised by some of the strange ideas that our historic heroes believed. God still blessed them, used them, and uses them still, but they did not have a complete picture of all of God's Word. Perhaps we are also a little blind to our own doctrinal faults, so much so that our errors will be more evident in the decades and centuries to come.

Why not let people who are new believers make mistakes early in their development, since this is the way all of us must grow? If we have to be perfect in our understanding from the very first day of our Christian life, then none of us is worthy. No wonder so many are afraid of opening their Bible; if they have to understand everything correctly all the time, it is a rather intimidating venture to merely open it up and read.

It is far safer to reinforce an attitude of humility and awareness of our own inadequacies as interpreters of Scripture than to be so confident that we know all that is true and can put every belief in its appropriate mental box. In my view, this overconfident attitude is more of a heresy than we realize. It is contrary to Scripture and produces a dull and unlearned church. A teacher who has many questions is far more desirable than one who has all the answers.

St. Jerome once said of the Scriptures, "They are shallow enough for a babe to come and wade in without fear of drowning and yet deep enough for theologians to plummet their depths without ever touching the bottom." Let's plummet the depths and also welcome everyone into the shallows!

We hold off on teaching basic Bible interpretation skills, until the disciples emerge as leaders and are preparing to facilitate the learning of others. Here is the amazing thing I have found in doing it this way: when I teach interpretive skills for the first time to a new leader, it is usually a refresher course for them. Because they have been reading an abundance of Scripture from the beginning, and reading entire books of the Bible repetitively and as a whole (a habit as part of the Life Transformation Group method we use), they have already picked up most of the rules of interpretation intuitively. I have found that the Holy Spirit is an outstanding teacher, and that He wants His Word understood better than we do. The best interpretive guidelines are simply a commonsense approach to a plain understanding of the Bible. By the time I show these guidelines to emerging leaders, they have already figured out much of it on their own. The ideas of context, style of literature, the voice of the biblical author, all of these principles behind sound Bible interpretation rise naturally within a student of the word, in whom the Holy Spirit dwells, and who reads the Bible often, extensively, and repetitively.

The problem in the church is not so much heresy in biblical interpretation or that we do not have good interpretive rules that we teach to others. Our problem in Christendom is that we do not have disciples who have a real appetite for God's word and regularly feast on it. If we had hungry disciples eager to consume God's word, we would not require teachers who monitor their interpretation. The Holy Spirit would do much of that over the course of their lifelong development. In our rush to make sure everyone has a teacher, we do not allow the Holy Spirit to be the Teacher He is meant to be. God has given some to be teachers, but they were never intended to supplant God Himself as a teacher. In fact, their job is to equip the saints to teach others. In all cases, the Holy Spirit is the Helper we all need.

what is real heresy, anyway?

The church has also been trained to think that the greatest threat she faces is heresy. That is why this is one of the first and most frequent questions asked of the organic church movement. Whenever this question is raised in my speaking, I often ask the audience to raise their hand if they know someone personally who has gone astray and actually has begun a cult. Usually two or three people do so (I suspect that this is an overestimated response from some who do not understand what it entails to actually be a cult). I then ask them to raise their hand if they know a Christian leader who has fallen into immorality. Without fail, everyone in the room raises a hand. My point is, "Why are we so afraid of *heresy*?" It seems that there are other, more formidable problems in our churches. The problem in the church of the West is not in believing the wrong things, but in not obeying the right things we do believe. We are all educated beyond obedience. More education will only push us farther away from actually obeying the simple truths we already know.

Some would argue that immorality is a result of wrong beliefs. In other words, if we can get our minds working properly, our actions will follow. Perhaps, to some degree, that is the case. These same people may argue that better teaching will result in better Christians. I am sorry, but our grand experiment of the past hundred years reveals that this assumption is incorrect. Ours is not a cognitive problem, but a moral and spiritual one. You cannot actually think your way into good behavior. In fact, you must often *act* your way into good thinking. We must recognize that our weakness is in the area of human will rather than the mind. We must make a choice to follow Christ, and not just accept that what He says is true cognitively. There are many people who know what they do is wrong but do it anyway (because, frankly, they want to). To continue teaching rebellious people who do not want to obey what they have learned is not just futile; it encourages disobedience and rewards lackadaisical spirituality.

We needn't continue this hundred-year experiment to see if good teaching corrects bad behavior. All we need to do is read the Scriptures we've been teaching from all along! As James writes:

> But prove yourselves doers of the word, and not merely hearers who delude themselves. For if anyone is a hearer of the word and not a doer, he is like a man who looks at his natural face in a mirror; for once he has looked at himself and gone away, he has immediately forgotten what kind of person he was [James 1:22–24].

According to James's writing, when we continue teaching people who are not doing what they have already been taught, we not only look ugly to the world—with wacky hair, blemished face, and dirty teeth—but we also deepen the deluding process of thinking we're all OK. This is serious. We are deceived into thinking we are better than we really are, and the result is we do not even begin to look for solutions because we never see the problems for what they truly are. Self-deception is a dangerous game, because when you have a serious problem you don't know it. For instance, if you knew you left your zipper open, you would do something about it. If you don't know it, you continue to look foolish to the world. This may be where we are today: exposed and ugly, and all the while thinking we look great!

the heretics in history are often heroes in the future

I also question what people label as heresy. What is heresy for one segment of the kingdom is often orthodox in another. Most claim that their doctrinal belief is closest to the historic and orthodox doctrines.

In my own denomination, I have been labeled a heretic by a few pastors. One time, a pastor publicly said I was a fraud and that I would die with nothing to show for my life. He accused me of only seeking a fast trip to recognition. Another pastor in my own denomination wrote an article intending to expose me as a heretic (along with George Barna and Frank Viola). He read this article at a round table in Oxford, England, and then he sent a copy to every church in our denomination. The article is full of misrepresentations and faulty interpretations of one of my books. He lumps Barna, Viola, and me together as if we were writing our books while all sitting at the same desk. The irony is that the heresy he accused me of was making God out to be in my own image, and yet there is a photograph on the cover of the article portraying the author as Jesus. He never contacted me to clarify anything or ask me to recant from my heretical ways. Some of my coworkers tried to talk to him, but he is not interested in two-way communication.

In both of these cases as well as the first one I mentioned, the charges were made publicly, not privately. In both cases, the one who was accusing me never asked for clarification or a chance to explain myself; this was not their interest. Although these words, coming from men I thought were friends, did hurt, they did not hurt nearly as much as the silence of others who did not challenge the other men in their conduct or lack of biblical procedure. When we allow this sort of evil, we are actually enabling sin and we all suffer for it. When we take these accusations at face value and do not question them, we not only enable such sinful practices but empower the ones responsible and give them cause to continue doing such things.

Proverbs is clear that it is a listening ear that promotes and enables all sorts of evil associated with the tongue, including slander, gossip, and boastfulness (Prov. 17:4; 18:8; 26:22). We are specifically instructed to not receive an accusation against an elder except on the basis of two or three witnesses (1 Tim. 5:19). It is shocking how we allow people to blatantly disregard Scripture in the name of defending it. The irony is that people can trample all over clear biblical teaching to accuse someone else of being biblically wrong and do so publicly and not face any consequence. Others usually suspect the one attacked without real cause, and allow the accuser to face little or no consequence. We have fostered an environment of fear where false teaching is considered the greatest of sins and all who would intend to go after such teachers can do so without reserve or recourse. I assure you, however, that when we publicly accuse and slander people without sound witness or documentation, and not approach the brother or sister first, we are the ones blatantly guilty of sin. It would be good to remind ourselves that our enemy is the accuser (Satan) and slanderer (devil) and when we practice such things we are not Christ-like, but like the devil himself.

In either case of public accusation, I have not tried to defend myself; I feel that doing such only empowers the attackers and increases the suspicion. Being labeled a heretic is not the worst thing that could happen.

Perhaps one of the most dire consequences of this type of unhealthy environment is that people are afraid to speak openly about theological questions they may have, for fear of being labeled a heretic. When we freely and publicly attack others without any biblical and ethical restraint, it creates an environment hostile to theological learning.

If you divided all the Christian leaders of history into two sides and put those labeled heretics on one side and those labeled orthodox on the other, looking down the aisle of history you might end up preferring the heretical side. There you will find some of the best people of history: Martin Luther, John Wesley, George Fox, John Hus, John Wycliffe, Galileo, the apostle Paul, and even Jesus Himself, to name but a few. You'd be hard pressed to recognize any on the other side of the aisle. Granted, you would also be aligning with some rather peculiar folks, but it would be far more interesting to spend eternity on that side of the aisle. The other side would be, frankly, boring. I think we should be less concerned with being called a heretic and more concerned with growing in the light.

The truth is that those we do consider great heroes of the faith in history all had some areas of theological, and even moral, concern that we would not endorse today. They were a product of their own time and culture, and this has a way of clouding our judgment on certain things. We would be foolish not to recognize this in ourselves as well. As Dallas Willard once insightfully pointed out, "You do not have to be right to be saved."[3]

If we all live a respectable and safe life, which others will say is correct, the world will never be changed. It is not an easy task to find even a small handful of world changers who were not labeled as heretical by some of their contemporaries.

Jesus may have had this in mind when he told his disciples, "Blessed are you when people insult you and persecute you, and falsely say all kinds of evil against you because of Me. Rejoice and be glad, for your reward in heaven is great; for in the same way they persecuted the prophets who were before you" (Matt. 5:10). In fact, it can be argued that unless you are being persecuted you are doing something wrong (2 Tim. 3:12). Paul seems to indicate that those who are trying to appeal to others as religious and avoid persecution are in fact false teachers themselves (Gal. 6:12). Jesus even predicted that the religious establishment would call those whom God has sent to set the stage for what is to come as heretics and persecute them under the premise that they are offering a service to God (John 16:1–4). As the Bible plays itself out, one thing is clear: those whom God sends to His people are most often rejected, labeled false, and cast out from the religious establishment. So maybe our goal should not be to be accepted as orthodox, but to be willing to endure whatever comes for the sake of truth and transformation.

This is not to say that there are not true heretics needing to be revealed as false teachers. Of course there are. Jesus confronted them, as did Paul, and so should we. I simply feel that more humility and less derision in our addressing of heresy would serve us well. If we were this way, we would be more introspective and vulnerable, willing to learn and much slower to attack others.

I remember talking with a missionary in Europe who was concerned that the French government might call them a "sect." After hearing this same concern being mentioned a few times, I eventually could ignore it no longer. I asked, "Why are you so concerned if the French government labels you as a sect?" He explained that the French people think much more socialistically than Americans. They will not question the government's verdict, and the Christians would lose a lot of potential influence. I finally said, "Listen, if a dark unbelieving government that has no spiritual light in it and is against all that is true thinks you are doing fine, then you must be doing something wrong! I wouldn't be concerned if they call you a sect, I'd be concerned if they *didn't*!" I then reminded him that anytime the kingdom of God has thrived and become a fast-growing, unstoppable movement it is labeled a sect, starting with the first Christians. It is equally true that any time the church has been approved of and endorsed by a government, it ended up in the wrong. The kingdom of God thrives always in the margins, not in the mainstream.

Rather than seeing heresy as the worst thing that could ever happen, I have actually started to think that it is a sign of doing something right. We are doing something wrong if Satan is not threatened by us. When he is threatened he will try to counterfeit a legitimate work with something that may appear true but is packed with lies—heresy. I'm not endorsing heresy, nor asking for it; I am simply saying that we should not live our lives worried about it so much that we are paralyzed in fear.

I am always upset when I see one Christian leader attacking another publicly because they disagree over a minor theological component. Using fear and hatred disguised as orthodoxy to denounce others who are not the same is not only small-minded but often the work of the enemy, not the Spirit of Jesus. It is good to have a conviction regarding doctrine, and even to have a lively discussion over your convictions, but to slanderously attack a fellow Christian is perhaps a greater sin than the faulty interpretation itself.

how do we screen people doctrinally?

This whole matter of heresy raises a question of whether or not we should screen people over doctrines. In our movement we consider the DNA of Christ's body as the code that dictates life, health, and fertility (here, DNA stands for *d*ivine truth, *n*urturing relationships, and *a*postolic mission). We want to see the DNA evident in every cell of the Body. It is what holds our movement together. Divine truth is crucial for health and unity in the church and in our own unique movement. Divine truth, of course, is found in the Scripture, but not just the Scripture. Jesus is also Divine Truth, as He is a revelation of God for humanity. So holding firmly to God's Word is of utmost importance to us all. Currently our movement consists of church planting associated with many denominations (from Reformed to Vineyard to Seventh Day Adventist to Lutheran). Now the question is which beliefs are crucial and which are not. Is there a point when we exclude fellowship with certain people over doctrine?

One way we keep unity among our diversity is to run people through what we call the "bullet test." We ask, "What would you do if someone held a gun to your head and said, 'Renounce this doctrine or I will shoot'?" If you say, "Pull the trigger" then it is a bullet doctrine. We agree on bullet doctrines. We can hold to doctrines that are not bullet doctrines, and even teach them with conviction, but we don't exclude or attack brothers and sisters over nonbullet doctrines. They are secondary doctrines that are enlightening but not worth dying over, and certainly not worth killing over.

For us, the bullet doctrines could consistently be summed up:

- One true God in three persons, the Father, the Son, and the Holy Spirit.
- The deity and incarnate humanity of Jesus and His redemptive work evident in His death, burial, resurrection, ascension, and imminent return.

- Salvation, as an ongoing regeneration and transformation of one's soul, is by grace through faith in the atoning work of Christ and not ever the results of our own works.
- The inspiration and power of God's written Word in all of its revelation, without error in its original manuscripts.
- All believers are redeemed to be significant in the cause of God's kingdom and granted the empowerment necessary to do so by the indwelling presence of the Holy Spirit.

Of course, the bullet test is not meant to be a fixed and static screening process. It is only a beginning to a relationship that will grow over time, built on much more than cognitive assent to a set of stated beliefs. The consequence of this form of doctrinal screening is that we have "unity on the essentials, liberty on the non-essentials, and love in everything."[4]

We understand that this is also not a foolproof method of screening out heresy. There were more than nine hundred people in 1978 in Guyana who took a "Kool-Aid test" over the wrong doctrines and gave their lives for false teaching. History is littered with people who have given their lives for a lie, so this is not considered a mistake-proof method by any means. It is just a starting point for those who have the Spirit of God and listen to His voice and join together over uncompromising truth.

We have found that any true multiplication movement of God's kingdom has some basic screening or filtering that occurs from the start and throughout development. Doctrine is only one thing to be filtered. Obedience, faithfulness, yieldingness, and fruitfulness are all equally essential to screen in developing disciples of the kingdom.

Doctrine is not the best path to unity anyway. In fact, when we use doctrine as the barometer of fellowship, we end up being quite divisive. Humility is the only true path to unity. Humility is defined by Paul as regarding one another as more important than ourselves and thinking of their interests above our own (Phil. 2:3–4). If we can't do this, we will never find a basis for being united. We are commanded to love our enemies (Matt. 5:44), so loving those who follow Jesus but disagree with us over some doctrinal issues should be a given.

how do you keep heresy from exploiting the organic church movement?

Although completely eliminating false teaching will not truly occur until Christ returns, we have an excellent immune system in the organic church movement. In fact, I believe it to be better, *much* better, than the solution in the traditional church system— an upgrade over the previous model of false doctrine prevention.

Heresy usually emerges because of three elements. First, a strong, opinionated leader wants the most followers he can rally. Second, a biblically illiterate group of Christians follow him. Finally, Scriptures are used out of context to construct a false doctrine.

With the Life Transformation Group (LTG) strategy,[5] we have addressed all of these issues at the cellular level of church life. This is where the war against infection is won or lost in the body.

In an LTG, men or women meet with one or at the most two others. This is hardly an attractive following for a future cult figure. All those in an LTG are reading large volumes of Scripture (approximately twenty-five to thirty chapters per week), and all in the group are reading the same book, in context, in its entirety and repetitively. For instance, if they are reading Romans they read the book twice a week. If by the time they meet that next week one or more of them do not finish the reading in its entirety, they read Romans twice again the next week. When all of them finish in the same week, they choose a different book. If they choose Acts or a Gospel, they read it one time. If the choice is Ephesians or Galatians, they read it about five times.

A manipulative leader cannot take advantage of LTG participants because they are not a biblically illiterate following. If it takes a group four weeks to finish reading Romans, some may well have read it eight times in that month. Imagine how much you would learn reading Ephesians twenty times in a month. It is hard to take the Scripture out of context because all three in the group who have the Holy Spirit in them are reading the same book, in its whole context, repetitively. If someone in the LTG says, "I think this is saying that I am god," the other two will likely respond, "I didn't get that." Heresy is cut off at the start because God's people are being immersed in God's Word.

For far too long, the church has thought that the solution to heresy was a well-educated preacher in the pulpit, when all along the real solution is instead to have the Word of God in the hearts of the people in the pews. A church is only as good as her disciples. Keeping the Word and its interpretation in the hands of professionals has actually created an environment more vulnerable to false teaching.

In conclusion, I firmly believe that the organic church movement is not merely tolerating heresy or taking a step down in combating it. We have a better way of addressing the problems of heresy in the church without reverting to static controls or gatekeepers of God's truth. Perhaps the very thing we have been threatened by most—releasing the Scriptures into the hands of common Christians—is indeed the very thing that will slow the threat of heresy. If everyone is reading God's word and listening to the Shepherd's voice, then there will be less opportunity for heretical doctrines to cause damage. On the other hand, perhaps creating an environment with controls and only a few responsible for everyone else's doctrinal thinking is more conducive to heretical influence. After all, if you can infect the few at the top with faulty thinking then everyone under them will be polluted and easily swayed to falsehood. If we create an environment where a single charismatic leader is trusted to tell us all what is right and wrong, we create just the kind of environment that is most vulnerable to heresy. Can it be that in our zeal to protect truth we have somehow managed to cause more damage than good?

12

what about finances?

from ten percent to the whole enchilada

Nothing that is God's is obtainable by money.
—TERTULLIAN

THE NEW TESTAMENT TALKS a great deal about money. The church also talks a great deal about it—but are they saying the same thing? I do not believe so.

Preachers are notorious for their appeals for money, especially some televangelists. The church has been the laughing stock of the culture and the punch line of too many jokes by late night talk show hosts. Living in a capitalistic culture that worships the dollar, we conclude some of that reaction can be attributed to an overprotective public that is uncomfortable with any appeal for money. We cannot really be let off the hook that easily, though.

To be fair, not all of us have been so unappealing; many of us have been so ashamed of the way we appear to the world that we are gun-shy of ever asking for money. I know I have been that way. Many of us have become so apologetic that we seem like shy little church mice when the subject comes up. I have even put off writing this chapter until last, procrastinating because of the difficult nature of discussing Mammon. Nevertheless, it has to be addressed; it's just too important to ignore.

I am often asked what we do in organic churches with our money. People want to know how we take offerings, where we spend our money, and how we organize for tax purposes. I address all of these concerns here, but first there are some other questions we must address—in our Bibles.

The subject of church finances is too large to treat exhaustively here. In a previous book I looked at some of the issues of supporting church leaders, so I will not go into much depth on that subject here.[1] I hope to address in this chapter the idea of collecting weekly tithes and offerings from the people of God to support the church.

old testament church practices

It seems strange to write of Old Testament "church practices," because there is no church in the Old Testament. When it comes to money I believe that we have Old Testament ideas and practices and we try to make the New Testament support them.

In the Old Testament, Israel was the people of God. It was a nation with a government, an army, and a market, but not a church. Israel was a theocracy, not a democracy, monarchy, or socialistic nation. As a theocracy, God was supposed to be the king, but the people suffered from potentate envy and decided they needed a human king like all the other nations. God warned that establishing this king would end badly and tax the people heavily, but that's what they wanted, so God obliged.

Part of the nation of Israel's economic system was the tithe, which was a kind of tax levied on the people to cover maintenance of the religious system (the temple and the priests). In a theocracy, the religious system is part of the state, not separate from it.

The Lord gave Israel specific instructions for how to handle the tithe (meaning a tenth). It was collected from the first fruits of God's people. Today, when we say we "tithe," we also assume that we are to pay 10 percent. In Israel, however, there was more than one tithe taken; in fact, if Israel followed the law strictly, they would collect 23.3 percent of the earnings from the people.

There are many in the church who still use the idea of tithing and others who have done away with the expression and simply refer to offerings. Of course there are some who still demand both! Most who favor tithing in the church today are quick to point out that Abraham paid a tithe from the spoils of a battle to Melchizedek before the formation of Israel, as evidence that tithing is not just for Israel. They assume from this that God instructed Abraham that tithing was what all godly people do, not just those under the Law of Moses. Actually, giving a voluntary tribute of a tenth of the spoils from a battle was a common practice prior to Moses, so Abraham may well have been following the Gentiles' pattern rather than God's.

From that tithe and the tithing system of ancient Israel, they make the leap to instructing people in the church to tithe 10 percent every week from their income. In my view, this is a stretch indeed. Not that giving 10 percent is a bad thing to do, but to read Malachi and then tell the church they are robbing God when they do not give their 10 percent is poor hermeneutics at best, and manipulative at worst. It certainly paints a strange picture of God.

Do we really think that God is paid off with 10 percent of our income, like some sort of loan shark who offers protection for a fee? If we fail to give Him 10 percent are we robbing Him of His just due? Of course not. For one thing, He is justly due everything. He already owns it all. He doesn't want a 10 percent tip for good service; He wants more than that. He wants everything from us, not because He needs it, but because He wants us to be completely His.

new testament tithing

It is just as strange to have a heading that reads "New Testament Tithing" as it is to have one that says "Old Testament Church Practices." The word *tithe* does not appear in the New Testament, for a number of reasons. Here are just a few.

First, we no longer have a temple building to maintain. In the New Testament, Christ is not so concerned with the temple as was previously understood. He proclaims that it is finished with His generation. Instead, He establishes a whole new way of understanding the temple: we are it. Now God dwells within us!

Second, we no longer have a special class of priest to support. The coming of Christ changes everything. Where once there were special priests who had the responsibility of representing the people before God, this is no longer the case. Instead, we are the priests. Every person in Christ is a priest before God.

Third, we are no longer under the law of Israel. Christ did not abolish the law; He fulfilled it and established a new covenant that writes God's law not on stone tablets but in our hearts. We are no longer under all the strict Mosaic laws with righteous standards that no one was able to live up to until Jesus fulfilled them. Instead, love rules in our hearts. We are to act in grace now, not under the law. To continue to operate under the law is to render Christ's death meaningless (Gal. 2:21).

Fourth, we are not a nation but a new kind of people that are part of His kingdom. The church is a body of Christ, not a government. Peter calls us a nation of priests, which is a way of showing how radically things have changed because of Christ. Paul calls us a new creation (2 Cor. 5:17). There were Adam and Eve, then fallen humans, and now there is *us*—a new kind of creature. We are now a people who have the Spirit of the living God within. This is remarkable. Why would anyone want to go back to the old system?

If tithing is not prescribed in the New Testament, why is it in our churches? I believe that the reason we emphasize tithing is because we look in our Bibles for teaching concerning the support of our buildings and our professional leaders and do not find much in the New Testament. We did the next best thing; we turned to the Old Testament. There we found a centralized religious institution that had leaders to support, buildings to maintain, and a financial system that made it all possible—called tithing. This is why we emphasize tithing in the church. Other than Jesus condemning the practice of the Pharisees, tithing is not mentioned, prescribed, or even described in the New Testament, but this is not to say that it does not speak of giving.

offerings

Offerings in the Old Testament were sacrifices made to God on the altar for a variety of reasons—for sin, for healing, for forgiveness. There were burnt offerings, drink offerings, free will offerings, guilt offerings, votive offerings, grain offerings, and peace offerings. An offering could be sacrificing a bird, a bull, or even a boy (as with Abraham and Isaac).

Rarely was the offering money. It was usually a sacrifice of something to the Lord as a picture of the atonement that was promised. In fact the tithe was always some sort of food in the Levitical Law, not money (Lev. 27:30–32; Deut. 12:17; 14:23).

When you get to the New Testament, the examples of offerings slim down considerably. Jesus always fulfilled the Law while He was on earth, so when He healed people He would often instruct them to go present their offering at the Temple (Matt. 8:4; Luke 5:14). He commended the widow for her sacrificial offering put into the treasury (Luke 21:1–5). After the Gospels, there are very few references to making offerings. Paul presented an offering at the Temple to appease the legalistic Christians in the Jerusalem church (Acts 24:17).

There is, however, one important offering presented in the New Testament that pretty much outshines all others: Jesus as our sin offering (Heb. 10:1–18). After this sacrifice, most of the uses of the term *offering* in the New Testament refer to people presenting themselves to God's service (Rom. 12:1–3; Phil. 2:17; 2 Tim. 4:6).

There is not a single prescription in the New Testament for the church to receive financial offerings from the people to support the church functions. Does this sound strange, given the centuries of church practices?

Some people reading this book will be concerned that if the church did away with the system of collecting tithes and offerings it would go out of business. I wonder. I suspect we would all be surprised if we called the people of God to surrender to Jesus completely as Master of their whole life; what would happen? I think many would follow the rich young ruler and turn to walk away, but the few that remain would be transformed to become generous people of faith. I suspect that the 10 percent we once settled for would seem like chump change compared to the new economy of a surrendered church life. We could do away with appeals for offerings in a church of surrendered followers because they would beg to be able to give.

So how is the church supposed to survive without tithes and offerings? Church 3.0, much like the first-century church, is not dependent on buildings or professional Christian leaders. Without overhead, it is a lot easier to not just survive but thrive.

new testament church finances

The church tries to reinforce a system of tithes and offerings with New Testament verses, but they are always taken out of context. For instance, we use 1 Corinthians 16:1–2 to support our practice of collecting weekly offerings on Sunday mornings. I wonder how many offering envelopes around the country have these two verses printed on them:

> Now concerning the collection for the saints, as I directed the churches of Galatia, so do you also. On the first day of every week each one of you is to put aside and save, as he may prosper, so that no collections be made when I come.

It seems obvious that Paul is speaking about our offerings and tithes, doesn't it? It's perfect. It is about collecting for the saints, it is directed at the churches, it is to be on the first day of the week, and it is something all the churches are supposed to do. There's just one problem. It doesn't say what we typically tell people that it does.

First, notice that Paul is not directing the saints to collect for the churches, but the other way around. The churches are to collect for the saints. Second, the church isn't collecting the money; the people, "each one," are saving and putting aside what they can as God blesses them. Third, the person receiving the saved money isn't the pastor or the ushers; it is the missionary who is coming through—Paul. Finally, the recipients are not the church where the collections are being made, but the struggling saints in Jerusalem who are in the midst of a famine. Yes, this is about famine relief, not tithes and offerings. In the next verses, Paul says:

> When I arrive, whomever you may approve, I will send them with letters to carry your gift to Jerusalem; and if it is fitting for me to go also, they will go with me.

The problem here is not what percentage we pay or how it is collected. It lies in what Jesus truly wants from us. Jesus speaks about money often, though what He demands is not 10 percent but the whole enchilada. I'm not talking about 100 percent of your income or 100 percent of all your possessions. More than that: He wants 100 percent of you. Just to be counted among His disciples, we must surrender our life. He says repeatedly, "If anyone wishes to come after me, he must deny himself, pick up his cross and follow me" (Matt. 16:24). The disciples knew what this meant. When they saw someone carrying a cross, it wasn't a 10 percent proposition; it was a dead man walking. It meant execution and nothing less. Jesus is not asking for 10 percent of your income; He is calling for your entire life.

There is a reason tithing is not included in the New Testament: it is irrelevant. Once you have already given your life, what's 10 percent of your money? It is virtually impossible to tithe after you have already given everything. You don't have 10 percent of anything left to give if you have chosen to follow Christ.

Jesus is less concerned with our money than He is with our souls. He says, "Where your treasure is, there will your heart be also" (Matt. 6:33). This is not meant to be a way of scrutinizing our giving habits as much as our heart's devotion. If you are holding on to all but 10 percent, then your heart is not with Christ; it is with the other 90 percent.

So does this mean we should give our whole paycheck to the church, as well as all our possessions? It's been done before (Acts 4:32–37), but I do not see this as a prescription—just a description of what took place in a specific moment.

Paul presents for us a perfect example of how the church is to respond to the subject of giving:

> Now, brethren, we wish to make known to you the grace of God which has been given in the churches of Macedonia, that in a great ordeal of affliction their abundance of joy and their deep poverty overflowed in the wealth of their liberality. For I testify that according to their ability, and beyond their ability, they gave of their own accord, begging us with much urging for the favor of participation in the support of the saints, and this, not as we had expected, but they first gave themselves to the Lord and to us by the will of God [2 Cor. 8:1–5].

This passage is used frequently to support the system of tithes and offerings in our churches, but it is also another passage about collecting for famine relief, not church budgets, pastors' salaries, or a mortgage on the building.

These Macedonians were not just low-income people, but people in the *depths of poverty*. During a time of prevalent emperor worship, it was common for Christians to be virtually unemployable in the marketplace. Nevertheless, these Christians gave in a surprising way. Whenever poor people give generously, we are surprised. But this is not the most surprising part; they were begging to be able to give! And give they did, abundantly beyond what could be expected or was possible at all.

It is always surprising when poor people give generously, but perhaps it shouldn't be. The reality is that they were so generous because they owned nothing. They already gave everything to Jesus, so passing it on to others was not hard at all; they simply were channels through which the Lord redistributed resources. They were slaves of the Lord, so when Jesus said give, they didn't ask questions. As slaves, they owned nothing. They were merely to obey their Master and trust Him to care for their own needs. It helps to remember that when the Lord places the order, He pays the bill!

Consistently in the New Testament we are told to give (Luke 6:38) and give generously (2 Cor. 9:6) and cheerfully (2 Cor. 9:7). Quoting something Jesus must have said that is not recorded in any of the Gospels, Paul says, "It is more blessed to give than to receive" (Acts 20:35). Our giving was to be motivated entirely out of our love for God and others, not under compulsion (2 Cor. 9:7). We are not to turn our back to the needy (Matt. 6:3). We are not to use our giving as a way of gaining attention (Matt. 6:1–4). We are not to honor wealthy people at the expense of the poor but to treat every person with equality (James 2:1–13). All of these ideas flow from a life that has already given its entirety to God.

Is it wrong to support church leaders financially? No, of course not; in fact, it can be wrong not to. Paul argues that it is the right of an apostle to derive a living from the church (1 Cor. 9:14). For this to be at all possible, there must be some channel for receiving and distributing funds. Whether it is weekly or not is unclear and not prescribed.

Not all apostles took advantage of this right, namely, Paul and Barnabas. Paul traveled around the first-century world, often at his own expense. He would make tents when needed. At other times, his associates would work to support the missionaries, releasing Paul to serve full-time.

Teaching elders were to receive an honorarium and in some cases a double honorarium, but it is hard to interpret that as a full-time salary. Twice the New Testament says the worker is worthy of his wages. Jesus said so in a sermon as He was sending the seventy out on a short-term mission trip without any financial resources (Luke 10:7). The idea in this sermon is to receive food and shelter while serving the Lord. Paul then quotes the saying in 1 Timothy 5:18, in reference to the "double honor" due to the elders who work hard at preaching and teaching. In both cases, the clear idea is that the people receiving the message are to provide for the needs of the leader while they are doing it. Paul also instructs the Galatians to "share all good things" with those who teach the church (Gal. 6:6). I see these ideas more as a day's wage, or twice a day's wage . . . but not a permanent salary. Our own idea of an honorarium is probably closer to the idea of these usages than our doctrine of tithes and offerings.

Another thing to consider in many of the passages about giving is that it was food that was given, not money. A "day's wage" in the context of Jesus' words was food and lodging. As I mentioned, the tithes in the Old Testament were all food products from agricultural work. Most, though not all, of the offerings in the Bible are also edible.

Practices that are not taught in the Bible are not necessarily wrong. Just because we do not find church offerings as we practice them in the Bible does not necessarily mean it is wrong to do them. What would be wrong is to command them with biblical authority and shame people into giving. To teach people that they are disobeying the Lord, are poor stewards, and are less spiritual if they do not give regularly is flat out wrong. Equally poisonous is to teach people that if they give God more, the floodgates of heaven will open up and He will bless them with more prosperity. There is the spiritual truth that we reap what we sow, but the idea that God will love us more and bless us more if we are giving to an organization is ugly, manipulative, and false. God's love and blessing are not contingent on our works in anyway whatsoever. Though we were yet sinners, He gave everything to us (Rom. 5:8).

A big problem we have is that we have set up practices that the church is completely dependent on, and we have therefore resorted to using our Bibles to defend them. This is abusive to God's people and to God's Word.

money in organic churches

To have a decentralized church multiplication movement, you cannot put forth commands for how to do things from a centralized headquarters. The churches must be able to hear the Lord's leading and make decisions out in the field that are best given their context. So in Church Multiplication Associates (CMA) we never mandated how money was to be used. We allow each church to figure it out for itself.

The more decentralized church networks, such as Awakening Chapels, allow each church to decide what the Lord is directing it to do with its resources. When a network is more centralized, the churches have more overhead and usually will take into a central bank account some or even all of the money given in the churches of the network to support the work.

Some networks look pretty much like a traditional church financially, with budgets, regular giving, and a checking account. Others may not even have an account or checks to write and simply take a collection for any specific need. Some churches have a box they take out for people to give as the Lord leads. Others may pass a basket or bag at each meeting.

I have seen generous people give in so many ways other than with a weekly check. I have seen people take others into their home, feed them, and treat them as family. I have seen some give their cars away. I have seen them give their service to others, which normally is their way of making a living. I have seen some buy groceries for others and leave them at the doorstep anonymously. These people are generous, because their Master is generous. They have first given themselves to the Lord so the things they have to manage in life are not theirs to own, but belong to Jesus.

tax laws and the church

In the United States churches are granted certain tax privileges. Not only is the church exempt from paying taxes on donations received, but those church members who contribute can write off the amount on their taxes. The IRS desires that the church be a nonprofit religious organization for this benefit, called 501(c)(3) tax-exempt status, and typically this means it has to file a comprehensive form with the government.

It is not actually required that a church have this status to enjoy the tax-exempt benefits. It is desired but not mandated. Donations to a church that does not have 501(c)(3) status are still tax-deductible, if you keep your receipts. It is true, however, that people will have more confidence in giving if the church does have 501(c)(3) status.

With a decentralized network it is often the case that churches function under the umbrella of another organization with 501(c)(3) status. If you do this, it is recommended that the money received be kept in an account under the parent organization's name.

awakening chapel's example

Awakening Chapel began with a "giving box" that was left on a shelf in the room where we met. People were told where it was so they could give as they felt led to do, and someone would take whatever was in there and deposit it into an account under the parent church that originally sponsored us. We had no rent to pay or pastor's salary to cover, nor missionaries that we supported, so the money accumulated for months at a time unused. Then the Lord would bring about a need and we would find the amount in the account to be just enough. Once, we replaced a visitor's transmission on his truck so he could return home. Other times, we helped buy a laptop computer for a church planter sent overseas (as a tentmaker). It was common for us to buy Bibles for those who came to Christ or were seeking to know more about Him. We also bought airline tickets for some we sent on short-term trips overseas. For more than a year, we bought food that was made into sack lunches and given away to the homeless every week. It seemed there was always enough for whatever need God brought our way.

Other churches we started usually practiced the same thing, but they had freedom to do whatever God led them to do. We never asked for money to be sent back to the mother church or to CMA either. In fact, CMA has never asked for donations, though some do give to us regularly. Somewhere along the line, while moving from one home to another, Awakening's box was lost. With time, we found that all of these types of needs were met even though the box went missing; people just "gave of their own accord" (2 Cor. 8:2) "to share with one who has need" (Eph. 4:28). If a general need arises now, we make it known and people give. We do not need an offering box, envelopes, or a bag that is passed around for people to be generous and fulfill God's desires. What we need is hearts surrendered to Him.

He held nothing back for us. Though He was as rich as heaven, He became poor for us so that we may gain the riches of heaven (1 Cor. 8:9). He gave everything for us, not just 10 percent; we ought to respond in the same way.

what about my church?

from being educated to being empowered

I've come to see institutional decline like a disease: harder to detect but easier to cure in the early stages; easier to detect but harder to cure in the later stages. An institution can look strong on the outside but already be sick on the inside, dangerously on the cusp of a precipitous fall.
—JIM COLLINS

IT IS ENTIRELY POSSIBLE that this book has offended you. I imagine it has at least provoked many. I do not mind if you think I am wrong; just don't do so without checking with the Word first. Is there a possibility that I am right and we have believed and passed on practices through the centuries that are really only the residue of the true expressions of church found in the New Testament, practices that have lost the real and powerful elements Jesus instituted that would ignite and accelerate a movement? Have we been ripped off?

I have challenged commonly held opinions on such things as children's Christian education, doctrinal purity, tithes and offerings, and even communion and baptism. Before you dismiss

what I have suggested, ask yourself if it is possible to read the
New Testament afresh and find some validity in what has been
espoused in this book. Push the mute button on the old song
that has been repeating in your head and listen to a true song
of the Scriptures, whether that song follows the tune within this
book or not. Certainly, as you read the New Testament and go to
Church 2.0 on Sunday morning, you will find a disparity between
the two experiences. Your emotions and traditions are not to be
a judge of such things.

But what if you go to the Bible and can't find true biblical
grounds to discount what I am saying in this book . . . what then?
This is the biggest question in the book and one that you must
answer for yourself. It is a question worthy of taking some time
to pray, think, meditate, listen, worship, and reflect on. You may
need to count the cost of accepting these ideas as true or rejecting
them as false.

If you've been able to read this far in the book, you probably
still have one other important question: What about my church?
What do I do now?

It amazes me that, for all the educating we do in Church 2.0,
how little we actually know about the things in this book. We are
the most educated people of God in any generation of history,
with access to seemingly limitless information, and yet we are still
so often left in the dark on some of the most important things.
Our problem, though, isn't really an education problem so much
as one of empowerment. You can hear all the information, but if
you are not able to do something with it all then the information is
meaningless. If we are not teaching people to obey the things Jesus
commanded, then we are not making disciples. It's that simple.
Teaching them to know His commands does not make a disciple.
Ultimately, we need to pass on life-transforming power, not just
ideas. For many, the solution is to start by making disciples who follow Jesus, and let all the other stuff develop from that place.

If I merely prescribe ten steps for you to take home and apply
today, I will have cheapened all that I have written of in this
book. It is not my place to tell you what to do. Rather, I am to let
you know that Jesus will lead and guide you in all He has for you.
Follow Him, and you will not be disappointed. I suspect, however, that Jesus has no intention of leading you to simply carry on

with an impotent spiritual life void of the true challenges of faith that are worthy of His sacrifice. One thing I know of our Lord is that He is always trying to take us further in our growth, and that requires that we let go of old things to move forward into the new: repentance, that is (changing your mind). This may not be a comfortable path, but it is one that leads to richer, deeper, and more fruitful significance for your life.

If you find yourself in a church that is still very much operating in the 2.0 system what can you do? Well, there are a few options, but ultimately for every one of us there are only two: whatever Jesus is telling you to do, and everything else. Here are five things to think through:

1. If all of this connects with you, do not run out and start condemning your pastor and denomination leaders. May I suggest you process this more reflectively and prayerfully? Remember that repentance really just means to change your mind (*your* mind, not everyone else's). Be humble and serve others, for that is the Jesus way. Remember, our true enemy is not made of flesh and blood.

2. Count the cost. Jesus recommended that we do so. For some of you, the cost could be incredibly high. This doesn't mean it isn't worth it, but you need to go into such a decision well informed and having weighed the consequences.

3. If you are in a place where it is quite impossible to change so radically, try small changes first. Most of the ways we have been doing church in the old system are not wrong or bad in and of themselves. If you still give 10 percent, you haven't done a bad thing; in fact, it is good. If you take communion with wafers and grape juice, sitting in rows next to people you have never met, you have not committed a sin. I am suggesting that you are missing out on the *best* stuff because you are so consumed with *good* stuff. Why not continue with the old, but let your mind download the new system and begin to do some of the really *great* things as well?

4. If you are an early adopter, and you realize you cannot go back to church as usual, then I suggest you find out more about organic church. There are lots of great books being written today by a wealth of experienced and capable authors. You can

come and be a part of a Greenhouse and get connected. You can start by visiting our Website and connecting from there with authors, other Websites, and training opportunities, if you want to go further (www.cmaresources.org).

5. If you don't like what I am saying, I suggest that you broadcast that this book is full of dangerous ideas, burn it, and blacklist it to protect your vested interest in Church 2.0.

Do you remember the "duck and cover" drill in school during the Cold War? In case of a nuclear bomb attack, when the alarm sounded we practiced hiding under our school desk. Everyone knew that hiding under a plywood desk is not sufficient protection against an actual bomb. The drill was really just to give the students the illusion that they had something they could do in a helpless situation to provide them with a false sense of control and hope.

Church 3.0 has arrived. It is spreading already. You can duck and cover, or you can run full speed ahead and join in what God is doing. What you probably can't do is stop it from coming.

notes

Introduction

1. Heath, C., and Heath, D. *Made to Stick: Why Some Ideas Survive and Others Die*. New York: Random House, 2007, pp. 19–20.
2. Ibid, p. 20.

Chapter One: What About the World We Live In?

1. Thom Wolf, lectures presented at Overlake Christian Church on October 20–21, 2005.
2. Friedman, T. L. *The World Is Flat: A Brief History of the Twenty-First Century*. New York: Picador, 2005.
3. Friedman delineates three eras of globalization. Globalization 1.0 was after America was discovered and nations started imperializing around the world. Globalization 2.0 was from 1800 to 2000 and was a period when corporations began to go global. Globalization 3.0 is when the individual begins to have a voice and becomes a player on the global scene, which has been made possible mostly by technological advances (Friedman, *World Is Flat*, pp. 9–10).
4. Ibid, p. 11.

Chapter Two: What About Our Changing Culture?

1. Stetzer, E., Stanley, R., and Hates, J. *Lost and Found: The Younger Unchurched and the Churches That Reach Them*. Nashville: B&H, 2009, p. 44.
2. Ibid, p. 45.
3. P. 43.
4. Pp. 36–37.
5. P. 38.
6. P. 43.
7. P. 32.

Chapter Three: What About the Church's Mission?

1. I am indebted to Daniel Brown, who first used this contrast of lake and river to describe churches.

2. Hall, C. "Missional Possible: Steps to Transform a Consumer Church into a Missional Church." *Leadership Journal,* Winter 2007, p. 35.

3. Hirsch, A. "Defining Missional." *Leadership Journal,* Fall 2008, p. 22.

4. Ibid., 22.

5. The Nicene Creed.

6. A report compiled by J. Slack: *Doing the Math! Analyzing the Growth and the Church Planting Task in USA.* August 2007. "Doing the Math: Looking at Lostness—Atlanta, GA."

7. Ibid., "Doing the Math: Looking at Lostness—New York (City)."

8. Brown, M., ed. *Giving USA 2009: The Annual Report on Philanthropy for the Year 2007.* Glenview, Ill.: Giving USA Foundation, 2009. You can find a pdf summary of the data here as a press release dated June 10, 2009: www.givinginstitute.org/press_releases/gusa.cfm, p. 3.

9. http://hirr.hartsem.edu/megachurch/definition.html.

10. http://www.gallup.com/poll/117409/easter-smaller-percentage-americans-christian.aspx.

11. Kosmin, B. A., and Keysar, A. *American Religious Identification Survey.* Hartford, Conn.: Trinity College, 2008.

12. Frost, M., and Hirsch, A. *The Shaping of Things to Come.* Peabody, Mass.: Henrickson, 2003, p. 72.

13. Cole, N. *Organic Church.* San Francisco: Jossey-Bass, 2005, p. 53.

14. Hirsch, A. *The Forgotten Ways.* Grand Rapids, Mich.: Brazos Press, 2006, p. 143.

15. Hirsch, "Defining Missional," p. 22.

16. Nunez, E. A., and Taylor, W. D. *Hope in Latin America: An Evangelical Perspective.* Chicago: Moody Press, 1989, pp. 332–333.

17. Cole, *Organic Church,* p. xxiii.

18. Ibid., 65.

Chapter Four: What About Church Growth?

1. Alan Hirsch frequently uses this analogy to demonstrate the latent "apostolic genius" that each Christian carries within. Used here by permission.

2. Hirsch, A. *The Forgotten Ways.* Grand Rapids, Mich.: Brazos Press, 2006, p. 19.

3. Yancey, P. "Discreet and Dynamic: Why, with No Apparent Resources, Chinese Churches Thrive." *Christianity Today,* July 2004, p. 72.

4. Garrison, D. *Church Planting Movements.* Midlothian, Va.: WIGTake Resources, 2004, p. 21.

5. Ibid., p. 172.

6. http://en.wikipedia.org/wiki/Social_movment.
7. Stetzer, E. "House Church Report: Excerpts from the Report, 'State of Church Planting in U.S. Today': Prepared for the Leadership Network." Leadership Network, 2008.
8. Schwarz and Schalk. *Implementation Guide to Natural Church Development.* Carol Stream, ChurchSmart Resources, 2003, p. 136.
9. Ibid., p. 136.
10. Cole, N. *Search & Rescue: Becoming a Disciple That Makes a Difference.* Grand Rapids, Mich.: Baker Books, 2008, p. 77.
11. Ibid., pp. 78–79.
12. Surratt, G., Ligon, G., and Bird, W. *A Multi-site Road Trip: Exploring the New Normal.* Grand Rapids, Mich.: Zondervan, p. 14.
13. Ibid., p. 14.
14. Pp. 210–215.

Chapter Five: What About Church Models? Part One

1. Myers, J. *Organic Community: Creating a Place Where People Naturally Connect.* Grand Rapids, Mich.: Baker Books, 2007.
2. Watts, D. J. *Six Degrees: The Science of a Connected Age.* New York: Norton, 2003, p. 27.
3. Buchanan, M. *Nexus: Small Worlds and the Groundbreaking Science of Networks.* New York: Norton, 2002, p. 19.
4. The first is called a dyad and is simply one person in relation to another, without any other groups added—in essence a network of two. We eliminate this from discussion for the sake of brevity and relevance in this chapter, but you will find this concept of utmost importance later in Chapter Seven.
5. Evan, W. M. "An Organization-Set Model of Interorganizational Relations." In M. Tuite, R. Chisholm, and M. Radnor (eds.), *Interorganizational Decision Making.* New Brunswick, Maine: AldieTransaction, 1972, pp. 181–200.
6. Arquilla, J., and Ronfeldt, D. "Networks and Netwars: The Future of Terror, Crime, and Militancy." Downloadable at http://www.rand.org/publications/MR/MR1382/.
7. Hirsch, *The Forgotten Ways*, pp. 200–202.
8. Arquilla and Ronfeldt, *Networks and Netwars*, p. 9.
9. Cole, *Organic Church*, p. 115.
10. It seems from Paul's words in 1 Corinthians 9 that the apostles were all supported full-time except for him and Barnabas.
11. The only cells without your whole DNA are your reproductive cells, which purposely only have half of your DNA so that they can merge with another's half and form a whole new person.

Chapter Six: What About Church Models? Part Two

1. Just to clarify, Curtis was using this analogy for years before the very popular book *The Starfish and the Spider* came out.
2. Brafman, O., and Beckstrom, R. *The Starfish and the Spider.* New York: Portfolio, 2006, p. 144.
3. Ibid.
4. Ibid., pp. 46–55.
5. Pp. 50–51.
6. Hirsch, A. *The Forgotten Ways.* Grand Rapids, Mich.: Brazo Press, 2007, pp. 142–143.
7. McCallum, D., and Lowery, J. *Organic Disciplemaking: Mentoring Others into Spiritual Maturity and Leadership.* Houston, Texas:TOUCH Publications, 2006.
8. Ibid., p. 80.
9. Cole, *Search & Rescue*, pp. 168–169.
10. You can purchase Life Transformation Group Cards that explain how these groups work and that contain these questions at www .cmaresources.org.

Chapter Seven: What About Larger Gatherings?

1. Shirky, C. *Here Comes Everybody: The Power of Organizing Without Organizations.* New York: Penguin, 2008, p. 17.
2. Shirky, *Here Comes Everybody*, p. 16.
3. "How to Design Small Decision Making Groups." At http://www .intuitor.com/statistics/SmallGroups.html. © 1996–2001, all rights reserved. Retrieved July 14, 2009.
4. Shirky, *Here Comes Everybody*, pp. 27–28.
5. Ibid.
6. The folks at Intuitor.com conclude their statistical study of small decision-making groups with these words: "Five [members in a group] takes advantage of the desirability of odd numbers for majority rules decisions. For the unanimous decision making style of a group of five a 99% accuracy assuming [sic] 60% individual accuracies and that a single person with the right answer can convince the others. Even with only 50% individual accuracies the group accuracy will average 96.9%. Adding additional members will not greatly improve accuracy. However, additional members will significantly increase group management problems since the number of possible social interactions increases rapidly."
7. Christopher Allen, writing about "The Science of Dunbar's Number" on his blog Life with Alacrity, says: "In my opinion it is at 5 that the feeling of 'team' really starts. At 5 to 8 people, you can

have a meeting where everyone can speak out about what the entire group is doing, and everyone feels highly empowered. However, at 9–12 people this begins to break down—not enough 'attention' is given to everyone and meetings risk becoming either too noisy, too boring, too long, or some combination thereof." At http://www .lifewithalacrity.com/2004/03/the_dunbar_numb.html.

8. Allen, C. "Community by the Numbers, Part One: Group Thresholds." Retrieved from Life with Alacrity, http://www.lifewithalacrity .com/2008/09/group-threshold.html, posted September 28, 2008.

9. This unique Website, developed by three self-proclaimed nerds in a family, takes on the physics and math behind a number of interesting questions: http://intuitor.com.

10. http://intuitor.com.

11. Allen, "Community by the Numbers."

12. Ibid.

13. http://hirr.hartsem.edu/research/fastfacts/fast_facts.html#sizecong.

14. Allen, "Community by the Numbers."

15. Ibid.

16. Granted, Dunbar has a strong evolutionary bias to all his work. Nevertheless, he does his homework to verify his hypothesis of our mental capacity to relate to a limited number of people.

17. Gladwell refers to it as the "magic number 150." *The Tipping Point: How Little Things Can Make a Big Difference.* New York: BackBay Books, 2002, pp. 169–192.

18. Buchanan, M. *Nexus: Small Worlds and the Groundbreaking Science of Networks.* New York: Norton, 2002.

19. Watts, D. J. *Six Degrees: The Science of a Connected Age.* New York: Norton, 2003.

20. Watts, D. J. *Small Worlds: The Dynamics of Networks Between Order and Randomness.* Princeton, N.J.: Princeton University Press, 1999.

21. Robb, "The Optimal Size of a Terrorist Network." March 24, 2004, at http://global guerillas.typepad.com/globalgueillas/2004/03/ what_is_the_opt.html.

22. http://hirr.hartsem.edu/research/fastfacts/fast_facts.html#sizecong.

23. Dunbar, R. "Coevolution of Neocortical Size, Group Size and Language in Humans." *Behavioral and Brain Sciences,* 1993, *16*(4), 681–735. http://www.bbsonline.org/documents/a/00/00/05/65/ bbs00000565–00/bbs.dunbar.html.

24. Ibid.

25. Allen, "Community by the Numbers."

26. Shirky, *Here Comes Everybody,* pp. 19–20.

27. Ross Mayfield's blog "Markets, Technology and Musings" at http:// radio.weblogs.coom/0114726/2003/02/12.html#a284.

28. Gladwell, *Tipping Point*, pp. 30–88.
29. Shirky, *Here Comes Everybody*, p. 21.

Chapter Eight: What About Evangelism?
1. Hirsch, *The Forgotten Ways*, p. 18.
2. Ibid., p. 18.
3. P. 274.
4. Hirsch, A., with Altclass, D. *The Forgotten Ways Handbook.* Grand Rapids, Mich.: Brazos Press, 2009, pp. 117–134.
5. His habits are (1) Pioneer and multiply; (2) Cultivate apostolic genius; (3) Foster community calling and uniqueness; (4) Develop ministry capacity; and (5) Catalyze.
6. Brafman and Beckstrom, *Starfish and the Spider*, pp. 109–131.
7. *Journeys to Significance* (Jossey-Bass), a forthcoming book I am writing, walks through each of Paul's journeys and demonstrates his own maturing as a leader and the perfecting of his apostolic gift.
8. Ibid., p. 133.
9. While Hirsch's writing on apostolic genius focuses on the contents of the node in a growing network, I wish to address what mathematics calls the edge, which is the link between the nodes. Both are important for network expansion to be accomplished and I believe are a part of the nature of apostolic genius (Figure 8.1). What is within the follower must also spread to release the same potency in another in such a way that it can spread to others beyond. That contagious spread is the focus of this chapter.
10. Godin, S. *Tribes: We Need You to Lead Us.* New York: Penguin, 2008, p. 23.
11. This is so important to all we do that I have yet to write a book that does not specifically expand on this concept. But in this book, we will go into some new details.
12. Heath and Heath, *Made to Stick*, p. 16.
13. Godin, *Tribes*, p. 79.
14. Godin, S. *Small Is the New Big: And 183 Other Riffs, Rants and Remarkable Business Ideas.* New York: Penguin, 2006.
15. Gladwell, *Tipping Point*, p. 9.
16. Godin, S. *Unleashing the Idea Virus.* New York: Hyperion, 2001, pp. 180–183.
17. Godin, *Tribes*, p. 81.
18. Heath and Heath, *Made to Stick*, p. 16.
19. Gladwell, *Tipping Point*, pp. 3–5.
20. Godin, *Unleashing the Idea Virus*, pp. 43–44.
21. Cole, *Organic Church*, p. xxviii; quote is from Sir Walter Moberly in his work *Crisis in the University.*

22. Ibid., pp. 159–169.

23. Godin, *Unleashing the Idea Virus*, pp. 49–51.

24. *Cultivating a Life for God* and *Organic Church* have been spread everywhere by my friend Carol. My other books have not had the same connection with her ... yet.

25. It is clear that although the Gospel of John follows Jesus' life it is not ordered strictly chronologically. It is put together more topically than the synoptic Gospels. The miracles that John writes about are placed in an intentional order. Therefore, following the order as John intended, though not absolutely necessary, has advantages.

26. Garrison, D. *Church Planting Movements*. Midlothian, Va.: WIGTake Resources, 2004, pp. 163–164.

27. I have an entire chapter in *Organic Church* detailing all five of these principles; see pp. 171–192.

28. Ma, J. *The Blueprint*. Ventura, Calif.: Regal, 2007, pp. 226–238.

Chapter Ten: What About Kids?

1. You can find out more at Campaignforcare.org and www.myspace.com/campaign_for_care.

Chapter Eleven: What About Heresy?

1. Some of the people behind this inquisition have moved on to other things, and I am glad to report that we are now in good relationship with many in this denominational office.

2. At this time, we became known, especially among leaders in that denomination, as the "pancake churches." This is not a practice we teach, nor was it repeated to my knowledge. So to label it a false teaching would be an overstatement. An error in judgment, perhaps, but to use it to call us false teachers is absurd. I do believe that church is to be a family, and I also believe that you should see your own family as a place to start living life as a church. I do not think this is heretical at all. That said, we do not count every nuclear family as a church and we never have. Even if we did, could one legitimately say this is a false doctrine?

3. D. Willard. From a lecture delivered at the Anaheim Vineyard in 2001.

4. This statement in various translations is attributed to the Moravians and also to Augustine.

5. You can find out more about LTGs in the books *Search & Rescue* and *Cultivating a Life for God*, available at www.cmaresources.org.

Chapter Twelve: What About Finances?

1. See Cole, *Organic Leadership*, pp. 280–292.

the author

Neil Cole is an experienced church planter and pastor. In addition to founding the Awakening Chapels, which are reaching young postmodern people in urban settings, he is also a founder of Church Multiplication Associates (CMA), which has grown to thousands of churches in more than' forty-five states and forty nations in only nine years. He is one of the key founding leaders of the simple church movement that is rapidly growing around the world. Currently Neil serves as CMA's executive director. He is responsible for resourcing church leaders with ministry tools to reproduce healthy disciples, leaders, churches, and movements. His responsibilities also include developing, training, and coaching church planters.

Neil is also an international speaker and has authored *Organic Church, Search & Rescue, Organic Leadership, Cultivating a Life for God,* and *TruthQuest.* He has coauthored *Raising Leaders for the Harvest* and *Beyond Church Planting: Pathways for Emerging Churches* with Dr. Robert Logan and *Organic Church Planters' Greenhouse* with Paul Kaak. He lives in Long Beach, California, with his wife, Dana, and their three children, Heather, Erin, and Zachary.

index

Organic Church

Growing Faith Where Life Happens

Neil Cole

ISBN 978-0-7879-8129-7
Cloth | 272 pp.

"This book is profound, practical, and a pleasure to read. It stretches our thinking and brings us to a place where we can see the Kingdom of God spread across the world in our generation. This book has come at the right time."

— **John C. Maxwell**, founder, INJOY, INJOY Stewardship Services and EQUIP

"I always listen when Neil Cole speaks. His breadth of understanding and practice of what he preaches is right on. Everyone should know or be aware of this guy that God is using in a powerful way."

— **Bob Roberts**, senior pastor, NorthWood Church

According to international church starter and pastor Neil Cole, if we want to connect with young people and those who are not coming to church, we must go where people congregate. Cole shows readers how to plant the seeds of the Kingdom of God in the places where life happens and where culture is formed — restaurants, bars, coffeehouses, parks, locker rooms, and neighborhoods. *Organic Church* offers a hands-on guide for demystifying this new model of church and shows the practical aspects of implementing it.

NEIL COLE is a church starter and pastor, and founder and executive director of Church Multiplication Associates, which has helped start over seven hundred churches in thirty-two states and twenty-three nations in six years.

Other Books of Interest

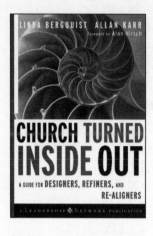

Church Turned Inside Out

A Guide for Designers, Refiners, and Re-Aligners

Linda Bergquist | Allan Karr

ISBN 978-0-470-38317-9
Cloth | 240 pp.

"What an extremely hopeful, heart-lifting, and practical book for anyone who loves the church. We must never be afraid to look at our church from the inside out as that is where true change will happen."

— **Dan Kimball**, author, *They Like Jesus but Not the Church*

There are no sacred models of church, no specific molds into which God pours blessings, and no special leadership styles that are holier than others. Too often, though, church leaders attempt to pattern their ministries after either tradition or the successes of a few prominent trendsetting congregations. In *Church Turned Inside Out*, Linda Bergquist and Allan Karr push back on the one-size-fits-all approach. They invite leaders of all kinds of churches—new and existing, megachurches and microchurches—to walk through an inside-out design process. Instead of starting with models and methods, they insist that every sphere of church life resonates with and communicates what you really believe.

LINDA BERGQUIST has been a church planter and church planting teacher for twenty-five years. She also has experience in the area of church consultations and urban ministry to the poor and assists her husband, who is a ministry center director in the Lower Haight district of San Francisco.

ALLAN KARR is currently an associate professor of missional/church planting at Golden Gate Baptist Theological Seminary and a practitioner of church planting and community development. Allan has also served for ten years as a national missionary of the North American Mission Board of the Southern Baptist Convention.

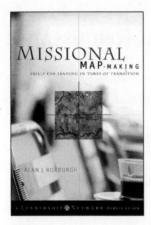

Missional Map-Making

Skills for Leading in Times of Transition

Alan Roxburgh

ISBN 978-0-470-48672-6
Cloth | 240 pp.

"This important book provides insightful historical perspective toward clarifying the contours of our present landscape, while also being deeply instructive for helping reflective and courageous Christians develop skills for creating new maps toward participating more faithfully in God's mission."

— **Craig Van Gelder**, Ph.D., Professor of Congregational Mission, Luther Seminary

In the burgeoning missional church movement, churches are seeking to become less focused on programs for members and more oriented toward outreach to people who are not already in church. This fundamental shift in what a congregation is and does and thinks is challenging for leaders and congregants. Using the metaphor of map-making, this book explains the perspective and skills needed to lead congregations and denominations in a time of radical change over unfamiliar terrain as churches change their focus from internal to external.

ALAN ROXBURGH is President of Missional Leadership Institute (MLI) and has pastored congregations in small towns, urban centers and the suburbs. He has served in denominational leadership as well as on the faculty of a seminary where he was responsible for teaching in the areas of leadership and domestic missional church leadership. Alan teaches in numerous seminaries as well as lecturing (including at the emergent church conventions) and consulting all over North America, Australia and Europe in the areas of leadership, transition, systems change and missional theology.

Other Books of Interest

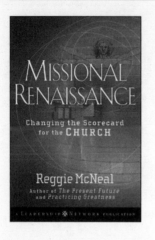

Missional Renaissance

Changing the Scorecard for the Church

Reggie McNeal

ISBN 978-0-470-24344-2
Cloth | 224 pp.

"This is Reggie McNeal's gift to the church of the twenty-first century and his finest and most thorough work to date. This book clearly defines the shifts necessary to gauge what matters most for the missional people of God."

— **Eric Swanson**, coauthor, *The Externally Focused Church* and *Living a Life on Loan*

The book is filled with in-depth discussions of what it means to become a missional congregation and important information on how to make the transition. With an understanding of the nature of the missional church and the practical suggestions outlined in this book, church leaders and members will be equipped to move into what McNeal sees as the most viable future for Christianity.

Missional Renaissance offers a clear path for any leader or congregation that wants to breathe new life into the church and to become revitalized as true followers of Jesus.

REGGIE MCNEAL serves as the Missional Leadership Specialist for Leadership Network of Dallas, Texas. McNeal is the author of *A Work of Heart: Understanding How God Shapes Spiritual Leaders* and the best-selling *The Present Future: Six Tough Questions for the Church* and *Practicing Greatness: 7 Disciplines of Extraordinary Spiritual Leaders* from Jossey-Bass.

Other Books of Interest

The Present Future

Six Tough Questions for the Church

Reggie McNeal

ISBN 978-0-470-45315-5
Paper | 176 pp.

"Christian leaders will find great questions being answered in this compelling and motivating work that unwraps what McNeal calls 'the realities of the present future' in the church today."

— **Kelvin Gardiner**, district superintendent, Christian and Missionary Alliance.

In *The Present Future*, McNeal identifies the six most important realities that church leaders must address including: recapturing the spirit of Christianity and replacing "church growth" with a wider vision of kingdom growth; developing disciples instead of church members; fostering the rise of a new apostolic leadership; focusing on spiritual formation rather than church programs; and shifting from prediction and planning to preparation for the challenges of an uncertain world. McNeal contends that by changing the questions church leaders ask themselves about their congregations and their plans, they can frame the core issues and approach the future with new eyes, new purpose, and new ideas.

REGGIE MCNEAL serves as the Missional Leadership Specialist for Leadership Network of Dallas, Texas. McNeal is the author of *Missional Renaissance*, *A Work of Heart*, and *Practicing Greatness* from Jossey-Bass.

The Tangible Kingdom

Creating Incarnational Community

Hugh Halter | Matt Smay

ISBN 978-0-470-18897-2
Cloth | 224 pp.

"No matter what kind of church you are seeking to participate in or plant, The Tangible Kingdom *will knock you out of your comfortable pew to follow the mission of Jesus to transform your community."*

— **Mark Driscoll**, author, *Confessions of a Reformission Rev.* and *The Radical Reformission*

Written for those who are trying to nurture authentic faith communities and for those who have struggled to retain their faith, *The Tangible Kingdom* offers theological answers and real-life stories that demonstrate how the best ancient church practices can re-emerge in today's culture, through any church of any size. In this remarkable book, Hugh Halter and Matt Smay—two missional leaders and church planters—outline an innovative model for creating thriving grass-roots faith communities.

HUGH HALTER is a specialist with Church Resource Ministries and the national director of Missio, a global network of missional leaders and church planters. He is also lead architect of Adullam, a congregational network of incarnational communities in Denver, Colorado (www.adullamdenver.com).

MATT SMAY co-directs both Missio and Adullam and specializes in helping existing congregations move toward mission. Halter and Smay direct the MCAP "missional church apprenticeship practicum," an international training network for incarnational church planters, pastors, and emerging leaders (www.missio.us).